T0301595

Quantifying Systemic Risk

A National Bureau of
Economic Research
Conference Report

Quantifying Systemic Risk

Edited by **Joseph G. Haubrich and Andrew W. Lo**

The University of Chicago Press

Chicago and London

JOSEPH G. HAUBRICH is a vice president of and an economist at the Federal Reserve Bank of Cleveland. ANDREW W. LO is the Charles E. and Susan T. Harris Professor, professor of finance, and director of the Laboratory for Financial Engineering at the Massachusetts Institute of Technology. He is a research associate of the National Bureau of Economic Research.

The University of Chicago Press, Chicago 60637
The University of Chicago Press, Ltd., London
© 2013 by the National Bureau of Economic Research
All rights reserved. Published 2013.
Printed in the United States of America

22 21 20 19 18 17 16 15 14 13   1 2 3 4 5
ISBN-13: 978-0-226-31928-5 (cloth)
ISBN-13: 978-0-226-92196-9 (e-book)

Library of Congress Cataloging-in-Publication Data

Quantifying systemic risk / edited by Joseph G. Haubrich and
    Andrew W. Lo.
       pages ; cm. — (National Bureau of Economic Research
  conference report)
   Includes bibliographical references and index.
    ISBN 978-0-226-31928-5 (cloth : alkaline paper) —
ISBN 978-0-226-92196-9 (e-book) 1. Financial risk—Mathematical
models—Congresses. 2. Risk assessment—Congresses.
3. Operational risk—Congresses. I. Haubrich, Joseph Gerard,
1958– II. Lo, Andrew W. (Andrew Wen-Chuan) III. Series:
National Bureau of Economic Research conference report.
  HG106.Q36 2012
  338.5—dc23
                     2012020450

Relation of the Directors to the
Work and Publications of the
National Bureau of Economic Research

1. The object of the NBER is to ascertain and present to the economics profession, and to the public more generally, important economic facts and their interpretation in a scientific manner without policy recommendations. The Board of Directors is charged with the responsibility of ensuring that the work of the NBER is carried on in strict conformity with this object.

2. The President shall establish an internal review process to ensure that book manuscripts proposed for publication DO NOT contain policy recommendations. This shall apply both to the proceedings of conferences and to manuscripts by a single author or by one or more co-authors but shall not apply to authors of comments at NBER conferences who are not NBER affiliates.

3. No book manuscript reporting research shall be published by the NBER until the President has sent to each member of the Board a notice that a manuscript is recommended for publication and that in the President's opinion it is suitable for publication in accordance with the above principles of the NBER. Such notification will include a table of contents and an abstract or summary of the manuscript's content, a list of contributors if applicable, and a response form for use by Directors who desire a copy of the manuscript for review. Each manuscript shall contain a summary drawing attention to the nature and treatment of the problem studied and the main conclusions reached.

4. No volume shall be published until forty-five days have elapsed from the above notification of intention to publish it. During this period a copy shall be sent to any Director requesting it, and if any Director objects to publication on the grounds that the manuscript contains policy recommendations, the objection will be presented to the author(s) or editor(s). In case of dispute, all members of the Board shall be notified, and the President shall appoint an ad hoc committee of the Board to decide the matter; thirty days additional shall be granted for this purpose.

5. The President shall present annually to the Board a report describing the internal manuscript review process, any objections made by Directors before publication or by anyone after publication, any disputes about such matters, and how they were handled.

6. Publications of the NBER issued for informational purposes concerning the work of the Bureau, or issued to inform the public of the activities at the Bureau, including but not limited to the NBER Digest and Reporter, shall be consistent with the object stated in paragraph 1. They shall contain a specific disclaimer noting that they have not passed through the review procedures required in this resolution. The Executive Committee of the Board is charged with the review of all such publications from time to time.

7. NBER working papers and manuscripts distributed on the Bureau's web site are not deemed to be publications for the purpose of this resolution, but they shall be consistent with the object stated in paragraph 1. Working papers shall contain a specific disclaimer noting that they have not passed through the review procedures required in this resolution. The NBER's web site shall contain a similar disclaimer. The President shall establish an internal review process to ensure that the working papers and the web site do not contain policy recommendations, and shall report annually to the Board on this process and any concerns raised in connection with it.

8. Unless otherwise determined by the Board or exempted by the terms of paragraphs 6 and 7, a copy of this resolution shall be printed in each NBER publication as described in paragraph 2 above.

We dedicate this book to all those who lost their jobs, their homes, or their savings because of the financial crisis. By developing better measures of systemic risk, we hope to learn from the mistakes of the past and build a more stable and robust future for the global financial system.

Contents

Acknowledgments

Any book—especially one associated with a conference—is the product of a great many people. Our greatest debt is, of course, to the conference participants, without whom there would be nothing to publish. But several others were also instrumental in making this volume possible. Jim Poterba of the NBER and Mark Sniderman and Stephen Jenkins of the Cleveland Fed immediately recognized the benefit of bringing together academics, policymakers, and practitioners to confront the issue of quantifying systemic risk in response to the financial crisis, and we thank them for their support and encouragement throughout this project. In Cambridge, Alterra Milone and Rob Shannon deftly handled local arrangements, while Kathy Popovich, Sereta Johnson, and Paula Warren managed various conference-related activities at the Cleveland Fed. In preparing the volume, Helena Fitz-Patrick of the NBER and David Pervin of the University of Chicago Press patiently guided us through the process, including revising the text according to the insightful comments of two anonymous reviewers. Lastly, we thank our families for putting up with us as we engaged in yet another project that took time away from them.

Introduction

Joseph G. Haubrich and Andrew W. Lo

Introduction

In the wake of the financial crisis of 2007 through 2009, many proposals have been put forward for its causes and the appropriate remedies. In response to an impatient and frustrated public, and several months before the Financial Crisis Inquiry Commission completed its analysis, Congress passed the 2,319-page landmark Dodd-Frank Wall Street Reform and Consumer Protection Act of 2010, setting the stage for seismic shifts in the regulatory landscape of the financial industry. Clearly, change is afoot, but are we ready?

In the context of such sweeping regulatory reform, one of the most urgent priorities is establishing the means to measure and monitor systemic risk on an ongoing basis. Even the most cautious policymaker would agree that attempting to eliminate all systemic risk is neither feasible nor desirable—risk is a necessary consequence of real economic growth. Moreover, individual financial institutions do not have the means or the motivation to address systemic risk themselves. Because risk is closely tied to expected returns in this industry, as both theory and practice suggest, in competing for market share and revenues financial entities will typically take on as much risk as

Joseph G. Haubrich is a vice president of and an economist at the Federal Reserve Bank of Cleveland. Andrew W. Lo is the Charles E. and Susan T. Harris Professor, professor of finance, and director of the Laboratory for Financial Engineering at the Massachusetts Institute of Technology. He is a research associate of the National Bureau of Economic Research.

The views expressed here are those of the authors only, and do not represent the views of the Federal Reserve Bank of Cleveland, the Board of Governors of the Federal Reserve System, AlphaSimplex Group, MIT, the National Bureau of Economic Research, or their affiliates and employees. For acknowledgments, sources of research support, and disclosure of the authors' material financial relationships, if any, please see http://www.nber.org/chapters /c12066.ack.

shareholders allow, without considering the consequences for the financial system as a whole. In much the same way that manufacturing companies did not consider their impact on the environment prior to pollution regulation, we cannot fault financial institutions for ignoring the systemic implications of their risk-taking in the absence of comprehensive risk regulation. Unless we are able to measure systemic risk objectively, quantitatively, and regularly, it is impossible to determine the appropriate trade-off between such risk and its rewards and, from a policy perspective and social welfare objective, how best to contain it.

However, the challenge is not just measuring systemic risk, but also implementing it within the existing regulatory infrastructure; at issue is institutional design as well as statistical inference. After all, the ultimate goal is not just prediction, but also prevention—failing that, intervention to mitigate the severity of an impending crisis. Achieving this lofty goal requires detailed knowledge of the dynamics of the financial sector.

The technical side of risk measurement has received the most attention, particularly from academics, but risk management involves three distinct elements according to Lo (1999)—prices, preferences, and probabilities—and we can frame the discussion of systemic risk in a similar fashion. Centuries of work by scientists and mathematicians have advanced the understanding of probability, but the practical difficulties in estimating the distribution of financial market data remain formidable. Estimating extreme events from everyday behavior can be seriously misleading. The space shuttle booster O-rings performed acceptably in cool temperatures, but failed disastrously in the freezing conditions of the *Challenger* launch on January 28, 1986 (Tufte, 1990). Though not as rare as we once thought, financial crises remain extreme events. Making the problem even harder, figuring the odds means aiming at a moving target. The past twenty-five years of finance have stressed how changes in variance affect stock prices, interest rates, and spreads (Engle, 2001). Recent financial crises, from the sovereign defaults of the late 1990s to the Panic of 2007 to 2009 to the current problems in Europe highlight how quickly the correlations between different investments can change, encapsulated in the folk wisdom that "in a crisis, all correlations go to one."

Decisions also require a way to rank different risks—investors, even regulators, must confront their own (or society's) preferences, which are inevitably subjective. Exactly how does a particular investor value different payoffs and probabilities? Still, as an aid to decision making, a variety of objective measures have been proposed, mainly variations of statistical concepts used to describe the "risk." These include traditional measures such as mean and variance, along with the various flavors of the popular value at risk (VaR) measure such as expected shortfall. Other notions such as stochastic dominance and its extensions, for example, the economic risk measure of Aumann and Serrano (2008) or the operational measure of Foster and Hart (2009), provide a way to think about the trade-off between risk and return but must ultimately involve preferences. A more mathematical approach postulates a set of axioms that any "good" risk measure must obey. As might be expected, however, different axioms can produce very different risk measures, producing such varying measures as expected utility, coherent measures of risk, or uncertainty aversion. Regulators face the problem on a higher level, seeking to implement the trade-offs that society prefers.

Finally, prices play a dual role in thinking about risk, as both the input and the output of the process. Price movements—the profits and the losses— drive the need for hedging and risk management. At the same time, prices are the output, the outcome of supply and demand expressed through preferences and probabilities. But it is when prices do not properly capture the economic value of the corresponding commodity that problems arise. As with air pollution, systemic risk arises when market prices do not reflect the full impact of a firm's decisions on the rest of the economy. This creates the need for something beyond business as usual.

Perhaps in an ideal world, market discipline alone would induce firms to measure and manage risk properly. But systemic risk, like other negative externalities, means that individual firms do not consider how their actions affect the system as a whole. There is a sense that we are not starting from the Garden of Eden. Safety nets such as deposit insurance or implicit too-big-to-fail policies reduce the incentive to manage risk. How supervision best responds is another matter. Recently, the conversation has shifted from the safety and soundness of individual banks to the appropriate level of "macroprudential" supervision; that is, the total risk in the system. An early proponent of macroprudential supervision, Claudio Borio of the Bank for International Settlements explains it as having both a cross-sectional (distribution of risk) and a time series (change over time) dimension (Borio 2003). Other regulators have also voiced the intent to make regulation more macroprudential (Tarullo 2010). One output of this philosophy is the Basel III proposal to require globally systemically important banks (G-SIBs) to hold additional capital buffers (BCBS 2011).

Clearly, macroprudential regulators need valid measures of systemic risk. Operationally, they need these measures to set capital requirements and to consider other aspects of supervision such as merger decisions. Measures that are not available on a timely basis, difficult to interpret, or easily manipulated are of little use. But if risk measurement needs change, so to do regulators. This "changing face of supervision" (FRBC 2010) is, in fact, becoming apparent in both the skill sets and organization of supervisors and regulators. One example is the horizontal reviews conducted by the Federal Reserve System and the Financial Stability Board, which has introduced cross-functional, horizontal reviews for capital (SCAP, CCAR) and executive compensation. These involve diverse groups of supervisors, economists, and lawyers, who make a point of comparing results across similar firms.

But reacting properly takes more than technical expertise. Will the regulators have the commitment to react as they should, forcing firms into resolution or requiring higher capital? How the public reacts to a crisis depends on how they expect the regulators to behave, and thus credibility and reputation become paramount. The best systemic risk measures should support this, and enable the public to hold regulators accountable. Ed Kane, among others, has called for the creation of a military-style academy for supervisors, as much to provide the *esprit de corps* needed to resist lobbying pressure as to provide advanced risk training (Kane 2011). But this also suggests that there are limits to what supervision and regulation can accomplish, even based on advanced measures of systemic risk. If so, the financial system should be designed to be robust to mistakes. But if finding the correct statistical measure of systemic risk is hard, redesigning the financial system is orders of magnitude more difficult (Haubrich 2001).

Of course, any successful attempt to measure and supervise systemic risk must be based on understanding the financial markets, on how actual institutions behave and interact. This is a tall order, as any list of the major players would include banks, brokers/dealers, hedge funds, exchanges, mutual funds, pensions plans, insurance companies, and government-sponsored enterprises. The financial crisis provided many examples of the byzantine connections between these players: consider the failure of AIG. They were writing credit protection in the form of credit default swaps (CDS) on tranches of collateralized debt obligations (CDOs) based on subprime mortgages (Stultz 2010). Risk was transferred from home lenders via the derivatives market to an insurance company. Uncovering such connections is difficult even for highly regulated entities such as banks. For example, a new, fairly priced swap arrangement has no effect on a company's balance sheet, as the two legs are priced to offset each other. Future price changes can shift the relative valuation of the legs, however, and so the swap does constitute risk to the balance sheet. The crisis has renewed discussions of more extensive data collection, but such collection is expensive and, inevitably, a trade-off must be made. In an ironic twist of fate, in 2006 the Federal Reserve stopped reporting the M3 monetary aggregate that contained a (limited) measure of repurchase aggreements (Repos, RPs), which, barely more than a year later, emerged at the center of the financial crisis of 2007 to 2009 (Gorton 2010).

The limits of accounting information have led some to look for connections via price information: Adrian and Brunnermeier (2010) propose conditional value at risk (CoVaR), Acharya et al. (2010) use the marginal expected shortfall, and Billio et al. (2011) use principal component analysis and Granger-causality networks. This brings the discussion back full circle, in that advancements on the technical side of measuring risk can uncover structural connections. Even here, the analysis does not eliminate the need for wisdom. The connections are dynamic and changing—there was no correlation between monoline insurers and mortgage-backed securities until the monolines started writing insurance on mortgage-backeds. The whole process might be compared to a card-counting blackjack player in Las Vegas trying to find patterns in a multideck sort. A few hands do not reveal much about the remaining cards, but now start swapping in decks with extra face cards, and on top of that, every once in a while let a Tarot card from the Major Arcana turn up.

This is the current challenge that faces policymakers and regulators—even after the passage of the Dodd-Frank bill—and the focus of this NBER conference volume on quantifying systemic risk. The chapters are based on papers presented at an NBER conference held in Cambridge, Massachusetts, on November 6, 2009, and jointly sponsored by the Federal Reserve Bank of Cleveland and the NBER. We were fortunate to have a remarkable and diverse array of participants drawn from academia, industry, and government agencies, and the breadth and depth of ideas contained in this volume is a clear testament to their unique expertise. Each paper presented at the conference was assigned two discussants, one from academia and the other from either industry or government, and we have included summaries of these insightful discussants' remarks after each contribution.

In "Liquidity Risk, Cash Flow Constraints, and Systemic Feedbacks," Sujit Kapadia, Matthias Drehmann, John Elliott, and Gabriel Sterne introduce a theme that reappears in several other conference papers: while outside shocks may touch off a financial crisis, the reaction of market participants determines the course of the disaster. In the model they develop, solvency concerns at one bank lead to liquidity problems as funding becomes more difficult. This forces the bank to take defensive actions, hoarding liquidity and reducing lending to other banks. In certain cases, the problem snowballs (or becomes contagious) and a crisis looms. As other banks find it harder to obtain liquidity, the problem can become systemic. The process illustrates, as do several other chapters in this volume, how the fallacy of composition can hold in the financial markets: individual defenses against risk lead to greater risk overall.

The chapter emphasizes the cash flow constraint: banks must have cash inflows that cover their cash outflows. Kapadia et al. go further, however, and quantitatively evaluate the systemic effects of this funding liquidity risk. To do so, the work builds on a broader project (RAMSI) under way at the Bank of England, using detailed balance sheet information from UK banks encompassing macrocredit risk, interest and noninterest income risk, network interactions, and feedback effects. Funding liquidity risk is introduced by allowing for rating downgrades and incorporating a simple framework in which concerns over solvency, funding profile, and confidence trigger the outright closure of funding markets to particular institutions. The detailed look at the network of counterparty transactions demonstrates how defensive actions on the part of some banks can adversely affect others. The model can accommodate both aggregate distributions and scenario analysis: large losses at some banks can be exacerbated by liability-side feedbacks, leading to system-wide instability.

In "Endogenous and Systemic Risk," Jon Danielsson, Hyun Song Shin, and Jean-Pierre Zigrand explore the feedback between market volatility and traders' perception of risk. Trading activity sets and moves prices, but traders also use the resulting price volatility to gauge risk. Equilibrium requires a consistency between the perceived and the actual risk. In a setting where traders operate under value at risk constraints (although the logic carries over to risk-based capital requirements and more), volatility can become stochastic, even as fundamental risk remains constant. Trader reactions amplify fluctuations, creating a spiral of even greater response. If the purpose of financial regulation is to shield the financial system from collapse, then basing regulation on individually optimal risk management may not be enough: in this case, the prudent behavior of individuals increases the aggregate risk.

Roughly speaking, a market shock (say, a decrease in prices or an increase in volatility) now makes the asset look riskier according to risk management rules, be they value at risk or some other method. This forces the firm to reduce risk by selling the asset. But of course other firms, also noting the increased risk, do the same, leading to an even larger drop in price, starting a downward spiral toward even more risk. A crisis can arise quickly, because the process is highly nonlinear, with larger movements appearing suddenly. The critical threshold depends on the specifics of each market: risk management strategies, leverage, and capital plans. The chapter applies this insight to a variety of markets, explaining the implied volatility skew for options, the procyclical impact of Basel II bank capital requirements, and the optimal design for derivatives clearing and lenders of last resort. Spelling out the precise mechanism, though a challenge, takes a vital first step in the design of more robust institutions and policies.

In "Systemic Risks and the Macroeconomy" Gianni De Nicolò and Marcella Lucchetta make a distinction between real and financial risk, and present a modeling framework that jointly forecasts both sorts of systemic risk. They emphasize that lost output and unemployment constitute the true costs of financial crises. Thus, their systemic version of VaR has two components: the 5 percent tail of a systemic financial indicator (market-adjusted return for the financial sector), and GDP at risk, the 5 percent tail on real GDP growth. This framework is implemented using a large set of quarterly indicators of financial and real activity for the G7 economies over the 1980Q1 to 2009Q3 period. They first use a dynamic factor model to check forecasting power, and then impose sign restrictions from a simple macromodel to identify the shocks. For example, an aggregate supply shock should increase output but decrease inflation.

They obtain two main results. First, the model can, with some accuracy, forecast large declines in real activity, showing promise as an early warning system or a risk monitoring tool. Second, in all countries aggregate demand shocks drive the real cycle, and bank credit demand shocks drive the bank lending cycle. These results challenge the common wisdom that constraints in the aggregate supply of credit have been a key driver of the sharp downturn in real activity experienced by the G7 economies from 2008Q4 to 2009Q1.

In "Hedge Fund Tail Risk" Tobias Adrian, Markus K. Brunnermeier, and Hoai-Luu Q. Nguyen estimate the tail dependence between the major hedge fund styles, such as long/short equity and event-driven funds. They use quantile regressions to document how the return of one strategy moves with the return on another. Quantiles can explicitly compare the dependencies between normal times (50 percentile) and stress periods (5 percentile). The tail sensitivities between hedge funds increase in times of crisis, some more than doubling.

The chapter identifies seven factors that explain this tail dependence; these risk factors include the overall market excess return, a measure of volatility, and the slope of the yield curve. Because the seven factors are effectively tradeable in liquid markets, it is possible to hedge, or offload that risk, which significantly reduces tail dependence. The chapter thus provides a built-in solution to the problem it uncovers. Implementing this solution may not be easy, however. In fact, the chapter demonstrates that individual hedge fund managers have no incentive to offload the tail risk, as funds that increase their exposure to the factors also increase their returns and their assets under management. Offloading the risk then lowers both sides of managers' expected compensation (the famous 2 and 20 rule).

In "How to Calculate Systemic Risk Surcharges," Viral V. Acharya, Lasse H. Pedersen, Thomas Philippon, and Matthew Richardson take the important step of tying a specific regulation to a quantitative measure of systemic risk. They explore the implications of taxing each firm based on its contribution to systemic risk. Specifically, the tax would depend on a firm's expected loss conditional on the occurrence of a systemic crisis. Note the dual trigger: both the individual firm and the financial sector must become undercapitalized. The tax is then just the fair-value premium of insurance against this event. Although they derive the pricing for such insurance, they also examine letting the market set the price. In such a scenario, individual firms would be required to purchase contingent capital insurance, that is, insurance against the losses they incur during systemic crises. The cost of this insurance determines the firm's systemic risk tax. In a true systemic crisis, however, it is not clear that private firms would be in a position to provide the insurance. Rather, joint private-public provision of such insurance (say, 5 percent to 95 percent) lets the government piggyback on the market's superior price-setting ability. The total insurance premium, or tax, should induce the financial sector to internalize the systemic risk. A further element of the design addresses the moral hazard problem: If the firm has insurance, why should it avoid the risk? In this setting, the payoff goes not to the firm, but to the regulator. This adds a measure of precommitment to the government rescue policy.

Applying this measure of systemic risk to the recent crisis provides some encouraging results. The chapter calculates both the tax and the insurance premium for major financial firms prior to the crisis, and Bear Stearns, Lehman Brothers, Fannie Mae, and Freddie Mac show up high on the list, although AIG is prominently missing. This suggests the intriguing possibility of an early warning system, but it is an entirely different question whether the tax would have been enough to reduce systemic risk in these firms—or the market—to a manageable level. A further consideration is how this type of contingent support compares with other related proposals such as forced debt-for-equity conversions.

In "The Quantification of Systemic Risk and Stability: New Methods and Measures," Romney B. Duffey approaches the problem of predicting financial systemic risk from the standpoint of a general theory of technical systems with human involvement. Discussions about the financial crisis often borrow terminology from meteorology or other physical sciences: we hear about "hundred-year floods" or "perfect storms." The analogy can be misleading, not only because it neglects the rich analysis of risk quantification, minimization, and management within the engineering profession, but also because it ignores the human element. Among other problems, the meteorological terminology puts an undue emphasis on calendar time. In human systems, failure instead depends on experience time. Airline crashes and automobile deaths, for example, depend on miles traveled. Just what best captures the experience time for financial markets is unclear, but quite likely involves something like volume or the dollar value of transactions, and those have increased. Between 1980 and 2009, monthly trading volume on the New York Stock Exchange increased by a factor of 100, from 1 billion shares to 100 billion.

Accumulating experience has contrasting effects on the probability of major failures, sometimes known as the learning paradox. Learning reduces risk, but learning requires taking the risk and experiencing the very events you seek to avoid. As learning brings risk down to acceptable levels, there is more time for the unknown and rare events to manifest themselves. Indeed, risk often looks low before a major crisis, as the obvious problems have gotten resolved, but not enough (experience) time has passed for the new, rare problems to occur. This interaction often makes it difficult for simple statistical models to capture the distribution of losses.

A related theme is emphasized in the keynote address by Henry Hu on "Systemic Risk and Financial Innovation: Toward a 'Unified' Approach." Hu argues that a proper understanding of systemic risk requires understanding financial innovation as a process, focusing less on particular products and more on how products are invented, introduced, and diffused through the marketplace. Any fixed classification or regulatory scheme quickly becomes obsolete, both because firms find ways around regulation and because the marketplace continually evolves. Such rapid evolution makes mistakes inevitable, because learning takes time, and while that occurs, the heuristic approaches and cognitive biases of market participants have room to operate. This human element again emphasizes the dangers of taking physical models of the market too literally: a market crash, the net result of many voluntary trades, is not a meteor strike, and indeed financial markets have an element of a self-fulfilling prophecy: if everyone trades according to a price rule, that rule really works, even if it is flawed.

As an example of this evolution, Hu emphasized financial decoupling: the ability of firms to separate the economic and legal benefits and rights and obligations that standard debt and equity bundle together. For example, a fund may buy stock and obtain voting rights in a corporation, but hedge the financial exposure with offsetting credit default swaps. Conversely, selling a CDS can allow economic exposure without voting rights, and more complicated examples abound. Reckoning with such possibilities clearly requires more than even the most sophisticated economic analysis, needing a unified, interdisciplinary approach drawing on both law and economics, each situated in the proper dynamic context.

Some of the most important themes of the day arose not from the paper presentations but from the discussions, both from the assigned discussants and comments from the floor. There were philosophical discussions about what it meant to understand: in biology, the question as to why polar bears are white has an answer from an adaptive/evolutionary standpoint (they blend in with the snow) or from a developmental standpoint (which genes create white fur). Others considered the differing roles of models used for description or for prediction. Regulators from different jurisdictions considered the merits of systems that discouraged risk as opposed to early warning systems, and of deeply understanding one market versus testing across many markets. Others argued over the relative merits of different risk measures: value at risk, simple leverage, even instinctive feelings of discomfort among traders.

However, there was widespread agreement that any serious effort at managing systemic risk must begin with measurement—one cannot manage what one does not measure. In the very best tradition of the NBER, these discussions, and the analytical foundations that the following chapters have begun developing, represent an important first step in our attempt to better understand the nature of financial crisis and systemic risk.

References

Acharya, Viral, Lasse H. Pedersen, Thomas Philippon, and Matthew Richardson. 2010. "Measuring Systemic Risk." Working Paper. New York University.

Adrian, Tobias, and Markus Brunnermeier. 2010. "CoVaR." Working Paper. Princeton University.

Aumann, Robert J., and Roberto Serrano. 2008. "An Economic Index of Riskiness." *Journal of Political Economy* 116:810–36.

Basel Committee on Banking Supervision (BCBS). 2010. *Basel III: A Global Regulatory Framework for More Resilient Banks and Banking Systems.* Basel: Bank for International Settlements, December. (Revised June 2011.)

Billio, Monica, Mila Getmansky, Andrew W. Lo, and Loriana Pelizzon. 2011. "Econometric Measures of Systemic Risk in the Finance and Insurance Sectors." Working Paper. MIT Sloan School.

Borio, Claudio. 2003. "Towards a Macroprudential Framework for Financial Supervision and Regulation?" *CESifo Economic Studies* 49 (2): 181–215.

Engle, Robert. 2001. "GARCH 101: The Use of ARCH/GARCH Models in Applied Econometrics." *Journal of Economic Perspectives* 15 (4): 157–68.

Federal Reserve Bank of Cleveland (FRBC). 2010. *Putting Systemic Risk on the Radar Screen.* Annual Report. Cleveland: Federal Reserve Bank of Cleveland.

Foster, Dean P., and Sergiu Hart. 2009. "An Operational Measure of Riskiness." *Journal of Political Economy* 117:785–814.

Gorton, Gary B. 2010. *Slapped by the Invisible Hand: The Panic of 2007.* New York: Oxford University Press.

Haubrich, Joseph G. 2001. "Risk Management and Financial Crises." *Economic Commentary,* February. Cleveland: Federal Reserve Bank of Cleveland.

Kane, Edward J. 2011. "Statement on Distortions in Systemic-Risk Measurement and Risk-Taking in the Financial Sector." Financial Institutions and Consumer Protection Subcommittee, US Senate Committee on Banking, Housing and Urban Affairs, Hearing on Debt Financing in the Domestic Financial Sector, August 3.

Lo, Andrew W. 1999. "The Three P's of Total Risk Management." *Financial Analysts Journal* 1999:13–26.

Stulz, Rene M. 2010. "Credit Default Swaps and the Credit Crisis." *Journal of Economic Perspectives* 24 (1): 73–92.

Tarullo, Daniel K. 2010. "Financial Regulatory Reform." Speech at the US Monetary Policy Forum, New York, February 26.

Tufte, Edward R. 1990. *Envisioning Information.* Cheshire, CT: Graphics Press.

Systemic Risk and Financial Innovation
Toward a "Unified" Approach

Henry T. C. Hu

Introduction

Three econometricians were on a hunting trip in the wilds of Canada. It was close to lunchtime, and they were getting hungry.

The first econometrician shoots, but misses, one meter to the left.
The second econometrician shoots, but misses, one meter to the right.

Henry T. C. Hu holds the Allan Shivers Chair in the Law of Banking and Finance at the University of Texas Law School and was the inaugural director of the Division of Risk, Strategy, and Financial Innovation at the US Securities and Exchange Commission (2009–2011).

Copyright © 2012 by Henry T. C. Hu. All rights reserved. This chapter represents solely my own views as an academic and does not necessarily represent the views of the SEC, individual Commissioners, or the Commission staff. The chapter is in the loose, informal style of my keynote address at the National Bureau of Economic Research–Federal Reserve Bank of Cleveland Research Conference on Quantifying Systemic Risk (November 2009, Cambridge), delivered solely in my academic capacity. My thanks go to Dr. Joseph Haubrich, Professor Andrew Lo, Professor James Poterba, and conference participants. The chapter is also in part based on Congressional testimony prior to my arrival at the SEC (House Agriculture Committee, October 2008, and Senate Banking Committee, June 2009) and pre-SEC presentations at, among other places, the ABA Section of Business Law Spring Meeting (April 2009, Vancouver); Commissione Nazionale per le Societa' e la Borsa Seminar on Disclosure of Cash-Settled Derivatives (May 2009, Rome); Duisenberg School of Finance Business Law and Innovation Conference (May 2009, Amsterdam); George Washington Law School Conference on the Panic of 2008 (April 2009, Washington); Harvard Law School–Sloan Foundation Corporate Governance Research Conference (February 2009, Cambridge); INSOL Eighth World Quadrennial Congress (June 2009, Vancouver—via video); International Finance Corporation SOS Conference (April 2009, Istanbul); PLI—Corporate Governance: A Master Class (February 2009, New York); University of Sydney Law School's Ross Parsons Address (June 2009, Sydney); and the Vanderbilt Law School Conference on Future of Federal Regulation of Financial Markets, Corporate Governance and Shareholder Litigation (March 2009, Nashville). This chapter speaks in part as of the time of the Cambridge conference, with some updating as of late 2010/early 2011, and, as to footnote 1, as of June 2012. For acknowledgments, sources of research support, and disclosure of the author's material financial relationships, if any, please see http://www.nber.org/chapters/c12053.ack.

The third econometrician doesn't shoot at all, but shouts "We got it! We got it!"[1]

It can be difficult to come up with a good model, much less a model that actually puts food on the table. This is certainly true for coming up with good models relating to "systemic risk," a widely-used term that remains resistant to well-accepted operational meaning.[2] Given this foundational looseness, the *quantification* of systemic risk—the theme of this conference—is a daunting task indeed. A better understanding of the relationship between systemic risk and modern financial innovation may facilitate the task.

Here, there is an overarching question: *What is the proper approach for understanding this critical relationship?* This keynote address revolves around that question. I do so almost exclusively from the narrow perspective of the past writings of an academic who had been peering through the window of the candy store. Then, very briefly, I do so from the perspective of someone who had been let into that store, and become a government regulator.

I make two basic claims. First, the approach must fully consider the underlying *process* of modern financial innovation through which new financial products and strategies are invented, introduced to the marketplace, and diffused. The process has significance independent of the specific products and strategies.

---

1. See, e.g., http://orion.it.luc.edu/~twren/econioke.htm. As noted in the introduction, this chapter's call for a "unified" approach to evaluating the relationship between financial innovation and systemic risk involves two basic themes: one involving the underlying process of financial innovation and the other involving eclecticism in terms of academic disciplines and "local knowledge" of marketplace realities. Hu (2012) analyzes, among other things, the relationship between financial innovation and the disclosure paradigm that has animated the US Securities and Exchange Commission since its creation. This 2012 article shows that financial innovation has substantially undermined that disclosure paradigm, thereby affecting investor interests, corporate governance, market efficiency, and systemic risk. It also offers ways forward. The 2012 article discusses in substantially greater depth a number of the themes briefly noted in this chapter. (Among other things, the 2012 article uses the JPMorgan Chase Chief Investment Office derivatives losses that started coming to light in May 2012, as well as asset-backed securities matters, to illustrate some of that article's ideas.)

2. The International Monetary Fund has noted that:

> "Systemic risk" is a term that is widely used, but is difficult to define and quantify. Indeed, it is often viewed as a phenomenon that is there "when we see it," reflecting a sense of a broad-based breakdown in the functioning of the financial system, which is normally realized, ex post, by a large number of failures of FIs (usually banks). Similarly, a systemic episode may simply be seen as an extremely acute case of financial instability, even though the degree and severity of financial stress has proven difficult, if not impossible, to measure. Systemic risk is also defined by the breadth of its reach across institutions, markets, and countries.

See International Monetary Fund (2009, 116), and Bliss and Kaufman (2005, 16, stating that "[n]o single generally-agreed definition of what constitutes systemic risk exists"). Recently, Billio et al. (2010) referred to systemic risk as:

> A concept originally intended to describe bank runs and currency crises, but which now applies to any broad-based breakdown in the financial system. Systemic risk can be realized as a series of correlated defaults among financial institutions, occurring over a short time span and triggering a withdrawal of liquidity and widespread loss of confidence in the financial system as a whole. (1)

Second, the approach must be highly eclectic in nature, in terms of academic disciplines and in terms of "local knowledge" of marketplace realities. The academic disciplines of economics and finance may offer the central theoretical insights, but other disciplines, such as law and psychology, as well as cross-fertilization across disciplines, can be surprisingly informative. Academic disciplines, no matter the range and the cross-fertilization, may fail to provide proper directions. Indeed, the baselines may have become obsolete. In financial innovation, local knowledge, an understanding of actual marketplace practices and institutions, may shed light on the limitations of academic learning and guide that learning along more promising paths.

In short, the approach must be highly inclusive—one that comprehends the underlying innovation process and an eclecticism as to academic and local knowledge. There is need for this very rich kind of interdisciplinary analysis—what can be characterized as a "unified" approach.

I use some of my academic writings to illustrate such a unified approach in relation to financial innovation and systemic risk. First, the innovation process itself can have significance for the nature of the regulatory response to the systemic risks posed by new financial products and strategies. For instance, the innovation process can quickly overwhelm the classification-based, "cubbyhole" technique so commonly used in law and regulation, including that used in the pioneering 1988 international response to the systemic risks posed by the derivatives revolution (1989, 1991, and 1993; see next section).

Second, the unified approach can contribute to a richer understanding of the financial innovation process and the systemic risks that can arise from the process. This unified approach, for instance, nearly two decades ago yielded reasons to believe that big, "sophisticated" financial institutions may well take excessive risks and make other mistakes as to derivatives and other complex financial products. Such factors as the "inappropriability" of benefits associated with financial RTD, banker incentive structures, cognitive biases, and the peculiar nature of "financial science can undermine bank and investor decision making and lead to systemic risk." (1993; see subsection "Understanding the Innovation Process and Its Role in Systemic Risk").

Third, one particular type of innovation process—"decoupling"—has put stress on the foundational architecture of corporate governance and debt governance. This new phenomenon has consequences for corporations, individual and corporate borrowers, and possibly for the stability of the financial system at large (2006–2009; see subsection "The 'Decoupling Process'").

I conclude this address with a few very brief comments on my current role. In September 2009, Securities and Exchange Commission (SEC) Chairman Mary Schapiro appointed me the inaugural Director of the "Division of Risk, Strategy, and Financial Innovation." The first new division at the SEC in nearly four decades, "Risk Fin," was created to provide sophisticated interdisciplinary analysis across the entire spectrum of SEC activities. This fresh interdisciplinary approach, and the new academic and local knowledge skill-sets Risk Fin brought in have been used, for instance, in helping the SEC respond to, and implement the landmark 2010 Congressional legislation that finally brought OTC (over-the-counter) derivatives squarely into the regulatory fold (see "Concluding Thoughts" section).

Academia: The Unified Approach and Systemic Risk

The Innovation Process and the Use of Classifications in Law and Regulation

The usual approach to addressing regulatory matters relating to financial innovation is to look at specific new financial products. Beginning in 1989, I have emphasized that modern financial innovation consists of two components: the products, and the underlying process of financial innovation through which such products are invented, introduced to the marketplace, and diffused.[3] At its most impressive, the process has many of the characteristics commonly associated with science-based industries like biotechnology. There is heavy reliance on PhDs with highly quantitative backgrounds— called "quants," "lightbulb heads," "rocket scientists," or something entirely different when there are big losses—and a reliance on formal models laden with incomprehensible Greek letters. The process is also institutionalized, central to the competition among major financial institutions. Tinkering by generalist bankers and the occasional introduction of new financial products have given way.

In 1989, the path-breaking (first) Basel Accord governing the capital adequacy of major banks worldwide had just been adopted. Currency and interest rate swaps, the first OTC derivatives, had emerged about a decade earlier and bank exposure to such derivatives was rising rapidly. Motivated in large part by the systemic risks posed by such exposure, the Basel Accord relied on the classification-based technique so characteristic of regulation and law. Regulators, at least in the first instance, decide mechanistically the capital required to be allocated to any given derivative by applying simple rules to a limited number of facts. The amount of capital presumptively required on account of a swap is simply determined by whether it is an interest rate or a currency swap, its maturity, its notional amount, and the general nature of the swap counterparty.

My 1989 article, "Swaps, the Modern Process of Financial Innovation and the Vulnerability of a Regulatory Paradigm," suggested that this "cubbyhole" approach was bound to fail in the face of the modern process of financial innovation. As with any classification-based system, there will be an incentive to "walk the line," to try to use the rules to one's own advantage.

3. See Hu (1989).

But the financial innovation process itself causes a far more fundamental problem—administrative and political realities prevented a more complex classification system and since the diversity of financial products will grow as financial innovation continues, the system will assign improper regulatory prices with increasing frequency. The institutionalization of change, as well as the operation of a highly dynamic marketplace, will cause serious problems of regulatory obsolescence.

In theory, updating the cubbyholes in response to changing products was the answer. However, "Regulatory Paradigm" pointed out numerous obstacles, including the extraordinary informational asymmetry between regulators and derivatives dealers. Among other things, banks generally may develop an OTC derivative without any clearance from or registration with banking authorities: a regulator may not even be aware of the existence of a swap, much less how to model its risk characteristics.

To address this informational asymmetry, in a 1993 article (and in testimony before the Senate Banking Committee in June 2009, prior to arrival at the SEC), I suggested the creation of a public informational clearinghouse relating to OTC derivatives with systematic data collection and analytical responsibilities.[4] Due in large part to the lobbying efforts of the Committee to Establish the National Institute of Finance, the Dodd-Frank Wall Street Reform and Consumer Protection Act (the Dodd-Frank Act), signed on July 21, 2010, provides for the creation of an Office of Financial Research within the Treasury Department, with various informational clearinghouse and other responsibilities.[5]

The same financial innovation process that undermined the cubbyhole approach in the bank regulatory context can undermine other areas of law. For instance, noted scholars and practitioners showed the applicability of this process-cubbyhole analysis to tax law.[6] And in a 1991 article, I showed its applicability to corporate law, in particular the difficulties posed by the process to fiduciary duties owed by directors to those who are classified as "shareholders."[7]

The concluding paragraph of "Regulatory Paradigm" argued that:

> Financial regulators must develop a mechanism to deal explicitly with this underlying process. The difficulties involved in devising such a mechanism are daunting. A brief overview of one of the simplest, most incremental of possible mechanisms suggests the dimensions of the task. Unless we begin now to intensify our efforts, incremental changes may ultimately

4. See Hu (1993, 1503–08); 2009a.
5. Dodd-Frank Act, Pub. L. No. 111-203, §§ 151–153 (2010). Although said committee was kind enough to include Hu (1993) and Hu (2009b) in the listing of "Documents and Readings" on the committee's website, the author was never affiliated with the committee. See Committee to Establish the National Institute of Finance—CE-NIF Documents, http://www.ce-nif .org/background-readings.
6. See, e.g., Strnad (1994, 570, n. 2).
7. See Hu (1991, 1292–300, 1311–12).

prove insufficient to ensure the continued stability of the world financial system. (435)

It is now more than twenty years after the initial Basel Accord. The challenges identified in the 1989 article remain. In discussing reform proposals advanced in 2010, *The Economist* stated as follows:

The proposals have already been dubbed "Basel 3"—which tells you regulators have been here twice before. Alas, the record of bank capital rules is crushingly bad. The Basel regime (European and American banks use either version 1 or 2) represents a monumental, decades-long effort at perfection, with minimal capital requirements calculated from detailed formulae. The answers were precisely wrong.[8]

Understanding the Innovation Process and Its Role in Systemic Risk

Financial institutions focused solely on shareholder interests would generally take on more risk than would be socially optimal. At least in the past, governments typically constrained risk-taking at financial institutions, but not elsewhere. This stemmed, of course, from concerns over the especially large negative externalities associated with financial institutions.

In 1993, I suggested that much more than a gap between shareholder- and social-optimality would likely be involved when it came to financial institution risk taking with respect to derivatives and other complex financial products. In "Misunderstood Derivatives: The Causes of Informational Failure and the Promise of Regulatory Incrementalism,"[9] I argued that a pattern of outright mistakes, harmful to shareholders and societies alike, was likely to occur even at major, presumptively "sophisticated" entities.

Why? From the standpoint of psychology, I discussed how cognitive biases might explain underproduction of information relevant to certain kinds of risks, especially legal ones. From the standpoints of marketplace realities and principal-agency theory, I showed how analysis that would normally imply excessive managerial aversion to risk taking could, when applied to the specific OTC derivatives context associated with complex banking organizations, lead to excessive risk taking even from the standpoint of diversified shareholders. From the standpoint of the law and economics of technological change, I applied "inappropriability" and other theories pertaining to commercial scientific research to illuminate allocative problems arising from the financial innovation production process. From the standpoint of traditional scientific norms, I showed how departures of financial "science" from such norms undermined decision making. I offered some possible responses.

I argued that one factor contributing to mistakes is cognitive bias in the derivatives modeling process. Humans often rely on cognitive shortcuts to solve complex problems. Sometimes these shortcuts are irrational.

8. See *The Economist* (2010a).
9. Hu (1993, *supra* note 4).

For instance, one of the cognitive biases undermining derivatives models is the tendency to ignore low-probability catastrophic events.[10] Psychologists theorize that individuals do not worry about an event unless the probability of the event is perceived to be above some critical threshold. The effect may be caused by individuals' inability to comprehend and evaluate extreme probabilities, or by a lack of any direct experience. This effect manifests itself in attitudes toward tornadoes, safety belts, and earthquake insurance.

The 1993 article suggested that in the derivatives context, rocket scientists are sometimes affirmatively encouraged, as a matter of model design, to ignore low-probability states of the world. I also showed how this tendency, along with other cognitive biases, may cause risks of a legal nature to be ignored. Rocket scientists are expert in all manner of financial risks and their quantification. Law itself is unfamiliar turf, and no rich tradition of incorporating legal risks into derivatives modeling exists. Under such circumstances, "expert" and "availability" effects are given a free hand to inhibit proper consideration of legal risks.

The foregoing relates to irrational behavior in connection with the innovation process that can contribute to decision-making errors. Behavior that is fully rational on the part of the humans involved in the process—responding to the incentive structure actually in the marketplace—contributes as well.

I also showed how the complexities associated with a bank's organization can cause excessive risk taking. One contributing factor is the fact that the incentive structure can be highly asymmetric in the derivatives industry.[11] True success—or the perception by superiors of success—can lead to enormous wealth. Failure or perceived failure may normally result, at most, in job and reputational losses. Thus, there may be serious temptations for the rocket scientist to emphasize the rewards and downplay the risks of particular derivatives activities to superiors, especially since the superiors may sometimes not be as financially sophisticated (and loathe to admit this). Moreover, the material risk exposures on certain derivatives can sometimes occur years after entering into the transaction. Given the turnover in the derivatives industry, the "negatives" may arise long after the rocket scientist is gone. The rocket scientist may have an especially short-term view of the risks and returns of his activities. Principal-agent issues within the bank organization abound here, and can lead to *too much* risk-taking from the standpoint of diversified shareholders, rather than *too little,* as may be the general case in normal situations.

The 1993 article also considered the inability to capture—to fully appropriate the benefits of their financial research and development.[12] The nature of the intellectual property law regime, and related legal and marketplace

---

10. Ibid., 1487–92. This 1993 discussion of this cognitive bias and its applicability to finance substantially predated writings of the related matter of "black swans."
11. Hu (1993, *supra* note 4, 1492–94 and 1512–13).
12. Ibid., 1481–87.

factors, effectively precluded this. This inappropriability could lead to the failure to devote enough resources to fully understand the risks and returns of these products.

More importantly, the peculiar nature of financial science at the heart of the innovation process also contributes to difficulties, for both financial institutions themselves as well as for regulators.[13] This matter goes beyond the "precisely wrong" tendency of financial science to fail exactly when it may matter most: in chaotic market conditions, the liquidity and other assumptions underlying the models do not hold.

Among other things, financial science departs radically from violations of the traditional scientific norm of "universalism." This raises profound questions as to the "true" value of complex financial products. Robert K. Merton, the great sociologist, suggested that "universalism" is that the truth of claims should be determined through the application of impersonal criteria without regard to the source's personal, social, or other attributes. As an example, Merton stated that "The Haber process cannot be invalidated by a Nuremberg decree nor can an Anglophobe repeal the law of gravitation" (1973, 270).

"Misunderstood Derivatives" suggested that the univeralism imperative did not entirely apply to financial science. The predictive power of any model depends on who is doing the thinking and on what others actually think of the thinker. This lack of universalism may be especially troublesome when a bank is a substantial factor in an esoteric product. For instance:

> If a derivatives dealer who dominates the market for a given derivative thinks a particular model is suitable for valuing that derivative, then his identity is relevant. Even if the model is seriously flawed as a theoretical matter, his importance alone makes the model at least temporarily relevant. Moreover, should the dealer decide to withdraw from the market for that derivative, liquidity may dry up and the pure "theoretical" value may be particularly irrelevant. There is no Mertonian universalism here. The impact of this is likely to be especially severe as to the more arcane instruments and products dominated by a few dealers and in chaotic market conditions.[14]

In view of my present role at the SEC, I will only sketch in very broad terms some of the ways in which the 1993 article may relate to, or explain, some subsequent developments in the real world. Others have been kind enough to intimate that the overarching thesis that "sophisticated" capital market participants were prone to make mistakes as to derivatives and other complex products foreshadowed the 1998 collapse of Long Term Capital Management[15] and matters associated with the current global financial crisis, including the near-collapse of the American International Group (AIG) in

---

13. Ibid., *supra* note 5, 1476–81 and 1496–502. See also Lo and Mueller (2010).

14. Hu (1993, *supra* note 4, 1501).

15. Roger Lowenstein was kind enough to use an extract from "Misunderstood Derivatives" as the epigraph to his classic book, *When Genius Failed: The Rise and Fall of Long-Term Capital Management* (2000).

2008.[16] And matters such as the inappropriability problem may be a factor in the excessive reliance on credit ratings in securitizations and inadequate due diligence.[17] Cognitive biases such as the tendency to ignore low probability/catastrophic events appear to have been demonstrated repeatedly during the global financial crisis. Departures from Mertonian universalism may help make more understandable current controversies over distinctions among mark-to-market, mark-to-model, and mark-to-myth.[18] In 2010, the points made in the incentive structure analysis in "Misunderstood Derivatives" were characterized by financial academics as "hardly mainstream" in 1993, but "[n]ow . . . arguably define the ground on which the debate takes place."[19] Concerns over banker incentive structures have motivated disclosure and substantive regulatory responses worldwide over the past year, including in the Dodd-Frank Act.

The "Decoupling" Process, the Foundational Architecture of Corporate Governance and "Debt Governance," and Systemic Risk

The foundational architecture of corporate law and finance—equity and debt—used to be clear.

Ownership of equity conveyed a package of economic rights, voting rights, and other rights. Such ownership also carried with it various obligations, such as disclosure obligations.

Similarly, ownership of debt conveyed a package of rights and obligations. A holder of debt had, for instance, economic rights (such as the right to principal and interest), the control rights given by contract (such as in the loan agreement or the bond indenture), and other legal rights (such as those flowing from bankruptcy, corporate, and securities law).

That is, classic understandings of *equity* and *debt* contemplated bundled packages of rights and obligations.

In a series of articles where I was the lead or sole author, I suggested that a new "decoupling" process had emerged. Because of rocket scientists, hedge funds, and other factors, one can easily break up these equity and debt packages, quickly and on a massive scale. And beyond equity decoupling and debt decoupling, there could also be hybrid decoupling across equity and debt categories.[20]

Consider, first, the decoupling process on the equity side, the simplest of these three basic types, and the subject of the initial May 2006 article.[21] And

16. See, e.g., Scannell (2010a, C1), For a brief, pre-SEC analysis of the possible applicability of cognitive bias and other factors identified in Hu (1993) might apply to AIG, see Hu (2009b, *supra* note 5).

17. For a pre-SEC analysis of this, see Hu (2009b, *supra* note 5).

18. As to the distinctions, see, e.g., Mizen (2008) and Sunder (2009).

19. See Bolton, Kogut, and Puschra (2010, 5).

20. See Hu and Black (2008a), available at http://www.efmaefm.org/eufm_450_corrected.pdf.

21. See Hu and Black (2006), available at http://ssrn.com/abstract=904004. Subsequent articles focusing on the equity decoupling side include: Hu and Black (2007), nearly final draft available at http://ssrn.com/abstract=874098; Hu and Black (2008b), available at http://ssrn.com/abstract=1030721.

I will just focus on one example of equity decoupling, the example the article dubbed "empty voting." I leave aside other examples of equity decoupling, including an example dubbed "hidden (morphable) ownership."[22]

Corporate governance, at almost all companies, is based on a proportional relationship between the number of shares held and shareholder voting rights. In other words, one share-one vote. All existing theories of corporate governance are based on this coupling of economic interest and voting power.

Today, however, the voting rights you have no longer need to depend on the economic stake you have. There is a variety of techniques for accomplishing this.[23] One way is to simply buy a lot of shares, and then hedge that exposure. You can buy 1,000,000 shares, and thus have 1,000,000 votes. Simultaneously, you can buy lots of put options. You still have 1,000,000 votes, but you may only have the economic equivalent of, say, 200,000 shares. This type of voter, we called an "empty voter": the votes have been emptied of a corresponding economic interest.[24]

Or consider an extreme type of empty voter. If you buy enough put options, you may actually have a *negative* economic interest. You could literally have a situation where the person who holds the highest number of votes could have a negative economic interest. That person may not use his votes as a monitoring device to make sure that the company does well, but may try instead to use his votes so that the company does badly. He may want to vote Inspector Clouseau or Maxwell Smart to the board.

The decoupling process on the debt side is more directly related to systemic risk matters that are the focus of this conference.[25] Let's begin with debt decoupling in the context of individual corporate borrowers.

Here the issues correspond to those on the equity decoupling side. On the equity decoupling side, I just referred to an "empty voter." That is, a shareholder by, for instance, buying equity derivatives, can have control rights—the vote—and yet have relatively little or no economic exposure.

Similarly, a creditor, by buying credit derivatives, can have control rights and also have little or no economic exposure. In August 2007, I coined the term "empty creditor" to refer to this scenario.

---

22. This hidden (morphable) ownership issue was first litigated in the United States in CSX Corp. v. Children's Investment Fund Management, 562 F. Supp. 2d 511 (S.D.N.Y. 2008), *aff'd in part, vacated in part, and remanded in part*, 654 F.3d 276 (2d Cir. 2011). See, e.g., Norris (2008, C1). For examples of types of equity decoupling other than empty voting and hidden (morphable) ownership, see Hu and Black (2008b, *supra* note 21, at Part V).

23. For instance, in the United Kingdom, Laxey, a hedge fund, used the stock lending market to engage in empty voting in relation to British Land. See Hu and Black (2006, *supra* note 21); and Scannell (2007, A1).

24. Although perhaps counterintuitive, as the decoupling articles cited in *supra* note 21 suggest, empty voting can, under certain circumstances, improve corporate governance.

25. Some of the key articles that address decoupling on the debt side are Hu and Westbrook (2007) available at http://papers.ssrn.com/sol3/papers.cfm?abstract_id=977582, Hu and Black (2008b, *supra* note 21); Hu and Black, (2008a, *supra* note 20); Hu (2009a, A13), online version available at http://online.wsj.com/article/SB123933166470307811.html.

One simple way of becoming an empty creditor is to take the long side of a credit default swap. But there are other coupled assets that the creditor could use. For instance, it could engage in strategies involving a company's shares (such as buying put options on the shares or taking the short side of equity swaps) or use related nonhost asset strategies (such as holding long or short positions in the shares or the debt of the company's competitors).

On the equity side, one can have an empty voter-with-a-negative-economic-interest. Similarly, on the debt side, creditors can also have control and legal rights, and yet have net negative economic exposure to the firm. For instance, a creditor could hold $100 million in loans or bonds, but have a credit default swap in the notional amount of $200 million.

What might some of the systemic risk effects be? Let me discuss a few. Both loan agreements as well as bankruptcy laws are premised on the assumption that creditors have an economic interest in the company's success and will behave accordingly. Thus, a troubled borrower may anticipate that its creditor may well agree to waive certain debt covenants because of the creditor's interest in the borrower's survival.

But empty creditors may act in ways inconsistent with these assumptions. A creditor with a negative economic ownership may have incentives that correspond to their equity counterparts. These creditors may seek to reduce the value of the debt class they hold as a formal matter. These creditors may oppose an out-of-court restructuring because they might prefer that the company fail (and thus trigger payments on its credit default swap positions). Even a creditor with zero, rather than negative, economic ownership may want a bankruptcy filing because such a filing may trigger an immediate contractual payoff in its credit default swap position.

Under such circumstances, the weakened incentives to help a debtor stay out of bankruptcy may contribute to systemic risk. This is to be distinguished from the issue of the overall impact of credit default swaps on the lending market or on systemic risk, matters beyond the intended scope of the analysis.

And if empty crediting is hidden, the problem gets worse. There is a problem of hidden nonownership or hidden noninterest. Outside of bankruptcy, a struggling company is in the dark as to the true incentives of its lender.

And in bankruptcy, disclosure and substantive complications can arise as well. In bankruptcy, when the voting rights of creditors depart from their economic exposure, proper decision making can sometimes be undermined. This gap can happen when the creditor's true economic stake is unclear. Problems with the efficient resolution of companies in bankruptcies can, in turn, sometimes pose systemic risk concerns.

In sum, debt decoupling, both in its substantive and disclosure aspects, can thus undermine what one can refer to as debt governance—the relationship between creditors and debtors, both in and outside of bankruptcy proceedings. This can raise systemic risk concerns.

Consider, for instance, the possibility of an empty creditor issue having occurred in connection with one of the signal events of the current global financial crisis—the bailout of AIG.

In an April 2009 *Wall Street Journal* op-ed, written prior to my arrival at the SEC,[26] I pointed to what may be referred to as *The Curious Incident of the Bank That Didn't Bark.* On September 16, 2008, as AIG was being bailed out, Goldman Sachs said its exposure to AIG was "not material." But on March 15, 2009, AIG disclosed that it had turned over to Goldman $7 billion of the federal bailout funds that AIG received.

The op-ed suggested that one reason Goldman Sachs did not express alarm in September was that it was an empty creditor. Having hedged its economic exposure to AIG with credit default swaps from "large financial institutions," Goldman had lessened concerns over the fate of AIG. Yet Goldman had control rights associated with the contracts that it had entered into with AIG (including rights to demand collateral). Perhaps not surprisingly, Goldman was apparently aggressive in calling for collateral from AIG—nothwithstanding the possible impact on AIG's solvency and the consequences for systemic risk.[27]

Recently, both Sheila Bair, the Chairman of the Federal Deposit Insurance Corporation, and Gary Gensler, Chairman of the Commodity Futures and Trading Commission Chairman, explicitly raised concerns as to empty creditor incentives.[28] In contrast, the International Swaps and Derivatives Association is more skeptical.

The foregoing debt decoupling discussion relates to the single borrower situation.

But debt decoupling relating to the multiple borrower context may also

---

26. Hu, 2009a, *supra* note 25. I emphasize that I have not here attempted to update the analysis in the op-ed. I do not mean to suggest here in any way the accuracy of the April 2009 op-ed, or other matters relating to the Goldman-AIG relationship, including subsequent reports such as Morgenson and Story (2010, A1).

27. I did not in any way suggest that Goldman did anything improper, and noted that Goldman had obligations to its own shareholders.

28. Chairman Bair stated:

> Well, I think this is, the empty creditor issue. . . . What kind of skewed incentives does the CDS market, the credit default swap market in particular, have [on] creditors of institutions when they start to get into trouble? Traditionally, if an institution starts to get into trouble, their creditors will work with them to restructure the debt, to stabilize them, to keep them out of bankruptcy.
>
> But if you have a large CDS position, even you might have some debt exposure, if you're to make more on our CDS if the institution fails, it can create very skewed incentives. (Bair 2010)

Chairman Gensler stated:

> Bondholders and creditors who have CDS protection that exceeds their actual credit exposure may thus benefit more from the underlying company's bankruptcy than if the underlying company succeeds. These parties, sometimes called "empty creditors," might have an incentive to force a company into default or bankruptcy. (Gensler 2010)

For views of others, see, e.g., *The Economist* (2009) and Mengle (2009).

raise systemic risk concerns. Consider the securitization process. By 2008, the moral hazard, informational asymmetry, modeling risk, and credit ratings agency concerns associated with securitization, and the consequent impact on systemic risk, had become familiar. Associated terms such as "skin in the game" came to be commonly used.

However, at that time, the role of debt decoupling as an additional way securitization might perhaps contribute to systemic risk was not part of the dialogue.[29] Consider the days before securitization. If a homeowner is having financial difficulties, he can approach his local banker—picture Jimmy Stewart in the film *It's a Wonderful Life*—and seek to renegotiate the terms of his mortgage. In many situations, such a loan modification may be better both for the borrower and for the creditor. There is a dynamic relationship between debtors and creditors, one sensitive to changing financial conditions and individual circumstances.

If, however, a loan has been securitized, such a dynamic debt governance system becomes difficult. The servicing agent holds the control rights, but has limited rights to modify the loan. In addition, since servicers typically have almost no ownership stake, they may have very little incentive to do so. The tranche holders usually have decision rights, but the economic interests of the tranches can differ widely. Tranche warfare is inevitable.

Thus the relationship between debtors and creditors may tend to get "frozen"; readjustments of the relationship between debtors and creditors may be difficult. If this issue involves just one or two debtors and creditors, there are no systemic risk concerns. But if there are thousands of debtors and creditors, the undermining of flexible "debt governance" through debt decoupling might contribute to systemic risk.

Concluding Thoughts: Risk Fin, Financial Innovation, and Systemic Risk

The SEC had long operated in large part through four "Divisions": the Division of Corporation Finance (handling such matters as public offerings), the Division of Enforcement (handling such matters as insider trading and fraud cases), the Division of Investment Management (handling such matters as mutual funds and closed-end frauds), and the Division of Trading and Markets (handling such matters as the stock exchanges and broker-dealers).[30] Substantially all of the professional staff at these divisions, as at the SEC as a whole, are traditional lawyers. At the initiative of then-Chairman Roderick Hills, the first professional economists of the modern era arrived at the SEC in the mid-1970s. As of August 2009, the SEC's economists were in organizational units called the

---

29. How the debt decoupling aspects of securitization may contribute to systemic risk was first set out in Hu & Black, 2008a, *supra* note 20.

30. This section relies in part on Hu (2011).

Office of Economic Analysis (OEA) and the Office of Risk Assessment (ORA).

In September 2009, the SEC created the Division of Risk, Strategy, and Financial Innovation, the first new division since 1972. Chairman Schapiro was kind enough to ask me to be Risk Fin's inaugural director. Concurrent with its creation, OEA and ORA became components of Risk Fin and so all staff at these two units (including the SEC's Chief Economist) immediately became part of my Risk Fin staff. With Risk Fin's subsequent adoption of an organizational structure consistent with its broad mandate, the OEA and ORA units disappeared, having been fully merged into the division. Shortly afterward, Risk Fin welcomed all of the financial data processing and analysis (e.g., "EDGAR") experts at the SEC's Office of Interactive Disclosure.

Risk Fin's overarching goal is to provide sophisticated, interdisciplinary analysis across the entire spectrum of SEC activities. In its think tank and other roles, Risk Fin is involved in policymaking, rule-making, enforcement, and examinations. Its responsibilities cover three broad areas: risk and economic analysis, strategic research, and financial innovation.

The SEC had excellent economists. But because of Risk Fin's broad, ambitious mandate, it needed to add to existing skill sets and try to deepen the bench. And, importantly, it had to do so within very severe SEC budgetary constraints. Risk Fin hired individuals who had financial, quantitative, and transactional experience in (i.e., local knowledge of) corporate governance, derivatives, risk management, and trading at major hedge funds, investment banks, and law firms. Moreover, Risk Fin hired individuals with advanced academic training in additional disciplines, including mathematics. Some Risk Fin staff had both local knowledge and a PhD. Some outside observers appear to have noticed the changes. *The Economist,* for example, has stated that this new division is "packed with heavyweight thinkers."[31]

To further cross-fertilization within Risk Fin, collaboration across disciplines and work experiences were encouraged. And, in terms of the SEC as a whole, Chairman Schapiro has talked about the division's role in "bor[ing] through the silos that for too long have compartmentalized and limited the impact of [the SECs] institutional expertise" and stated that Risk Fin "already is proving crucial to the mission of the agency, and will continue to do so."[32]

Risk Fin has been involved in a wide variety of matters relating to financial innovation and systemic risk. Most notably perhaps, Risk Fin has been actively involved in connection with the landmark Congressional efforts to bring the largely unregulated OTC derivatives market into the regulatory fold.[33] Though the OTC market only emerged about thirty years ago, at $490

31. See *The Economist* (2010b); Norris (2010, B1); Scannell (2010a, *supra* note 16).
32. See Schapiro (2010).
33. See, e.g., Hu (2009c).

trillion dollars in notional amount terms (as of June 2009), the market is no longer a sideshow. Now that the Dodd-Frank Act has passed, Risk Fin has been working closely with others at the SEC in trying to implement the legislative mandates. Matters such as clearinghouses for OTC derivatives, the regulation of OTC market participants, and hedge fund regulation, are central to the future of financial innovation and systemic risk.

Risk Fin has also been heavily involved in financial innovation and systemic risk matters outside of this derivatives legislation context. These include efforts relating to the asset-backed securities, hedge funds, and money market funds that help make up the "shadow banking system" at the root of many current systemic risk concerns. Its computer, economic, quantitative, and local knowledge expertise contributed to analysis of securitization matters, even prior to the Dodd-Frank Act.[34] Risk Fin and our SEC colleagues have worked closely with the UK Financial Services Authority with respect to hedge funds, including the gathering and sharing of information.[35] Risk Fin has worked with our Division of Investment Management colleagues on recent disclosure and substantive reforms with respect to regulation of money market funds.[36]

Risk Fin has also been involved in other matters that some believe implicate systemic risk issues. These include pension funding, disclosure, and other issues relating to the state of municipal securities markets.[37] Issues relating to high frequency trading and other innovative trading strategies have been decidedly more high tech in nature; Risk Fin staff contributed to a pertinent "concept release" issued on January 21, 2010,[38] and to both of the joint CFTC-SEC (Commodity Futures Training Commission-Securities and Exchange Commission) reports issued in the wake of the subsequent May 6 "flash crash."

Some financial innovation issues do not have obvious systemic risk implications, but are nevertheless important. Risk Fin has contributed to the SEC's most comprehensive review of the shareholder voting infrastructure in thirty years, especially with respect to the review's "empty voting"-related aspects.[39] In the enforcement context, it has worked on such matters as credit derivatives-based insider trading litigation.

Both those in academia and those in government have problems coming up with good models. As an academic, I have been interested in the multidimensional relationship between financial innovation and systemic risk. As a government technocrat, I am enormously appreciative of Chairman

34. See, e.g., Securities and Exchange Commission (2010a).
35. See, e.g., SEC (2010f), available at http://www.sec.gov/news/press/2010/2010-17.htm.
36. See, e.g., SEC (2010e).
37. See, e.g., SEC (2010g), transcript, available at http://www.sec.gov/spotlight/municipal securities/092110transcript.txt.
38. SEC (2010b).
39. See, e.g., SEC (2010c); Scannell (2010b, C3).

Schapiro having been kind enough to say that, with Risk Fin, the SEC has been set "on a new path," and that "[i]nterdisciplinary thinking is no longer a novelty at the SEC.[40]

I believe that a very comprehensive form of interdisciplinary approach, what I've referred to as the "unified approach," is necessary in approaching issues involving financial innovation and systemic risk, in academic thinking as well as in governmental regulation. Risk Fin is, and hopefully will always be, a work in progress, one as dynamic as today's capital markets.

Let's go back to those three hunters in the wilds of Canada. With either the academic or governmental hat on, if you ever hear me shouting, "We got it! We got it!", I ask that you approach me with the appropriate degree of skepticism.

References

Bair, Sheila. 2010. "Testimony, Hearing of the Financial Crisis Inquiry Commission—Part I." *Federal News Service,* January 14.

Billio, Monica, Mila Getmansky, Andrew W. Lo, and Loriana Pelizzon. 2010. "Measuring Systemic Risk in the Finance and Insurance Sectors." MIT Sloan School Working Paper 4774-10.

Bliss, Robert R., and George G. Kaufman. 2005. "Derivatives and Systemic Risk: Netting, Collateral, and Closeout." Federal Reserve Bank of Chicago, Working Paper 2005-03. May 10.

Bolton, Patrick, Bruce Kogut, and Werner Puschra. 2010. "Governance, Executive Compensation, and Excessive Risk in the Financial Services Industry." Executive summary of research symposium presented by the Friedrich-Ebert-Stiftung and the Sanford C. Bernstein & Co. Center at Columbia Business School, New York. May 28–29.

Campbell, Alexander. 2011. "The Fin Man." *Risk Magazine,* January.

Committee to Establish the National Institute of Finance. *CE-NIF Documents.* Available from http://www.ce-nif.org/background-readings/.

CSX Corp. v. Children's Investment Fund Management. 562 F. Supp. 2d 511 (S.D.N.Y. 2008), *aff'd in part, vacated in part, and remanded in part,* 654 F.3d 276 (2d Cir. 2011).

Dodd-Frank Wall Street Reform and Consumer Protection Act. 2010. Public Law 111-203. Washington, DC: GPO.

The Economist. 2009. "CDSs and Bankruptcy." June 20.

———. 2010a. "Base Camp Basel: Reforming Banking." January 23.

———. 2010b. "Fingers in the Dike—What Regulators Should Do Now." February 13.

Gensler, Gary. 2010. "Keynote Address." Markit's Outlook for OTC Derivatives Markets Conference. March 9.

Hu, Henry T. C. 1989. "Swaps, the Modern Process of Financial Innovation, and

40. See SEC (2010d), available at http://www.sec.gov/news/press/2010/2010-226.htm, on my anticipated return to academia in 2011; and Campbell (2011, 132).

the Vulnerability of a Regulatory Paradigm." *University of Pennsylvania Law Review* 138 (2): 333–435.

———. 1991. "New Financial Products, the Modern Process of Financial Innovation, and the Puzzle of Shareholder Welfare." *Texas Law Review* 69:1273–317.

———. 1993. "Misunderstood Derivatives: The Causes of Informational Failure and the Promise of Regulatory Incrementalism." *Yale Law Journal* 102 (6): 1457–513.

———. 2009a. "'Empty Creditors' and the Crisis—How Goldman's $7 Billion Was Not 'Material.'" *Wall Street Journal,* April 10.

———. 2009b. "The Modern Process of Financial Innovation and The Regulation of OTC Derivatives—OTC Derivatives: Modernizing Oversight to Increase Transparency and Reduce Risks." US Senate Banking Committee—Subcommittee on Securities, Insurance, and Investment. Testimony, June 21.

———. 2009c. "Testimony Concerning the Over-the-Counter Derivatives Market Act of 2009." The House Committee on Financial Services. Testimony, October 7.

———. 2011. "Keynote Address: The SEC, Dodd-Frank, and Modern Capital Markets." *New York University Journal of Law and Business* 7 (2): 427–37.

———. 2012. "Too Complex to Depict? Innovation, 'Pure Information,' and the SEC Disclosure Paradigm." *Texas Law Review* 90:1601–715. http://papers.ssrn.com/abstract=2083708.

Hu, Henry T. C., and Bernard Black. 2006. "The New Vote Buying: Empty Voting and Hidden (Morphable) Ownership." *Southern California Law Review* 79: 811–908.

———. 2007. "Hedge Funds, Insiders, and the Decoupling of Economic and Voting Ownership: Empty Voting and Hidden (Morphable) Ownership." *Journal of Corporate Finance* 13:343–67.

———. 2008a. "Debt, Equity, and Hybrid Decoupling: Governance and Systemic Risk Implications." *European Financial Management* 14 (4): 663–709.

———. 2008b. "Equity and Debt Decoupling and Empty Voting II: Importance and Extensions." *University of Pennsylvania Law Review* 156:625–739.

Hu, Henry T. C., and Jay Lawrence Westbrook. 2007. "Abolition of the Corporate Duty to Creditors." *Columbia Law Review* 107:1321–403.

International Monetary Fund. 2009. *Global Financial Stability Report: Responding to the Financial Crisis and Measuring Systemic Risk.* April. Washington, DC: IMF.

Lo, Andrew W., and Mark T. Mueller. 2010. "WARNING: Physics Envy May Be Hazardous to Your Wealth!" Draft of March 19, MIT Sloan School of Management and MIT's Center for Theoretical Physics.

Lowenstein, Roger. 2000. *When Genius Failed: The Rise and Fall of Long-Term Capital Management.* New York: Random House.

Mengle, David. 2009. "The Empty Creditor Hypothesis." *ISDA Research Notes* No. 3.

Mizen, Paul. 2008. "The Credit Crunch of 2007–2008: A Discussion of the Background, Market Reactions, and Policy Responses." *Review—Federal Reserve Bank of St. Louis,* September/October.

Morgenson, Gretchen, and Louise Story. 2010. "Quiet Conflict with Goldman Helped Push AIG to Precipice—Questions of Bank's Role in Fall of Insurer." *New York Times,* February 7.

Norris, Floyd. 2008. "Hedge Funds Can Vote at CSX Meeting." *New York Times,* June 12.

———. 2010. "A Window Opens on Pay for Bosses." *New York Times,* January 15.

Scannell, Kara. 2007. "How Borrowed Shares Swing Votes." *Wall Street Journal,* January 26.

―――. 2010a. "At SEC, Scholar Who Saw It Coming." *Wall Street Journal,* January 25.

―――. 2010b. "SEC Delves into 'Proxy Plumbing': Biggest Review in 30 Years Puts Empty Voting, Adviser Conflicts, Other Issues under the Microscope." *Wall Street Journal,* July 15.

Schapiro, Mary L. 2010. "Testimony before the Subcommittee on Financial Services and General Government." House Committee on Appropriations. March 17.

Securities and Exchange Commission (SEC). 2010a. "Asset-Backed Securities." SEC Release No. 33-9117, 2010 SEC Lexis 1493, May 3.

―――. 2010b. "Concept Release on Equity Market Structure." SEC Release 34-61358, 2010 SEC Lexis 334, January 21.

―――. 2010c. "Concept Release on the US Proxy System." SEC Release No. 34-62495, 2010 SEC Lexis 2407, July 22.

―――. 2010d. "Henry T. C. Hu, Inaugural Director of Division of Risk, Strategy, and Financial Innovation to Return to University of Texas." SEC Press Release 2010-226, November 18.

―――. 2010e. "Money Market Fund Reform." SEC Release No. IC-29132, 2010 SEC Lexis 462. February 23.

―――. 2010f. "SEC and UK FSA Hold Fifth Meeting of the SEC-FSA Strategic Dialogue." SEC Press Release 2010-17, February 1.

―――. 2010g. "Securities and Exchange Commission Field Hearing on the State of the Municipal Securities Market." San Francisco, CA, September 21.

Strnad, Jeff. 1994. "Taxing New Financial Products: A Conceptual Framework." *Stanford Law Review* 46 (3): 569–605.

Sunder, Shyam. 2009. "IFRS and the Accounting Consensus." *Accounting Horizons* 23 (1): 101–11.

Liquidity Risk, Cash Flow Constraints, and Systemic Feedbacks

Sujit Kapadia, Mathias Drehmann, John Elliott,
and Gabriel Sterne

1.1 Introduction

The global financial crisis has served to reiterate the central role of liquidity risk in banking. Such a role has been understood at least since Bagehot (1873). This chapter develops a framework that promotes an understanding of the triggers and system dynamics of liquidity risk during periods of financial instability and illustrates these effects in a quantitative model of systemic risk.

The starting point of our analysis is the observation that although the failure of a financial institution may reflect solvency concerns, it often manifests itself through a crystallization of funding liquidity risk. In a world with perfect information and capital markets, banks would only fail if their

Sujit Kapadia is a senior economist at the Bank of England. Mathias Drehmann is a senior economist in the Monetary and Economic Department of the Bank for International Settlements. John Elliott is a senior manager at Pricewaterhouse Coopers LLP (the UK firm). Gabriel Sterne is director and economist at Exotix Limited.

This research was undertaken when John Elliott, Sujit Kapadia, and Gabriel Sterne all worked at the Bank of England, and when Mathias Drehmann worked at the Bank of England and the Bank for International Settlements. The views expressed in this chapter are those of the authors, and not necessarily those of the Bank of England, Financial Policy Committee members, the Bank for International Settlements, or of any other entities above.

We are grateful to the following people who have provided valuable contributions and comments: David Aikman, Piergiorgio Alessandri, Niki Anderson, Richard Barwell, Emily Beau, Geoff Coppins, Jason Dowson, Bruno Eklund, Prasanna Gai, Harry Goodacre, Simon Hall, Andy Haldane, Joseph Haubrich, Andrew Lo, Elizabeth Martin, Emma Mattingley, Will Kerry, Nada Mora, Emma Murphy, Mikhail Oet, James Purchase, Matthew Willison, and two anonymous referees. We would also like to thank seminar participants at the Bank of England and the NBER-Federal Reserve Bank of Cleveland Research Conference on Quantifying Systemic Risk (Cambridge, November 6, 2009) for helpful comments and suggestions. For acknowledgments, sources of research support, and disclosure of the authors' material financial relationships, if any, please see http://www.nber.org/chapters/c12049.ack.

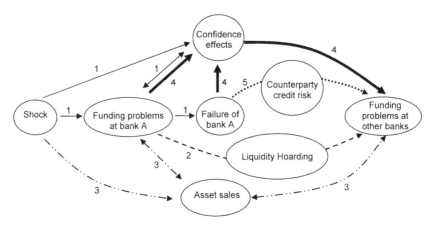

Fig. 1.1   Funding crises in a system-wide context

underlying fundamentals rendered them insolvent. In such a world, provided valuations are appropriate (e.g., adjusted to reflect prospective losses), then examining the stock asset and liability positions would determine banks' health, and solvent banks would always be able to finance random liquidity demands by borrowing, for example, from other financial institutions. In reality, informational frictions and imperfections in capital markets mean that banks may find it difficult to obtain funding if there are concerns about their solvency, regardless of whether or not those concerns are substantiated. In such funding crises, the stock solvency constraint no longer fully determines survival; what matters is whether banks have sufficient cash inflows, including income from asset sales and new borrowing, to cover all cash outflows. In other words, the cash flow constraint becomes critical.

The lens of the cash flow constraint also makes it possible to assess how banks' defensive actions during a funding liquidity crisis may affect the rest of the financial system. Figure 1.1 provides a stylized overview of the transmission mechanisms. For simplicity, it is assumed that the crisis starts with a negative shock leading to funding problems at one bank (bank A). The nature of the shock can be manifold—for example, it could be a negative earnings shock leading to a deterioration of the bank's solvency position or a reputational shock. After funding problems emerge, confidence in bank A may deteriorate further, either endogenously or linked to concerns about the shock (channel 1 in figure 1.1).

In an attempt to stave off a liquidity crisis, the distressed bank may take defensive actions, with possible systemic effects (channels 2 and 3). For instance, it may hoard liquidity. Initially, it may be likely to start hoarding (future) liquidity by shortening the maturities of the interbank market loans it provides. This is advantageous to bank A as shorter-term loans can be realized more quickly and hence may be used as a buffer to potential liquidity shocks. More extremely, the distressed bank could also cut the provision of interbank loans completely, raising liquidity directly. Both these actions could create or intensify funding problems at other banks that were relying on the distressed bank for funding (channel 2). The distressed bank could also sell assets, which could depress market prices, potentially causing distress at other banks because of mark-to-market losses or margin calls (channel 3). In addition, funding problems could also spread via confidence contagion, whereby market participants decide to run on banks just because they look similar to bank A (channel 4) and, in the event of bank failure, through interbank market contagion via counterparty credit risk (channel 5).

The main innovation of this chapter is to provide a quantitative framework showing how shocks to fundamentals may interact with funding liquidity risk and potentially generate contagion that can spread across the financial system. In principle, one might wish to construct a formal forecasting framework for predicting funding crises and their spread. But it is difficult to estimate the stochastic nature of cash flow constraints because of the binary, nonlinear nature of liquidity risk, and because liquidity crises in developed countries have been (until recently) rare events, so data are limited. Instead, we rely on a pragmatic approach and construct plausible rules of thumb and heuristics. These are based on a range of sources, including behavior observed during crises. This carries the advantage that it provides for a flexible framework that can capture a broad range of features and contagion channels of interest. Such flexibility can help to make the model more relevant for practical risk assessment, as it can provide a benchmark for assessing overall systemic risk given a range of solvency and liquidity shocks.

Our modeling approach disentangles the problem into distinct steps. First, we introduce a "danger zone" approach to model how shocks affect individual banks' funding liquidity risk. This approach is simple and transparent (yet subjective) as we assume that certain funding markets close if the danger zone score crosses particular thresholds. The danger zone score, in turn, summarizes various indicators of banks' solvency and liquidity conditions. These include a bank's similarity to other banks in distress (capturing confidence contagion) and its short-term wholesale maturity mismatch—since the latter indicator worsens if banks lose access to long-term funding markets, the framework also captures "snowballing" effects, whereby banks are exposed to greater liquidity risk as the amount of short-term liabilities that have to be refinanced in each period increases over time. Second, we combine the danger zone approach with simple behavioral reactions to assess how liquidity crises can spread through the system. In particular, we demonstrate how liquidity hoarding and asset fire sales may improve one bank's liquidity position at the expense of others. Last, using the RAMSI (Risk Assessment Model for Systemic Institutions) stress testing model presented in Aikman et al. (2009), we generate illustrative distributions for bank profitability to show how funding liquidity risk and associated contagion may exacerbate overall systemic risk and amplify distress during financial crises. In particular, we demonstrate how liquidity effects may generate pronounced fat tails even when the underlying shocks to fundamentals are Gaussian.

The feedback mechanisms embedded in the model all played an important role in the current and/or past financial crises. For example, the deterioration in liquidity positions associated with snowballing effects was evident in Japan in the 1990s (see figures 14 and 15 in Nakaso 2001). And in this crisis, interbank lending collapsed from very early on. Spreads between interbank rates for term lending and expected policy rates in the major funding markets rose sharply in August 2007, before spiking in September 2008 following the collapse of Lehman Brothers (figure 1.2, panels A through C, thick black lines). Throughout this period, banks substantially reduced their lending to each other at long-term maturities, with institutions forced to roll over increasingly large portions of their balance sheet at very short maturities. Figure 1.3 highlights these snowballing effects between 2007 and 2008. At the same time, the quantity of interbank lending also declined dramatically and there was an unprecedented increase in the amounts placed by banks as reserves at the major central banks, indicative of liquidity hoarding at the system level.

In principle, the collapse in interbank lending could have arisen either because banks had concerns over counterparty credit risk, or over their own future liquidity needs; it is hard to distinguish between these empirically. But anecdotal evidence suggests that, at least early in the crisis, banks were hoarding liquidity as a precautionary measure so that cash was available to finance liquidity lines to off-balance sheet vehicles that they were committed to rescuing, or as an endogenous response to liquidity hoarding by other market participants. Interbank spread decompositions into contributions from credit premia and noncredit premia (fig. 1.6, panels A through C), and recent empirical work by Acharya and Merrouche (2012) and Christensen, Lopez, and Rudebusch (2009) all lend support to this view.

It is also clear that the reduction in asset prices after summer 2007 generated mark-to-market losses that intensified funding problems in the system, particularly for those institutions reliant on the repo market who were forced to post more collateral to retain the same level of funding (Gorton and Metrick 2010). While it is hard to identify the direct role of fire sales in contributing to the reduction in asset prices, it is evident that many assets were carrying a large liquidity discount.

Finally, confidence contagion and counterparty credit losses came to the fore following the failure of Lehman Brothers. The former was evident in the severe difficulties experienced by the other US securities houses in the following days, including those that had previously been regarded as relatively safe. Counterparty losses also contributed to the systemic impact of its failure, with the fear of a further round of such losses via credit derivative

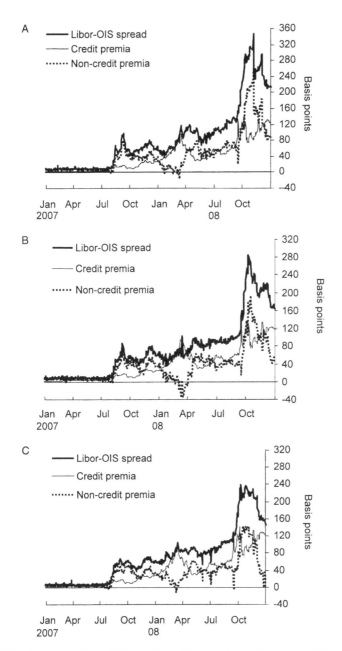

Fig. 1.2 Decomposition of the sterling, dollar, and euro twelve-month interbank spread: *A*, sterling; *B*, dollar; *C*, euro

Sources: British Bankers' Association, Bloomberg, Markit Group Limited, and Bank of England calculations.

Notes: Spread of twelve-month Libor to twelve-month overnight index swap (OIS) rates. Estimates of credit premia are derived from credit default swaps on banks in the Libor panel. Estimates of noncredit premia are derived by the residual. For further details on the methodology, see Bank of England (2007, 498–99).

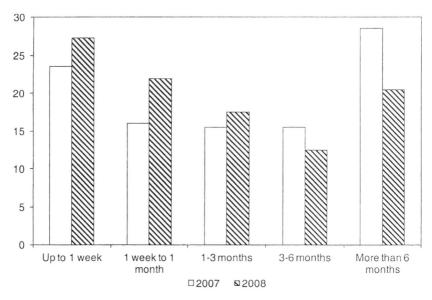

Fig. 1.3   Snowballing in unsecured markets

Source: European Central Bank.

Note: Maturity-weighted breakdown for average daily turnover in unsecured lending as a percentage of total turnover for a panel of 159 banks in Europe. Based on chart 4, section 1.2 of ECB (2008).

contracts being one of the reasons for the subsequent rescue of American International Group (AIG).

There have been several important contributions in the theoretical literature analyzing how liquidity risk can affect banking systems, some of which we refer to when discussing the cash flow constraint in more detail in section 1.2. But empirical papers in this area are rare. One of the few is van den End (2008), who simulates the effect of funding and market liquidity risk for the Dutch banking system. The model builds on banks' own liquidity risk models, integrates them to system-wide level, and then allows for banks' reactions, as prescribed by rules of thumb. But the paper only analyzes shocks to fundamentals and therefore does not speak to overall systemic risk.

Measuring systemic risk more broadly is in its infancy, in particular if information from banks' balance sheets is used (Borio and Drehmann 2009). Austrian National Bank (OeNB 2006) and Elsinger, Lehar, and Summer (2006) integrated balance-sheet based models of credit and market risk with a network model to evaluate the probability of bank default in Austria. Alessandri et al. (2009) introduced RAMSI and Aikman et al. (2009) extend the approach in a number of dimensions. RAMSI is a comprehensive balance-sheet model for the largest UK banks, which projects the different items on banks' income statement via modules covering macro-credit risk, net interest income, noninterest income, and operating expenses. Aikman et al.

(2009) also incorporate a simplified version of the danger zone framework developed more fully in this chapter. But in their model, contagion can only occur upon bank failure due to confidence contagion, default in the network of interbank exposures (counterparty risk), or from fire sales, which are assumed to depress asset prices at the point of default. In particular, they do not allow for snowballing effects or incorporate banks' cash flow constraints, and do not capture behavioral reactions such as liquidity hoarding or predefault fire sales, all of which are key to understanding the systemic implications of funding liquidity crises.

The chapter is structured as follows. Section 1.2 provides the conceptual and theoretical framework for our analysis, focusing on the potential triggers and systemic implications of funding liquidity crises through the lens of banks' cash flow constraints. Sections 1.3 and 1.4 focus on our quantitative modeling. Section 1.3 provides details on how the danger zone approach captures the closure of funding markets to individual institutions, and section 1.4 presents details and partial simulation results of how behavioral reactions and the danger zone approach interact to create systemic feedbacks. Section 1.5 integrates these effects into RAMSI to illustrate how shocks to fundamentals may be amplified by funding liquidity risk and systemic liquidity feedbacks. Section 1.6 concludes.

1.2 Funding Liquidity Risk in a System-Wide Context: Conceptual and Theoretical Issues

1.2.1 The Cash Flow Constraint

Liquidity risk arises because inflows and outlays are not synchronized (Holmström and Tirole 1998). This would not matter if agents could issue financial contracts to third parties, pledging their future income as collateral. But given asymmetric information and other frictions, this is not always possible in reality. Hence, the timing of cash in- and outflows is the crucial driver of funding liquidity risk, and a bank is liquid if it is able to settle all obligations with immediacy (see Drehmann and Nikolaou 2012).[1] This is the case if, in every period, cash outflows are smaller than cash inflows and the stock of cash held, along with any cash raised by selling (or repoing) assets:

$$\text{Liabilities}_{(\text{Due})} + \text{Assets}_{(\text{New/Rolled over})}$$
$$\leq$$
$$\text{Net Income} + \text{Liabilities}_{(\text{New/Rolled over})} + \text{Assets}_{(\text{Due})}$$
$$+ \text{Value of Assets Sold/Repoed.}$$

1. Drehmann and Nikolaou (2012) discuss how this definition of funding liquidity risk relates to other definitions commonly used.

Breaking down these components further:

(1)
$$WL_{\text{Due}} + RL_{\text{Due}} + WA_{\text{New,Ro}} + RA_{\text{New,Ro}}$$

$$\leq$$

$$\text{Net Income} + WL_{\text{New,Ro}} + RL_{\text{New,Ro}} + WA_{\text{Due}} + RA_{\text{Due}} + LA^S$$

$$+ \Sigma p_i * ILA_i^S$$

where:

- WL are wholesale liabilities and WA are wholesale assets
- RL are retail liabilities and RA are retail assets
- LA^S are the proceeds from the sale of liquid assets such as cash or government bonds,
- ILA_i^S is the volume of illiquid asset i sold or used as collateral to obtain secured (repo) funding
- p_i is the market price of illiquid asset i, which may be below its fair value and possibly even zero in the short run
- subscripts $_{\text{Due, New}}$, and $_{\text{Ro}}$ refer to obligations that are contractually due, newly issued or bought, and rolled over, respectively.

We note several issues. First, assessing funding liquidity risk through a cash flow constraint is common in practice (for a recent overview see Matz and Neu 2007) and also forms the basis of elements of proposed new liquidity regulations (Basel Committee 2010). Nonetheless, the literature has tended to model funding liquidity risk differently, even though most theoretical models can be recast in the cash flow constraint as discussed later.

Second, the flow constraint is written in terms of *contractual* maturities as these are the ultimate drivers of funding liquidity risk in crises. But in normal times, the constraint might reasonably be thought of in terms of behavioral maturities that may differ from contractual ones. For example, many retail deposits are available on demand. In normal conditions, a bank can expect the majority of these loans to be rolled over continuously, so RL_{Due} may roughly equal RL_{Ro}. But, in times of stress, depositors may choose to withdraw, so the behavioral maturity may collapse closer to the contractual one.

Third, equation (1) still makes some simplifying assumptions. For example, contingent claims are an important driver of funding liquidity risk. In particular, firms rely heavily on credit lines (see, e.g., Campello et al. 2010). Equally, banks negotiate contingent credit lines with other banks. We do not include off-balance sheet items separately because once drawn they are part of new assets or liabilities. Repo transactions are also an important component of banks' liquidity risk management. Even though technically different, we treat them as part of the asset sales category because in both cases, the market price broadly determines the value that can be raised from the underlying asset, which may or may not be liquid.[2] Transactions with the central bank are also included under repo. These occur regularly, even in normal conditions, as banks obtain liquidity directly from the central bank during open market operations.[3]

Beyond this, different funding markets split into several submarkets such as interbank borrowing, unsecured bonds, securitizations, commercial paper, and so forth. And there is clearly also a distinction between foreign and domestic funding markets.[4] These separate markets may have quite different characteristics that make them more or less susceptible to illiquidity. Not all factors relevant to funding market dynamics can be easily incorporated into a model of systemic risk. But there are two that we judge to be sufficiently important as well as empirically implementable to split them out separately. First, we differentiate retail funding, secured markets, and unsecured markets. Second, we split unsecured funding into longer-term and shorter-term markets. We discuss these in more detail later in the chapter.

Finally, note that ex post, liquidity outflows will always equal inflows. If the bank is unable to satisfy the flow constraint, it will become illiquid and default. Conversely, if the bank has excess liquidity, it can sell it to the market, for example, as WA_{New}, or deposit it at the central bank. Ex ante, however, banks are uncertain as to whether the flow constraint will be satisfied in all periods (i.e., they face funding liquidity risk). The right-hand side of equation (1) shows that this risk is influenced by banks' ability to raise liquidity from different sources for different prices, which will also change over time. The possibilities and implications of their choices are discussed in detail following. Before doing so, it is important to highlight a simple fact that is clear from equation (1): the maturity mismatch between (contractually) maturing liabilities and assets is a key driver for funding liquidity risk. It follows that, ceteris paribus, a bank with a larger share of short-term liabilities faces greater funding liquidity risk.

1.2.2 The Trigger for Funding Problems at Individual Institutions

Under normal business conditions, banks are able to meet their cash flow constraints in every period, as they can always obtain new wholesale funding or sell assets in a liquid market. But this may not be the case in a crisis. To understand crisis dynamics better, we first discuss the trigger events for

2. In repo transactions, there may also be an additional haircut applied, which would mean that the cash lent on the trade would be lower than the current market value of the security used as collateral. In principle, the flow constraint could be augmented to account for this.
3. Throughout this chapter, we abstract from extraordinary policy intervention in crises, so the cash flow constraint presumes that there is no intervention to widen central bank liquidity provision in a way that would allow banks to obtain more cash from the central bank than they could obtain through asset sales or repo transactions in the market.
4. McGuire and von Peter (2009) identify a shortage of dollar funding as a key driver of non-US banks' funding problems during the current crisis.

funding problems at an individual institution before analyzing how funding crises can spread through the system.

Many theoretical models can be cast in terms of the flow constraint. For example, Diamond and Dybvig (1983) assume there is only one illiquid investment project ILA_i, which pays a high, certain payoff in period 2 but a low payoff p_i if liquidated early in period 1 (the high period 2 return guarantees that the bank is always solvent). The bank is entirely funded by demand deposits (RL_{Due}). It is known that a fraction of (early) depositors only care about consumption in period 1, while other (late) agents (which cannot be distinguished by the bank) are patient and prepared to wait until period 2, though they can withdraw in period 1 if they wish. To satisfy withdrawals of early depositors, the bank invests a fraction of its deposits into liquid assets LA^S. For simplicity, the bank has to pay no costs and interest payments are subsumed into liabilities to depositors (i.e., net income = 0). Given that all other terms in the cash flow constraint are also assumed to be zero, equation (1) in period 1 for the Diamond and Dybvig bank looks like:

$$RL_{Due}^{early} + RL_{Due}^{late} \leq RL_{Ro}^{late} + LA^S + p_i * ILA_i.$$

Under normal circumstances, late depositors roll over their demand deposits ($RL_{Due}^{late} = RL_{Ro}^{late}$) and the bank can meet its cash flow constraint as the investment in the short-term asset is sufficient to pay back early depositors. But if late depositors are unwilling to roll over and start a run on the bank ($RL_{Ro}^{late} = 0$), the bank is forced to start selling its illiquid assets at p_i, which is below the fair value of the asset. Given that the bank is fundamentally sound, bank runs should not happen. But, as payoffs are low when all late depositors run, an equilibrium exists in which it is optimal for all agents to run. This generates the possibility of multiple equilibria, whereby fundamentals do not fully determine outcomes and confidence has an important role.

Even though very stylized, this model captures several key features of liquidity crises. First, contractual maturities matter in a liquidity crisis as the "behavioral" maturities of late depositors collapse in stressed conditions from two periods to the contractual maturity of one period. Second, funding and market liquidity are closely related. If the bank's assets were liquid, so that p_i equaled its fair value, the bank could always sell assets to satisfy unexpected liquidity demands and would never be illiquid but solvent. Third, confidence and beliefs about the soundness of an institution and the behavior of others play an important role in the crystallization of funding liquidity risk.

The result that confidence effects can, in isolation, drive self-fulfilling bank runs is not particularly realistic: runs only tend to occur when there are strong (mostly justified) doubts about the fundamental solvency of a bank, or the bank has a very weak liquidity position. Chari and Jagannathan (1988) therefore introduce random returns and informed depositors in the model, which can induce bank runs driven by poor fundamentals. More recently, global game techniques have been applied to this problem (Rochet and Vives 2004; Goldstein and Pauzner 2005). Our empirical strategy is in the spirit of these papers: liquidity crises only tend to occur in our simulations when bank fundamentals are weak, even though banks can still be illiquid but solvent.

1.2.3   System Dynamics of Funding Liquidity Crises

The main focus of our work is to capture the system-wide dynamics of liquidity crises. Figure 1.1 identified several channels through which a funding crisis at one bank could spread to the rest of the financial system. We now relate these dynamics to existing literature and, where appropriate, to the cash flow constraint.

Confidence contagion (channel 4 in fig. 1.1) could be interpreted through fundamentals, whereby a liquidity crisis in one institution reveals some information on the likelihood of insolvency of other banks with similar investments (Chen 1999).[5] Alternatively, it could simply reflect panic, whereby investors decide to run on similar banks purely because of sentiment. More generally, system confidence effects can contribute to liquidity hoarding. For example, Caballero and Krishnamurthy (2008) show that (Knightian) uncertainty may be triggered by a small shock, which is not necessarily a funding problem at one bank but could simply be a downgrade of an important market player. Anticipating potential funding needs in the future, banks start to hoard liquidity.[6]

The possible systemic consequences of liquidity hoarding (channel 2 in fig. 1.1) are made clear by considering cash flow constraints. For example, if a (stressed) bank hoards liquidity (either by shortening the maturity of loans it offers in the interbank market or withdrawing funding altogether), the flow constraints of counterparties will be tightened or put at greater future risk via a reduction in $WL_{\text{New,Ro}}$. This may intensify funding problems at institutions that are already stressed. And small banks may find it difficult to access alternative sources of funding even if they are not stressed: indeed, the potential loss of a major funding source for small regional US banks was one of the reasons for the bailout of Continental Illinois in 1984. Yet, despite its potential importance, this "funding contagion" channel has only received limited attention in the literature, though recent theoretical work by Gai, Haldane, and Kapadia (2011) has shown how this type of action, especially if associated with key players in the network, can cause an interbank market collapse in which all banks stop lending to each other.

---

5. Contagious bank runs can also affect the investment incentives of banks, making system-wide banking crises even more likely (see Drehmann 2002, and Acharya and Yorulmazer 2008).
6. Liquidity hoarding by surplus banks may also be a result of asymmetric information and heightened counterparty credit risk following adverse shocks (Heider, Hoerova, and Holthausen 2009).

By contrast, asset fire sales (channel 3 in fig. 1.1) have been widely discussed. The potential feedback loop between distress selling and falling asset prices was first highlighted by Fisher (1933). After the failure of Long-Term Capital Management (LTCM) and the resulting liquidity crisis for Lehman Brothers in 1998, this idea was formalized by a wide range of authors (see Shim and von Peter, 2007, for a survey). Cifuentes, Ferruci, and Shin (2005) illustrate how mark-to-market losses associated with falling asset prices could raise solvency concerns at highly exposed institutions And Brunnermeier and Pedersen (2009) show how downward spirals between asset fire sales and increased funding liquidity risk can emerge. Such a spiral can, for instance, start if a bank (or broker, as in the Brunnermeier and Pedersen model) is short of funding liquidity, cannot obtain it from the interbank market, and has to sell assets. If asset markets are characterized by frictions, (large) asset sales induce a fall in prices and thus the value of collateral. This, in turn, implies that the bank has to post higher margins, increasing liquidity outflows. To remain liquid banks have to sell even more assets, depressing market prices further.[7] Their model can also be recast in terms of the flow constraint: higher margin calls are equivalent to higher liquidity demands ($WL_{\text{New,Ro}}$) while at the same time, lower asset prices, p_i, reduce available liquidity.[8]

Interbank market contagion via counterparty credit risk (channel 5 in fig. 1.1) has also been widely discussed in the literature (Allen and Gale 2000; Freixas, Parigi, and Rochet 2000; Gai and Kapadia 2010; Upper 2011). Clearly, this may weaken the solvency and thus overall funding position of other banks. But it is also evident from the flow constraint that a loss of WA_{Due} could lead to a direct short-term funding problem at a bank even if it remains solvent.

Thus far, we have focussed on the negative system-wide effects of funding liquidity crises. But it is important to note that when funds are withdrawn from a stressed bank, they must be placed elsewhere. So, unless the funds end up as increased reserve holdings at the central bank, some banks are likely to *strengthen* as a result of funding crises through an increase in WL_{New} and, possibly, RL_{New}. Indeed, Gatev and Strahan (2006) and Gatev, Schuermann, and Strahan (2009) identify this effect in the US banking sector, especially for larger institutions.[9] However, the strength of this countervailing effect

7. Related papers on the amplification role of shocks to margins and haircuts on the securities that serve as collateral in repo transactions include Adrian and Shin (2010), Geanakoplos (2010), and Gorton and Metrick (2010).
8. Shocks to margins or haircuts could also be modeled more directly in the flow constraint by scaling down the value of the $\Sigma p_i * ILA_i^S$ term when interpreted as applying to repo transactions.
9. It should, however, be noted that Pennacchi (2006) finds that demand deposit inflows cannot be observed prior to the introduction of deposit insurance, indicating that this effect may be driven by regulatory interventions rather than by the underlying structure of banks' balance sheets.

is likely to be highly dependent on the type of crisis: in a crisis precipitated by an idiosyncratic shock to one institution, we may expect it to be fairly strong; if much of the banking system is in distress, central bank reserves may end up increasing, as has happened to a certain extent during this financial crisis. Moreover, such redistributional effects can only occur if funds are actually withdrawn—they do not help if there is a systemic shortening of the maturity of interbank lending across the system. Therefore, to maintain simplicity, we do not take these effects into account in our model.

1.3   Modeling Liquidity Risk for Individual Banks—A "Danger Zone" Approach

Modeling the liquidity risk of an individual bank quantitatively presents significant challenges. One might wish to construct a formal forecasting framework for predicting funding crises. But we do not have full information on the underlying cash flow constraints, and it would be difficult to estimate the stochastic nature of each component because of the binary, nonlinear nature of liquidity risk, and because liquidity crises in developed countries have been (until recently) rare events for which data are limited. Instead, we adopt a simple, transparent (yet subjective) danger zone approach, in which we assume that certain funding markets close if banks' solvency and liquidity conditions—summarized by a danger zone score explained following—cross particular thresholds. In some respects, this is consistent with the broad methodological approach, advocated by Gigerenzer and Brighton (2009), that simple heuristics can sometimes lead to more accurate inferences than approaches that use more information and computation.

Our approach to modeling the closure of funding markets is somewhat stylized. In particular, as discussed in section 1.2.1, we take a high level view of the flow constraint and do not consider all different markets for liquidity. But we differentiate between retail, short-term unsecured wholesale, and long-term unsecured wholesale markets. The closure of secured funding markets does not play an explicit role because it is assumed that banks will always be able to raise the same amount of cash by disposing the collateral at prevailing market prices. In reality, however, sudden closures of secured funding markets may make it impossible to sell all of the collateral at a sufficiently high price to meet immediate funding needs.

We also only consider normal and crisis times for each funding market. Figure 1.4 illustrates this point. In normal times, funding is available in all markets. But banks with weaker fundamentals have to pay higher costs. Interbank markets usually do not differentiate widely between different banks (see Furfine 2002 or Angelini, Nobili, and Picillo 2011). As a first-order approximation, we therefore assume that, in "normal" times, funding costs equal a market rate plus a credit risk premium, which increases as ratings deteriorate.

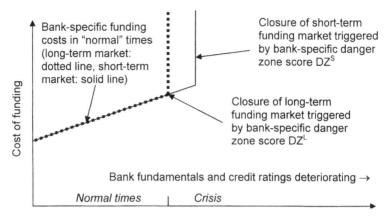

Fig. 1.4   A stylized view of funding liquidity risk for an individual bank

Once liquidity risk crystalizes, the process in different markets is inherently nonlinear and may occur at different ratings and funding costs. We model the nonlinearity especially starkly, but in line with practitioners (see Matz and Neu 2007): once fundamentals (as summarized in the danger zone [DZ] score) fall below certain thresholds, the bank faces infinite costs to access the relevant market (i.e., the market is closed for this bank). Crises have, however, shown that different funding markets close at different times. For example, as discussed earlier, it may be rational for lenders to provide short-term funding even if they are not willing to grant long-term loans. Given this, we assume that a danger zone score above DZ^L will lead to a closure of long-term wholesale markets, whilst short-term wholesale markets remain open until the bank breaches the danger zone score DZ^S.

The previous discussion highlights that there is not one simple trigger for a funding liquidity crisis at an individual bank. For practical purposes, we supplement the insights from theory with information from summaries of individual banks' liquidity policies and contingency plans (European Central Bank [ECB 2002]; Bank for International Settlements [BIS 2006]; Institute of International Finance [IIF 2007]), and evidence from case studies of funding liquidity crises from this and past crises. As shown in figure 1.5, we assume that a set of eight indicators can proxy the three broad areas that theory and experience suggest are important: (1) concerns about future solvency; (2) a weak liquidity position / funding structure; and (3) institution-specific and market-wide confidence effects, over and above those generated by solvency concerns or weakness in liquidity positions.

Solvency concerns are captured through a forward-looking Tier 1 capital ratio, based on regulatory measures. Weak liquidity positions and funding structures are captured through two metrics. First, short-term wholesale maturity mismatch compares short-term wholesale liabilities with short-

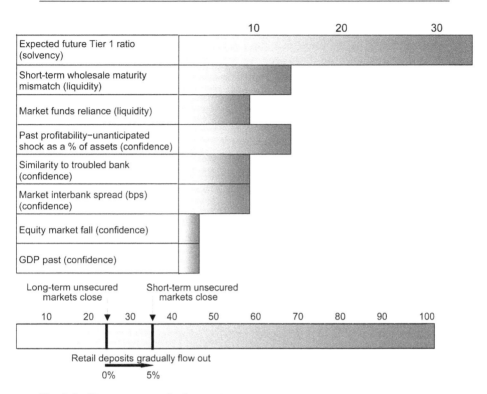

Fig. 1.5   **Danger zones—basic structure**

term wholesale assets (including maturing wholesale loans and liquid assets). Second, longer-term funding vulnerability is captured through a metric that measures reliance on market funds and shares some similarities to the (inverse of the) core funding ratio applied as a policy tool in New Zealand (Ha and Hodgetts 2011). These metrics assume funds from wholesale counterparties and markets to be flightier than retail deposits. Confidence concerns are captured through a number of metrics: unexpected shocks to the previous quarter's profitability (distinct from solvency concerns, which are longer-term in focus); the possibility of confidence contagion, which is captured through an assessment of how similar the institution is to other troubled banks; and three metrics looking at market prices and real economy data (the cost of interbank funding, the size of recent movements in equity markets, and the size of recent movements in GDP).

Note that the danger zone approach allows for some feedback effects. In particular, the closure of long-term funding markets to an institution: (a) may worsen that bank's liquidity position through snowballing effects, whereby the bank becomes increasingly reliant on short-term funding; and (b) may adversely affect similar banks through a pure confidence channel.

Figure 1.5 also presents the aggregation scheme and the thresholds at which short-term and long-term unsecured funding markets are assumed to close the bank. Noting that equal weights can predict almost as accurately as, and sometimes better than, multiple regression (Dawes and Corrigan 1974; Dawes 1979), we place roughly equal weight on the three main factors (solvency, liquidity, and confidence) that can trigger funding crises. In the aggregation, we allow for the possibility that a run could be triggered either by extreme scores in any of the three areas, or by a combination of moderate scores across the different areas. The judgments underpinning more specific aspects of the calibration and weighting schemes were informed by analysis of a range of case studies. As an example, the appendix in this chapter shows the danger zone approach ahead of the failure of Continental Illinois.

Funding options become more restricted as a bank's position deteriorates. At a score of $DZ^L = 25$ points, long-term unsecured funding markets close to the bank. The bank is also assumed to start experiencing gradual retail deposit outflows at this point (0.5 percent for every danger zone point above 25), intended to reflect the behavior of well-informed investors rather than representing a widespread (Northern Rock style) run. We refer to this as Phase 1 of funding market closure. There is no default during this phase since the bank is able to refinance in short-term unsecured funding markets and banks are assumed to have access to an infinite supply of short-term unsecured funding. Once the DZ score reaches $DZ^S = 35$, short-term funding markets close to the bank, and the bank enters Phase 2 of funding market closure. But even a very high DZ score does not in itself trigger the failure of the bank—this only occurs if the bank's capital falls below the regulatory minimum or if it is unable to meet its cash flow constraint.

1.4   Modeling Systemic Liquidity Feedbacks

As banks' liquidity position deteriorates, they may undertake increasingly extreme defensive actions to try to bolster it. As noted before, such actions may have an adverse effect on other banks. In this section, we provide illustrative simulations using the RAMSI balance sheets to highlight these dynamics quantitatively.

The RAMSI balance sheets cover the largest UK banks and are highly disaggregated, with a wide range of different asset and liability classes. Each of the asset and liability classes is further disaggregated into a total of eleven buckets (five maturity buckets and six repricing buckets) and these are interpolated so that maturity information for each asset and liability class is available in a series of three-month buckets (zero to three months, three to six months, six to nine months, etc.). Given the structure of these data, we define short-term assets and liabilities to be those with less than three months' maturity throughout the simulations. RAMSI also exploits large exposure data to construct a matrix of bilateral interbank assets and liabilities for the major UK banks.[10]

In general, the balance sheet data are mainly extracted from published accounts but supplemented from regulatory returns. As some balance sheet entries are unavailable, rules of thumb based on other information or extrapolations on the basis of similarities between banks are used to fill in the data gaps. As the simulations in this chapter are purely intended for illustrative purposes, they use balance sheet data for the ten largest UK banks as at end-2007.[11]

1.4.1   Phase 1: Closure of Long-Term Wholesale Markets

The closure of long-term wholesale markets implies that the bank has to refinance a larger volume of liabilities in short-term wholesale markets each period. This increases the short-term wholesale maturity mismatch danger zone score (MM_t):

$$MM_t = \frac{LA_t + WA_t^{0-3} - WL_t^{0-3}}{TA_t}.$$

The mismatch is constructed using liquid assets (LA_t), and wholesale assets (WA_t^{0-3}) and liabilities (WL_t^{0-3}), which have a remaining contractual maturity of less than three months, normalized by total assets (TA_t).[12] The danger zone scores for the short-term maturity mismatch indicator are shown in table 1.1.

We demonstrate some of the feedback dynamics embedded in the model by presenting results from a stressed scenario in which various transmission channels are introduced in turn. Results are presented relative to a baseline in which no effects are switched on. We focus on three banks from the RAMSI peer group. The "distressed" bank is initially set to have a DZ score exceeding 25, implying it is shut out of long-term funding markets. We also show the impact on two other banks (banks A and B). Both are connected

---

10. The techniques adopted are similar to those discussed by Wells (2004); Elsinger, Lehar, and Summer (2006); and OeNB (2006).

11. Membership of the major UK banks group is based on the provision of customer services in the United Kingdom, regardless of country of ownership. At the end of 2007, the members were: Alliance & Leicester, Banco Santander, Barclays, Bradford & Bingley, Halifax Bank of Scotland, HSBC, Lloyds TSB, Nationwide, Northern Rock, and Royal Bank of Scotland.

12. Liquid assets are defined as: cash and balances at central banks, items in the course of collection, Treasury and other eligible bills, and government bonds. Wholesale assets are defined as loans and advances to banks and other financial companies, financial investments available for sale (excluding items that are recognized as liquid assets), and reverse repos. Wholesale liabilities are defined as deposits from banks and other financial companies, items in the course of collection due to other banks, debt securities in issue, and repos. Short-term is defined as less than three months due to the constraints of RAMSI's balance sheet structure. Ideally, we would embellish the model with a more granular maturity split of liabilities, but the same key dynamics and feedbacks would apply.

Table 1.1   Points score for short-term wholesale maturity mismatch

Calculated maturity mismatch	Danger zone points
Less than −5%	0
−5% to −8%	0–3
−8% to −11%	3–6
−11% to −14%	6–9
−14% to −17%	9–12
−17% to −20%	12–15

to the distressed bank though the interbank network and we demonstrate how the degree of connectivity affects the magnitude of the spillovers. To simplify the analysis, we hold the size of balance sheets constant as time progresses, and also hold all other DZ scores constant apart from the short-term wholesale maturity mismatch score.

Snowballing into Shorter-Term Maturities (fig. 1.6, panel A)

Once the distressed bank loses access to long-term unsecured wholesale funding markets and starts to experience gradual retail deposit outflows, it substitutes lost funding for short-term wholesale unsecured funding. This is the snowballing effect. Panel A of figure 1.6 illustrates that snowballing worsens the distressed bank's short-term wholesale maturity mismatch each quarter as more of its liabilities mature and are rolled over only at short-term maturity. After three years, it deteriorates by around 4 percentage points. But most of the snowballing occurs in the first four quarters, with the effect tailing off over time, reflecting the concentration of liabilities in the shorter maturity buckets. By design there is no impact on the other banks.[13]

Liquidity Hoarding by Shortening Lending Maturities (fig. 1.6, panel B)

As argued by Acharya and Skeie (2011), a bank that is nervous about its liquidity position may hoard (future) liquidity by only providing wholesale lending at short-term maturities. This has two effects. First, the additional short-term wholesale assets improve the distressed bank's short-term wholesale maturity mismatch position as extra liquidity will be available on demand if needed. Abstracting from the snowballing effect, panel B of figure 1.6 illustrates how such hoarding can improve the maturity mismatch position of the distressed bank by nearly 5 percentage points over the simulation. Second, this behavior leads to a shortening of the interbank liabilities of other banks to which the distressed bank is lending—as the distressed bank hoards liquidity, some other banks effectively suffer a snowballing

---

13. This includes a simplifying assumption that there is no corresponding shortening of the maturity of assets of other banks, since this is likely to be of only second-order importance in its impact on funding conditions.

A Impact of Snowballing only

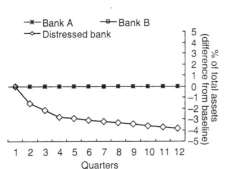

B Impact of Liquidity Hoarding only

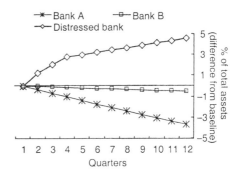

C Impact of snowballing and liquidity hoarding

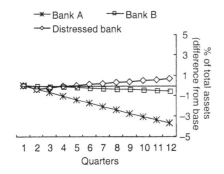

Fig. 1.6   The evolution of maturity mismatch under different assumptions: *A*, impact of snowballing only; *B*, impact of liquidity hoarding only; *C*, impact of snowballing and liquidity hoarding

effect on a portion of their interbank liabilities. As the bottom two lines in panel B illustrate, this worsens other banks' short-term wholesale maturity mismatch position. It thus serves to increase their DZ points scores—hence, this type of liquidity hoarding has clear adverse spillovers for other banks in the system. Note that bank A's position deteriorates by more than bank B. This is because more of bank A's interbank liabilities are sourced from the distressed bank (based on data from the matrix of bilateral interbank exposures).

Snowballing and Liquidity Hoarding by Shortening Maturities (fig. 1.6, panel C)

Allowing for both snowballing and liquidity hoarding is represented as a combination of the two previous subsections. In this case, after worsening initially, the distressed bank's maturity mismatch position eventually improves as the impact of liquidity hoarding becomes stronger than the impact of snowballing. Note that this is due to the specific balance sheet structure of this bank—in other cases, snowballing may prove to be the stronger effect. At the same time, other banks' maturity mismatch worsens, since they only experience the negative impact of the distressed bank's liquidity hoarding, identical to the case in the previous subsection.

In most circumstances, a stressed bank will survive this phase of a funding crisis, since it can still access short-term funding markets. But if its mismatch position worsens, its danger zone score will increase. Therefore, the bank may be accumulating vulnerabilities that place it at greater risk of losing access to short-term funding markets in future periods.

1.4.2   Phase 2: Closure of Short-Term Wholesale Markets

The second phase of the liquidity crisis occurs when funding conditions deteriorate to such an extent that the bank is frozen out of both short- and long-term funding markets. In our model, this occurs when a bank's DZ score exceeds 35 (see fig. 1.5). Although the bank's insolvency is not inevitable at this point, it becomes increasingly difficult for it to meet its cash flow constraint. Therefore, it may need to take further defensive actions.

The possible systemic consequences of funding crises are made clear by considering the short-term (i.e., one-period) cash flow constraint of a bank experiencing funding problems. In particular, suppose that a bank faces a liquidity crisis and cannot, or anticipates not being able to, access new funding from wholesale markets ($WL_{\text{New,Ro}} = 0$ in equation [1]). Then, short of defaulting, the bank has four options affecting the left- or right-hand side of the cash flow constraint. It can:

1. Use profits (net income) earned over the period to pay off maturing liabilities.
2. Choose not to roll over or grant new funding to other financial institutions ($WA_{\text{New,Ro}}$) (liquidity hoarding by withdrawal of funding).
3. Sell or repo liquid assets.
4. Sell illiquid assets ($\Sigma p_i * ILA_i^S$).

Note that, in practice, banks have further options, which we exclude in our simulations. First, they could draw down committed credit lines with other banks. In principle, this may be a preferred option, but experience in this and previous financial crises has demonstrated that a stressed bank cannot always rely on being able to draw on such lines. And any such drawdown may, in any case, send an adverse signal to the markets, further undermining confidence. Second, as set out in many contingency plans (see Matz and Neu 2007), banks could securitize assets. However, this requires some time as well as previous presence in these markets. As the current crisis has demonstrated, it may not be possible in systemic crises. Third, banks could contract lending to the real economy. This will improve the flow constraint but with potentially severe repercussions for the macroeconomy.[14] However, this is a very slow means of raising liquidity. And as Matz and Neu (2007, 109) put it, a strategic objective of liquidity risk management is to "ensure that profitable business opportunities can be pursued." Given this, we assume that banks continue to replace maturing retail assets with new retail assets ($RA_{New} = RA_{Due}$).

It is unclear how banks would weigh up the relative costs of options 1 through 4. For a start, banks' choice set is not as coarse as can be captured in the model. For example, banks hold a multitude of assets, some of which are less or more illiquid and therefore less or more costly to sell. Actions may also depend on specific circumstances. But we sequence defensive actions in our simulations as ordered earlier. As discussed following, this reflects an intuitive judgement of the costs imposed on the bank in distress by each action, information from summaries of banks' contingency planning documents, and an assessment of the defensive actions actually taken by banks during this financial crisis.

Simulating the Implications of the Various Funding Options

Continuing from phase 1 of funding distress, we now explain how a bank's reaction to losing access to short-term wholesale funding markets may be simulated by using its cash flow constraint. A preliminary check is made to determine if the bank can meet its cash flow constraint in the complete absence of wholesale funding but without accounting for any net income earned over the period, and assuming that banks aim to roll over interbank lending and avoid eroding liquid asset buffers or undertaking fire sales. If so, the constraint is satisfied and the bank survives to the next period. If not, then we consider the following sequence of defensive actions (options 1 through 4). Any bank that does not satisfy the flow constraint after all options are exhausted is defined as defaulted.[15]

Option 1: Using Profits (Net Income) Earned over the Period to Repay Liabilities. In normal times, profits boost bank equity and may be matched on the asset side by higher lending. But banks may also use these proceeds to repay maturing liabilities. This is unlikely to have a significant adverse effect on funding markets' confidence in the bank, and so is ordered first. But banks are only likely to be able to raise limited funds in this way, especially in circumstances in which low profitability has contributed to funding difficulties.

14. For the impact of liquidity shocks on real lending during the current crisis see, for example, Ivashina and Scharfstein (2010). Huang (2009) provides evidence that distressed banks reduced the availability of precommitted credit lines to nonwholesale customers.
15. Throughout the simulation, we also assume that all retail liabilities can be refinanced beyond the 5 percent outflow already captured between 25 and 35 points (i.e., $RL_{New} = RL_{Due}$).

Option 2: Liquidity Hoarding by Withdrawal of Funding ($WA_{New,Ro} = 0$). In practice, liquidity hoarding has probably been the most frequently observed defensive action during this financial crisis. From the perspective of individual banks in distress, it allows funds to be raised quickly and may be perceived as only having a limited impact on franchise value. Furthermore, although such hoarding may involve some reputational costs, these may be seen as less severe than those resulting from other options.

In phase 1, a bank that loses access to long-term funding hoards liquidity by shortening the maturity of its wholesale lending. But at this stage, we now suppose that it stops rolling over or issuing new wholesale loans completely. The proceeds from the maturing assets are used to repay maturing wholesale liabilities. The balance sheet shrinks as a result. For simplicity, this version of the model assumes that there is no direct impact on counterparties—we assume that those that are below 35 DZ points can replace the lost funding with new short-term wholesale liabilities in the interbank market, while those that are above 35 points will already have lost access to short-term wholesale funding markets in any case. It should, however, be noted that in practice, such liquidity hoarding behavior is likely to have adverse systemic consequences by tightening overall funding conditions and causing a deterioration in confidence.

Option 3: Sale or Repo of Liquid Assets. If the cash flow constraint still cannot be met, we assume that banks look to sell liquid assets or use them to obtain repo funding to replace liabilities due. Sales or repo of highly liquid assets are usually possible even in the most severe of crises, but are generally not the first line of defense. Their use depletes buffers, making banks more susceptible to failure in subsequent periods, when other options are exhausted (see Matz 2007). That said, selling or repoing liquid assets is likely preferable to selling illiquid assets, due to the real costs imposed by the latter course of action.

In the simulations, this step is implemented by assuming liquid assets are repoed so that the size of the balance sheet does not change. But banks' liquid assets are recorded as encumbered rather than unencumbered and remain so for the next quarter, meaning that they can no longer be counted as liquid assets in the danger zone measures and can no longer be used in a defensive way if the bank experiences further outflows in subsequent periods.

Option 4: Asset Fire Sales. Finally, banks may raise liquidity by selling assets in a fire sale. Fire sales are likely to be associated with a real financial loss and a corresponding hit to capital. They may also be easily observable in the market, potentially creating severe stigma problems. Given this, we assume that they represent the last course of action.

In principle, fire sales could apply across a wide range of asset classes, including in the trading book. But in the simulations, we restrict them to the bank's pool of available-for-sale (AFS) assets due to data limitations. If the bank does not have enough assets to sell to meet its flow constraint, then it fails. The restriction of fire sales to AFS assets makes individual bank failure more likely at this stage than may be the case in practice. But it also limits the extent of contagion to other banks.

The asset-side feedbacks associated with fire sales are modeled by assuming that other banks suffer temporary (intraperiod) mark-to-market losses. This can increase their DZ score via the solvency indicator. In extreme circumstances, these banks may then also suffer funding liquidity crises. The pricing equations used to determine mark-to-market losses on different types of assets follow Aikman et al. (2009)—the key difference with that approach is that fire sales and associated contagion occur *before* rather than upon bank failure.

Crisis Funding, a Graphical Illustration

Figure 1.7 illustrates the aforementioned mechanisms with a simulation representing an outcome for one bank. Its cash flow constraint is estimated using the RAMSI balance sheet data. Following a particular shock to fundamentals, the bank does not initially meet the flow constraint once it has been excluded from short- and long-term funding markets. In the example, the bank has a shortfall of around 5 percent of total assets (the first bar in the chart). Hence the bank moves to option 1. In the simulation example, the bank is not able to ameliorate its funding position from profits since it makes losses, which actually imply that it is further from meeting its flow constraint. The solid line in figure 1.7 illustrates that the bank gets closer to meeting its

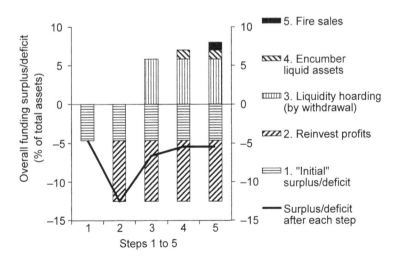

Fig. 1.7   Steps in flow constraint when wholesale funding withdrawn

flow constraint by withdrawing all maturing wholesale assets and using them to pay off liabilities due (option 2), by encumbering its liquid assets (option 3), and by selling illiquid assets in a fire sale (option 4). But in this example, the combined effect of these actions is insufficient for the bank to meet its flow constraint and the bank fails.

1.4.3   Phase 3: Systemic Impact of a Bank's Failure

If, after exhausting all potential options, a bank cannot meet its flow constraint, it is assumed to default. When a bank defaults, counterparty credit losses incurred by other banks are determined using a network model. This model operates on RAMSI's interbank matrix and is cleared using the Eisenberg and Noe (2001) algorithm. This returns counterparty credit losses for each institution.

Both fire sales and network feedbacks affect other banks' danger zone points scores by weakening their solvency position. If any of the banks reach 25 points as a result, then they suffer snowballing and start to hoard liquidity by shortening maturities, and this affects balance sheets in the next quarter as outlined under phase 1. If the score of any bank crosses 35 points, then that bank enters phase 2, in which case their defensive actions or failure may affect other banks. This process is continued in a loop until the system clears.

1.4.4   Summary of Systemic Feedback Effects

To summarize, we can see how the framework captures all of the feedback effects depicted in figure 1.1. Confidence contagion is modeled directly within the danger zone scoring system, while liquidity hoarding by shortening maturities is an endogenous response to a weak danger zone score that can, in turn, worsen other banks' danger zone scores. Pre-default fire sales can occur as a bank tries to meet its cash flow constraint when it is completely shut out of funding markets, and counterparty credit risk crystallizes upon default.

1.5   Shocks to Fundamentals and Liquidity Risk: Simulations in RAMSI

So far we have analyzed liquidity risk and associated systemic feedbacks in an isolated fashion. To illustrate the impact of introducing liquidity risk and systemic feedbacks on overall system risk, measured here by the system-wide asset and loss distribution, we now integrate these mechanisms into the RAMSI stress testing model, which simulates banks' profitability from fundamentals. Figure 1.8 provides a high-level overview of RAMSI. We only provide a very brief discussion here—for further details, see Aikman et al. (2009).

A key input into RAMSI are future paths of macroeconomic and financial variables. In the following experiments, these have been generated by a large-scale Bayesian VAR (BVAR). This is the only source of shocks, thereby

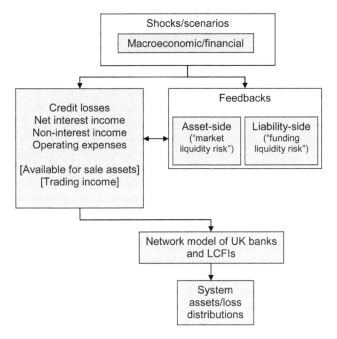

Fig. 1.8   RAMSI framework

preserving a one-for-one mapping from macroeconomic variables to default risk (as well as liquidity risk). The credit risk model treats aggregate default probabilities (PDs) and loss given default (LGD) as a function of the macroeconomic and financial variables from the BVAR. For most of the loan book, interest income is modeled endogenously. Banks price their loans to households and corporations on the basis of the prevailing yield curve and the perceived riskiness of their debtors: an increase in actual or expected credit risk translates into a higher cost of borrowing. For other parts of the balance sheet, including all of the liability side, spreads are calibrated based on market rates and other data. On certain liabilities, spreads also depend on the credit rating of the bank in question, which is, in turn, endogenous to its fundamentals. RAMSI also includes simple models for nontrading income and operating expenses, but for simplicity the version used in this chapter assumes that trading income is fixed and excludes portfolio gains and losses on AFS assets. Net profits are then computed as the sum of all sources of income, net of expenses, credit losses, and (when profitable) taxes and dividends.

At this point, we have all the information we need to assess the danger zone score—for example, the projected profit and loss for each bank drives its solvency score and balance sheet characteristics its liquidity scores. We then simulate the sequence of events described in section 1.4. In the absence of bank failures, or after the feedback loop has completed, we update the balance sheets of profitable surviving banks using a rule of thumb for reinvestment behavior. Banks are assumed to target prespecified capital ratios, and invest in assets and increase liabilities in proportion to their shares on their initial balance sheet, unless the bank faces high liquidity pressures and diverts some or all of its reinvestment funds to meet liquidity needs (step 2 in phase 2).

For the simulations, we use data up to 2007 Q4 (so that all balance sheets are on the basis of end-2007 data) and draw 500 realizations on a three-year forecast horizon stretching to the end of 2010. The BVAR is the only source of exogenous randomness in the stochastic simulations; each realization is thus driven by a sequence of macroeconomic shocks drawn from a multivariate normal distribution.[16] The results are purely intended to be illustrative rather than being the authors' view of the likely impact on the banks in question.

Figure 1.9 shows the simulated distributions of some key profit and loss items, when systemic liquidity feedbacks are not included. For each variable, we calculate aggregate cumulative figures for the first year by adding over banks and quarters, and normalize by aggregate 2007 (beginning of period) capital. The vertical line represents the corresponding figures from the 2007 published accounts, normalized by 2006 capital levels.

The top left-hand panel shows that credit risk is projected to increase in 2008, reflecting a worsening of the macroeconomic outlook. Net interest income is projected to be weaker than in 2007, reflecting higher funding costs and contractual frictions that prevent banks from instantaneously passing on these costs to their borrowers. The variance of net interest income may be unrealistically high as the version of the model used does not incorporate hedging of interest rate risk.[17] Noninterest income (bottom left-hand panel) remains high, with a median projection above the reported 2007 level; this variable is procyclical but adjusts relatively slowly to macroeconomic changes. The net impact on banks' profitability is summarized in the net profit chart (bottom right-hand panel). As can be seen, profits were projected to be weaker than in 2007.

Figure 1.10 shows the distribution of total assets in the last quarter of the simulation and the average *quarterly* aggregate return on assets (RoA) over the whole three-year horizon with funding liquidity risk and systemic liquidity feedbacks excluded from the model. This implies that institutions can only default if they become insolvent because their capital falls below the regulatory minimum. It also implies that there is no contagion. As can be

---

16. In other words, we draw 500 realizations of the macroeconomic risk factors in the first quarter. In subsequent periods, we draw a single set of macroeconomic risk factors for each of the 500 draws.

17. Banks can be penalized under Pillar 2 of Basel II for not hedging interest rate risk in their banking book.

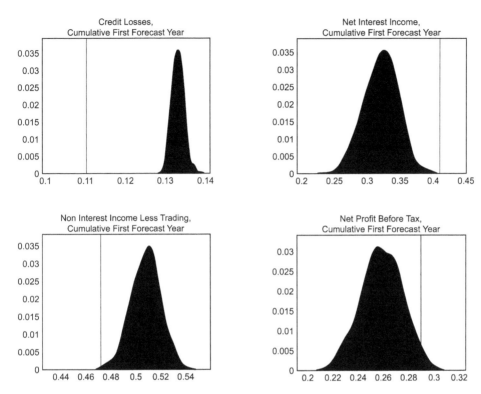

Fig. 1.9   Simulated distributions for profit and loss items: No liquidity effects
Note: In percent of aggregate 2007 capital. Vertical line represents the corresponding figures from the 2007 published accounts, normalized by 2006 capital levels.

seen, the RoA chart has negative skew and some observations in the extreme tail. The negative skew reflects cases where one institution defaults for pure solvency reasons; the extreme observations reflect cases where more than one institution defaults for pure solvency reasons.

Figure 1.11 presents the results incorporating funding liquidity risk and systemic liquidity feedbacks. It is immediately evident that the final projected outcomes are considerably worse. This is partly driven by a higher incidence of failure due to the possibility that an institution may default because it is unable to meet its cash flow constraint. But the charts also highlight the role of contagion due to the systemic feedbacks. The distributions have a long left-hand tail, which is a direct consequence of the feedbacks, which can in some cases cause several institutions to default. This fat tail emerges in spite of the Gaussian nature of the underlying shocks to macroeconomic fundamentals. These illustrative results point toward the importance of considering funding liquidity risk and systemic feedbacks in quantitative models of systemic risk.

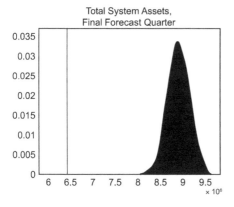 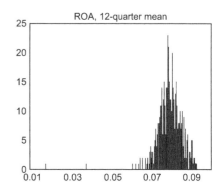

Fig. 1.10   Total system assets—final quarter: No liquidity effects

Note: Vertical line represents total system assets from the 2007 published accounts. RoA on a quarterly basis, in percent.

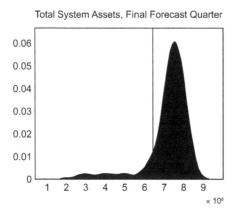 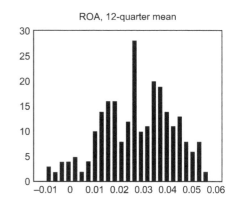

Fig. 1.11   Total system assets—final quarter: With liquidity effects

Note: Vertical line represents total system assets from the 2007 published accounts.

By adding on various components individually, the model can be used to identify how different mechanisms contribute to the profile of systemic risk. For example, the introduction of the danger zone framework permits failure even if a bank's capital does not fall below the regulatory minimum and thus worsens the loss distribution. Confidence contagion, counterparty defaults, liquidity hoarding, and asset fire sales all amplify distress in the tail, but allowing for hoarding and fire sales, increases the survival chances of individual banks. It is possible to dissect the tail to identify the particular contributions of these different feedbacks—for an exercise in this spirit that tries to disentangle the effects of (post-failure) fire sales and counterparty default, see Alessandri et al. (2009).

1.6 Conclusions and Future Work

The main contribution of this chapter has been to discuss and model how systemic risk may escalate and contagion may spread to other institutions as a bank's funding conditions deteriorate, irrespective of whether the bank ultimately survives or fails. Quantitative simulations illustrate how liquidity feedbacks can amplify other sources of risk.

Our model captures several channels of systemic funding liquidity crises. By using simple indicators and analyzing bank-specific cash flow constraints, we assess the onset and evolution of liquidity stress in various phases. As distressed banks lose access to longer-term funding markets, their liabilities snowball into shorter maturities, further increasing funding liquidity risk. Stressed banks take defensive actions in an attempt to stave off a liquidity crisis, which may, in turn, have a systemic impact. In particular, liquidity hoarding shortens the wholesale liability structure of other banks, while asset fire sales may affect the value of other banks' assets, which in turn can affect their funding conditions. Beyond this, spillovers between banks may occur due to confidence contagion or via default cascades in the interbank network.

The model could be extended in several ways. For example, rather than generating all shocks from a macroeconomic model, it would be interesting to allow for direct shocks to banks' cash flow constraints, perhaps linked to some underlying aggregate liquidity shock. It would also be helpful to capture the evolution of systemic liquidity crises on a more granular basis, incorporating more developed behavioral assumptions. With sufficient data, more detailed analysis of liquidity feedbacks over a time period of less than three months should be possible in this framework. But further extensions are likely to be more challenging, as modeling the optimal endogenous response to shocks is a highly complex problem—banks would need to optimize over different asset classes and maturity structures, taking account of shocks to fundamentals and behavioral reactions of all other market participants. Finally, it would be interesting to use the framework to explore the role that macroprudential policies such as time-varying liquidity buffers (see Bank of England 2011) might be able to play in containing systemic risk.

Appendix

An Example of a Danger Zone Calibration Using Continental Illinois

Case studies indicate that the danger zone approach performs relatively well, especially in terms of capturing the ranking of institutions under most stress. We have considered case studies beyond the current crisis. An example

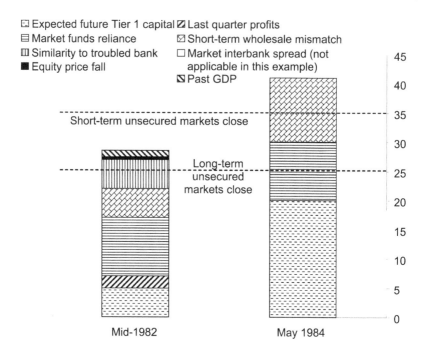

Fig. 1A.1   Applying danger zones to the failure of Continental Illinois

is the case of Continental Illinois, which, at least in terms of funding liquidity pressure, can be divided into two periods: the closure of longer-term domestic funding markets to it in July 1982 and the global run in May 1984. Figure 1A.1 scores Continental Illinois in each of these periods.

Reflecting its high dependence on wholesale funding, Continental scores highly on the market funds reliance indicator. But solvency concerns also played a crucial role for Continental. In particular, the July 1982 run may be identified with mild concerns over future solvency stemming from anticipated losses on risky speculative loans to the energy sector. Many of these loans had been originated by Penn Square, a much smaller bank that failed earlier that month. Aside from rising solvency concerns, Continental scores points following Penn Square's failure both because of its similarity and because of a significant unanticipated loss due to a direct exposure. Overall, Continental scores enough points for the first danger zone threshold to be crossed.

After 1982, Continental had greatly reduced access to long-term funding markets. Therefore, increased reliance on short-term funding served to increase Continental's DZ score over the next couple of years (the snowballing effect). But the final trigger for the second run was the fallout from the Latin American debt crisis—this substantially raised future solvency concerns during the first part of 1984 so that by May, Continental exceeds the second danger zone threshold and ultimately fails.

References

Acharya, V., and O. Merrouche. 2012. "Precautionary Hoarding of Liquidity and Inter-Bank Markets: Evidence from the Sub-Prime Crisis." *Review of Finance*, forthcoming.

Acharya, V., and T. Yorulmazer. 2008. "Information Contagion and Bank Herding." *Journal of Money, Credit and Banking* 40:215–31.

Acharya, V., and D. Skeie. 2011. "A Model of Liquidity Hoarding and Term Premia in Inter-Bank Markets." *Journal of Monetary Economics* 58 (5): 436–47.

Adrian, T., and H. S. Shin. 2010. "Liquidity and Leverage." *Journal of Financial Intermediation* 19 (3): 418–37.

Aikman, D., P. Alessandri, B. Eklund, P. Gai, S. Kapadia, E. Martin, N. Mora, G. Sterne, and M. Willison. 2009. "Funding Liquidity Risk in a Quantitative Model of Systemic Stability." Bank of England Working Paper no. 372. London: Bank of England.

Alessandri, P., P. Gai, S. Kapadia, N. Mora, and C. Puhr. 2009. "Towards a Framework for Quantifying Systemic Stability." *International Journal of Central Banking* 5 (3): 47–81.

Allen, F., and D. Gale. 2000. "Financial Contagion." *Journal of Political Economy* 108 (1): 1–33.

Angelini, P., A. Nobili, and C. Picillo. 2011. "The Interbank Market after August 2007: What Has Changed, and Why?" *Journal of Money, Credit and Banking* 43 (5): 923–58.

Bagehot, W. 1873. *Lombard Street: A Description of the Money Market*. London: HS King.

Bank of England. 2007. "An Indicative Decomposition of Libor Spreads." *Bank of England Quarterly Bulletin* 47 (4): 498–99.

Bank of England. 2011. "Instruments of Macroprudential Policy." Discussion Paper, December.

Bank for International Settlements. 2006. "The Management of Liquidity Risk in Financial Groups." *The Joint Forum of the Basel Committee on Banking Supervision*. Basel: BIS, May.

Basel Committee on Banking Supervision. 2010. *Basel III: International Framework for Liquidity Risk Measurement, Standards and Monitoring*. Basel: Bank for International Settlements, December.

Borio, C., and M. Drehmann. 2009. "Towards an Operational Framework for Financial Stability: 'Fuzzy' Measurement and Its Consequences." BIS Working Paper 284. Basel: Bank for International Settlements.

Brunnermeier, M. K., and L. H. Pedersen. 2009. "Market Liquidity and Funding Liquidity." *Review of Financial Studies* 22 (6): 2201–38.

Caballero, R. J., and A. Krishnamurthy. 2008. "Collective Risk Management in a Flight to Quality Episode." *Journal of Finance* 63:2195–236.

Campello, M., E. Giambona, J. R. Graham, and C. R. Harvey. 2010. "Liquidity Management and Corporate Investment during a Financial Crisis." NBER Working Paper no. 16309. Cambridge, MA: National Bureau of Economic Research, August.

Chari, V., and R. Jagannathan. 1988. "Banking Panics, Information, and Rational Expectations Equilibrium." *Journal of Finance* 43 (3): 749–61.

Chen, Y. 1999. "Banking Panics: The Role of the First-Come, First-Served Rule and Information Externalities." *Journal of Political Economy* 107 (5): 946–68.

Christensen, J., J. Lopez, and G. Rudebusch. 2009. "Do Central Bank Liquidity Facilities Affect Interbank Lending Rates?" Working Paper Series no. 2009-13, Federal Reserve Bank of San Francisco.

Cifuentes, R., G. Ferrucci, and H. S. Shin. 2005. "Liquidity Risk and Contagion." Bank of England Working Paper no. 264. London: Bank of England.

Dawes, R. M. 1979. "The Robust Beauty of Improper Linear Models in Decision Making." *American Psychologist* 34:571–82.

Dawes, R. M., and B. Corrigan. 1974. "Linear Models in Decision Making." *Psychological Bulletin* 81:95–106.

Diamond, D., and P. Dybvig. 1983. "Bank Runs, Deposit Insurance, and Liquidity." *Journal of Political Economy* 91:401–19.

Drehmann, M. 2002. "Will an Optimal Deposit Insurance Always Increase Financial Stability?" Bonn Econ Discussion Paper 28/2002, University of Bonn, Germany.

Drehmann, M., and K. Nikolaou. 2012. "Funding Liquidity Risk: Definition and Measurement." *Journal of Banking and Finance*, forthcoming.

European Central Bank. 2002. *Developments in Banks' Liquidity Profile and Management.* Frankfurt: ECB, May.

———. 2008. *Euro Money Market Survey.* Frankfurt: ECB, September.

Eisenberg, L., and T. Noe. 2001. "Systemic Risk in Financial Systems." *Management Science* 47 (2): 236–49.

Elsinger, H., A. Lehar, and M. Summer. 2006. "Risk Assessment for Banking Systems." *Management Science* 52:1301–41.

Fisher, I. 1933. "The Debt-Deflation Theory of Great Depressions." *Econometrica* 1 (4): 337–57.

Freixas, X., B. M. Parigi, and J. C. Rochet. 2000. "Systemic Risk, Interbank Relations, and Liquidity Provision by the Central Bank." *Journal of Money, Credit, and Banking* 32 (3): 611–38.

Furfine, C. 2002. "The Interbank Market during a Crisis." *European Economic Review* 46:809–20.

Gai, P., A. Haldane, and S. Kapadia. 2011. "Complexity, Concentration and Contagion." *Journal of Monetary Economics* 58 (5): 453–70.

Gai, P., and S. Kapadia. 2010. "Contagion in Financial Networks." *Proceedings of the Royal Society A* 466 (2120): 2401–23.

Gatev, E., and P. E. Strahan. 2006. "Banks' Advantage in Hedging Liquidity Risk: Theory and Evidence from the Commercial Paper Market." *Journal of Finance* 61 (2): 867–92.

Gatev, E., T. Schuermann, and P. E. Strahan. 2009. "Managing Bank Liquidity Risk: How Deposit-Loan Synergies Vary with Market Conditions." *Review of Financial Studies* 22 (3): 995–1020.

Geanakoplos, J. 2010. "Solving the Present Crisis and Managing the Leverage Cycle." *Federal Reserve Bank of New York Economic Policy Review* 2010 (August): 101–31.

Gigerenzer, G., and H. Brighton. 2009. "Homo Heuristicus: Why Biased Binds Make Better Inferences." *Topics in Cognitive Science* 1 (1): 107–43.

Goldstein, I., and A. Pauzner. 2005. "Demand-Deposit Contracts and the Probability of Bank Runs." *Journal of Finance* 60 (3): 1293–327.

Gorton, G., and A. Metrick. 2010. "Haircuts." *Federal Reserve Bank of St. Louis Review* 92 (6): 507–20.

Ha, Y., and B. Hodgetts. 2011. *Macro-Prudential Instruments for New Zealand: A Preliminary Assessment.* Wellington: Reserve Bank of New Zealand.

Heider, F., M. Hoerova, and C. Holthausen. 2009. "Liquidity Hoarding and Interbank Market Spreads: The Role of Counterparty Risk." European Central Bank Working Paper no. 1126. Frankfurt: ECB.

Holmström, B., and J. Tirole. 1998. "Private and Public Supply of Liquidity." *Journal of Political Economy* 106:1–40.

Huang, R. 2009. "How Committed Are Bank Lines of Credit? Experiences in the

Subprime Mortgage Crisis." Federal Reserve Bank of Philadelphia Working Paper no. 10-25.

Institute of International Finance. 2007. *Principles of Liquidity Risk Management.* Washington, DC: IIF, May.

Ivashina, V., and D. S. Scharfstein. 2010. "Bank Lending during the Financial Crisis of 2008." *Journal of Financial Economics* 97 (3): 319–38.

Matz, L. 2007. "Contingency Planning." In *Liquidity Risk: Measurement and Management,* edited by L. Matz and P. Neu, 121–45. Singapore: Wiley Finance.

Matz, L., and P. Neu. 2007. *Liquidity Risk: Measurement and Management.* Singapore: Wiley Finance.

McGuire, P., and G. von Peter. 2009. "The US Dollar Shortage in Global Banking." *BIS Quarterly Review* March:47–63.

Nakaso, H. 2001. "The Financial Crisis in Japan during the 1990s: How the Bank of Japan Responded and the Lessons Learnt." BIS Papers, no. 6. http://www.bis .org/publ/bppdf/bispap06.pdf?noframes=1.

Oesterreichische Nationalbank [Austrian National Bank] (OeNB). 2006. "Systemic Risk Monitor: Risk Assessment and Stress Testing for the Austrian Banking System." Available from http://www.gwu.edu/~gefri/PDF/SrmModelBook.pdf.

Pennacchi, G. 2006. "Deposit Insurance, Bank Regulation and Financial System Risk." *Journal of Monetary Economics* 53:1–30.

Rochet, J.-C., and X. Vives. 2004. "Coordination Failures and the Lender of Last Resort: Was Bagehot Right After All?" *Journal of the European Economic Association* 2 (6): 1116–47.

Shim, I., and G. von Peter. 2007. "Distress Selling and Asset Market Feedback: A Survey." Bank for International Settlements Working Paper 229. Basel: BIS.

Upper, C. 2011. "Simulation Methods to Assess the Danger of Contagion in Interbank Markets." *Journal of Financial Stability* 7 (3): 111–25.

van den End, J. W. 2008. "Liquidity Stress-Tester: A Macro Model for Stress-testing Banks' Liquidity Risk." DNB Working Paper 175. Amsterdam: De Nederlandsche Bank.

Wells, S. 2004. "Financial Interlinkages in the United Kingdom's Interbank Market and the Risk of Contagion." Bank of England Working Paper no. 230. London: Bank of England.

Comment   Mikhail V. Oet

Summary

Let me open by summarizing the main points of the chapter. The chapter describes a liquidity feedback model (hereafter, LFM) within a quantitative

Mikhail V. Oet is an economist in the Supervision and Regulation Department of the Federal Reserve Bank of Cleveland.

I would like thank the conference organizers, Andrew Lo and Joseph Haubrich, for inviting me. The chapter "Liquidity Risk, Cash Flow Constraints, and Systemic Feedbacks," by Sujit Kapadia, Matthias Drehmann, John Elliott, and Gabriel Sterne, is a very important and interesting study in the context of systemic feedbacks. I have followed several versions of this chapter to its current state with pleasure and am honored to be given an opportunity to comment.

The content represents the views of the author and is not to be considered as the views of the Federal Reserve Bank of Cleveland or the Federal Reserve System. For acknowledgments, framework of systemic risk.[1] The LFM simulates balance sheets and funding interactions of a population of banks within a financial system[2] to assess shock-induced feedback effects on the individual banks and the represented financial system. The model represents the systemic interactions through five contagion channels and analyzes collapse mechanics in a financial system due to propagation of liquidity risk through bank balance sheets. The LFM offers a well-thought-out analysis of the mechanics of cash flow constraints and liquidity effects and institutional actions and reactions through a set of network relationships.

Model Framework

The liquidity feedback model can be described as a progressive simulation of the following three stages:

1. Institutional liquidity risk assessment
2. Feedback (systemic) effects
3. Retesting of system solvency

As a component of a quantitative framework of systemic risk, the LFM is complemented by modules that at a minimum allow (a) the application of shocks, (b) attribution of effects to institutional balance sheets and income statements, and (c) reinvestment to maintain solvency and to manage institutional assets and liabilities.[3]

In the initial stage, the LFM projects individual bank ratings[4] to determine future funding costs and whether the institution falls into a danger zone. The latter is determined via a separate model of deterioration of the bank credit ratings and their funding costs.

In the second stage, the LFM analyzes feedback systemic effects. Certain funding markets close to a bank when its danger zone score exceeds specified thresholds.[5] The bank fails when it is no longer able to meet its cash flow constraints or when its capital falls below the regulatory minimum. As funding markets close or as the bank fails, the remaining banks in the financial

sources of research support, and disclosure of the author's material financial relationships, if any, please see http://www.nber.org/chapters/c12050.ack.

1. The LFMs originated as an important component of the Bank of England Risk Assessment Model for Systemic Institutions (RAMSI). Current development of the LFM allows for stand-alone modeling of liquidity feedbacks suitable for alternative quantitative approaches to systemic risk.

2. The specific analysis is performed on the RAMSI population of the ten largest UK banks as of 2007 year-end.

3. For example, RAMSI framework utilizes the following modules in addition to its LFM core: (a) macroeconomic BVAR model for macro/financial shocks, (b) credit risk model for bank PDs and LGDs, (c) institutional balance sheet and income statement model, and (d) reinvestment model.

4. In RAMSI, the LFM is supplied via modules (a) and (b). Outside of RAMSI, the inputs may be obtained through the supporting quantitative framework for systemic risk.

5. Long-term unsecured funding markets close when danger zone score reaches 25. Short-term funding markets close when danger zone score reaches 35.

network absorb the financial effects of the LFM systemic feedbacks, specifically: bankruptcy costs (through counterparty interbank lending losses), asset fire sales (through mark-to-market losses), general confidence slide (through increased funding costs for the remaining market participants), and snowballing and liquidity squeeze effects (through defensive actions by the distressed institution).

In the third stage, the LFM retests system solvency. If a particular bank fails, the model adjusts counterparty credit losses and mark-to-market available-for-sale (AFS) assets, updates danger zone scores, and retests individual banks for survival.

Model Evolution

It is important to note that the RAMSI framework is modular, and that the LFM is designed to fit a set of specific objectives within RAMSI. It is also instructive to view the LFM through its evolution within RAMSI. Originally, bank failure occurred when a bank was shut out of funding markets.[6] Therefore, the failure mode did not include the bank's flow constraint, and the contagion channels were "rational"; that is, they only operated after one or more banks had failed. The current LFM reflects the progressions of RAMSI from a stability model to a model of systemic conditions. In its original form as a funding liquidity model, the LFM looked at the effects stemming from a four-element mechanism: rating downgrades, solvency concerns, funding profile, and confidence. The current LFM extends the original mechanism by simulating additionally certain defensive actions by the banks, specifically (a) cash flows from defensive actions by banks, and (b) effects of the defensive actions on funding pressures. In both the original and the extended model, the combined effects of the feedback factors would trigger closure of markets to particular institutions. Therefore, through its extension to the present form, the model focus remains consistent. The main research question of the LFM remains as follows: is failure likely through a liquidity-based transmission mechanism?

Comparative Feedback

In this section I will offer some comparative feedback. The current version of the chapter identifies a number of pending modeling improvements. Therefore, this feedback would be conceptual and comparative in nature, raising some questions and offering some alternative approaches. Largely, this feedback expresses a perspective that I developed through work on an alternative quantitative framework of systemic risk at the Federal Reserve Bank of Cleveland.

---

6. Aikman et al. (2009, 3).

What Is the Systemic Motivation: Institutional Stability or Systemic Risk?

The motivation for this comparison is as follows. The chapter describes a model of liquidity feedbacks in a quantitative model of systemic risk (RAMSI). RAMSI's original motivation is a quantitative model of systemic stability. Thus, it is fair to recognize first, that the origins of the LFM lie within a stability model, and second, that stability is inherently a structural question. Why is this important?

RAMSI framework is taking balance sheet data for top UK financial institutions individually and then constructing a network model between these institutions based on *interbank exposures.*

The constructed network model then is considered to define the financial system. The model sends simulated shocks through the network to study feedback-induced collapse mechanisms of individual institutions and the resulting collapse path through the network. What is useful to note here is that the constructed network is just one example of the possible representations of the financial system, based on two assumptions:

Assumption I: Top banks are necessary and sufficient to represent all financial institutions in the system.

Assumption II: Aggregated interbank exposures are necessary and sufficient to represent the top banks.

Therefore, a violation of any of the previous two assumptions will prompt the need for the financial system to be described by more than one type of network. In the event that Assumption I is violated, the financial system may need to be represented by other types of participants in the financial services industry that contribute to systemic effects.[7] Violation of Assumption II will lead to representations that include a number of different asset classes. In general, it can be reasonably expected that due to concentrations within the financial system, the networks can vary quite widely by asset class and be dynamic in nature, both through attrition of the market players and through willful redistribution of assets by financial system participants to optimize returns.

Representing the financial system through the interbank lending network is only one possible representation of the financial system. A different set of institutions might be engaged and a different set of concentrations might be envisioned in networks represented by different asset classes. Since different representations could lead to the population change, the results of the simulated shocks might actually differ from the results based on the interbank

---

7. For example, thrift institutions, insurance firms, investment companies including hedge funds and mutual funds, pension funds, finance companies, securities brokers and dealers, mortgage companies, and real estate investment trusts. See Kroszner (1996).

lending-based network. Therefore, one possible direction to enhance the model would be to allow for collapse originating in an asset class. A second possible direction would be to enhance the model by extending the typological representation of the financial system from banks to a wider set of market participants. The 2007 crisis provides evidence that a propagation mechanism can initiate within a narrow set of asset class exposures with specific characteristics[8] and only later expand to the interbank market.[9]

Given the evolution of RAMSI and the LFM as a stability framework, it is not surprising to find that the stability is tested through simulation. Inherent within this simulation is an estimator for danger zones, that is, areas where probability of institutional instability is sufficiently high so that they can be hypothesized to represent likely or imminent failure states. Thus, running an effective systemic stability simulation would presuppose ability to effectively identify the institutional and systemic danger zones. A suggested refinement of the LFM therefore deals with the clarity and validity of this inherent identification. Thus, in order for the LFM and RAMSI to be successful in identifying systemic stability, the two must effectively embed an identification system, similar to an early warning system (EWS) that defines the variety of modes of failure. To the extent that these systemic failure modes stem from liquidity-induced feedbacks, the LFM should be able to accommodate the range of causal drivers effectively. In the LFM, the danger zones approach serves as the identification system with failure states defined a priori. Thus, support of the LFM identification system may be enhanced through further discussion of the parameterization and validation of the danger zone thresholds. One possible direction for clarifying the identification basis of a stability simulation is through the alternative methodology of an early warning system, for example, via empirical support for selection of danger zone thresholds.

In its present state, the LFM as part of RAMSI is clearly a simulation model that results in institutional and system distributions of assets and losses, so the resulting outcome may be considered to represent solvency. RAMSI exemplifies one type of quantitative framework of systemic risk (stability based) that benefits from the LFM. Alternative quantitative frameworks of systemic risk would similarly benefit from the LFM simulation model. As a stability framework, RAMSI asks two key questions: "Is an institution or system solvent?"; and "Is failure likely through a liquidity-based transmission mechanism?" An alternative key question that may be asked is: "Are there imbalances (potential expectations shocks) and network structural weaknesses that increase the probability of systemic stress?" This alternative question in fact arises within an early-warning system approach

---

8. For example, valuation uncertainty in mortgage-backed securities and structured finance exposures.

9. For example, through collateral assets tied to counterparty-risk exposures.

for systemic stress.[10] The shared technical challenge for both types of approaches is incorporation of uncertainty in the identification problem. In a simulation approach, the assessment depends on the success of capturing uncertainty in the simulated propagation mechanism. Omission of uncertainty will bias the correct estimation of placement within a danger zone. Similarly, a bias in estimating the effect of uncertainty will likely result in a biased estimation of EWS parameters.[11]

It is also useful to consider the formulation of shocks in the two alternate approaches. For the LFM and RAMSI, the only source of shocks is the Bayesian VAR module that captures the evolution of macroeconomic and financial variables. Therefore, a reasonable question might be: "Can the model allow for shocks originating within the financial system?" For example, in the SAFE approach, shocks can be triggered by imbalances, stemming from failure of expectations about return, risk, and liquidity in a wide variety of asset classes on- and off- institutional balance sheets.[12]

Another useful comparison is the causal framework behind the model. The LFM is fed and simulated through a clear schema: "systemic risks stem from the connectivity of bank balance sheets via interbank exposures (counterparty risk); the interaction between balance sheets and asset prices (fire sale effects); and confidence effects that may affect funding conditions."[13] In addition, effects of institutional defensive actions (hoarding and snowballing) are incorporated. This schema is essentially causal, feeding a simulation model of funding conditions that are affected by five factors: connectivity through interbank exposures, fire sale effects, confidence effects, liquidity hoarding, and snowballing. Thus, the research questions to extend the LFM can be formulated as follows:

- "Are the above factors sufficient to fully represent the possible liquidity-related propagation mechanism?"
- "Are there additional propagation mechanisms that can be tested using the LFM?"

10. Dependent variable in such an EWS can be a continuous measure calibrated to provide signals of probability and severity of systemic stress in the financial markets. The theoretical foundations for such an approach to identification are established in Borio and Drehmann (2009), Hanschel and Monnin (2005), and Illing and Liu (2003; 2006). An example of this approach can be seen in a model developed at the Federal Reserve Bank of Cleveland, dubbed SAFE for Systemic Assessment of Financial Environment (see Oet et al. 2011), that also asks if supervisory institutional data can help forecast the probability of a systemic stress in financial markets. The primary objective of such an early warning system is to serve as a supervisory monitoring tool enabling consideration of specific ex ante regulatory policy alternatives for systemic stress. SAFE EWS is implemented as a scenario-based optimal-lag regression model.

11. SAFE provides an alternative approach to accommodating "an uncertainty function" within a systemic stress early-warning system, where an uncertainty factor drives assessment scenarios.

12. The authors discuss that incorporation of shocks originating within financial institutions would be an interesting extension to the LFM. Presently, the LFM does not implement this extension.

13. Aikman et al. (2009, 3).

By extension, a larger quantitative framework of systemic risk might ask a broader question: "Are there additional propagation mechanisms that are relevant?" The LFM is a rich simulation environment for the analytical study of the path to collapse. However, in the event that additional propagation mechanisms are relevant, it is the responsibility of the feeder modules of a quantitative framework of systemic risk to test a variety of shocks. Hence, the LFM should be able to accommodate a variety of shock sources. Presently, the LFM primarily looks to liquidity-relevant "transactions," but leaves open by what factors the interbank exposures, asset prices, and confidence are motivated. Thus, relevant propagation mechanisms are "hidden" behind the transaction-based perspective of the LFM. For comparison, it is again useful to refer to the early warning system approach used in the Cleveland Fed's SAFE model. The EWS approach allows a variety of propagation mechanisms through several distinct classes of variables. For example, shocks in the model are allowed through three distinct types of asset-class imbalances in (1) return, (2) risk, and (3) liquidity. In addition, shocks are possible through structural weaknesses in the system. These structural weaknesses can stem from three types of structural imbalances: connectivity, concentration, and contagion.[14] Conceptually, this approach to structural factors largely parallels the theoretical precedent set by James Thomson (2009).

Path to Collapse

An important output of the Liquidity Feedback Model is path to collapse. This path is deterministic once the LFM establishes the BVAR shocks, their effects on the composition of the institutional balance sheet, and the interbank lending-based network. This leads to the following five questions:

1. Is there possibly a variety of failure modes affecting liquidity?
2. Is there a variety of propagation mechanisms?
3. If the structure is not static and underlying drivers have an irrational element, is a precise network important?
4. Are interbank exposures more representative of network effects than asset-class based associations?
5. How else can these networks be modeled?

Significantly, an alternative EWS-based quantitative framework may allow a systemic risk researcher to remain agnostic as to a particular precise path to collapse and particular institutions affected. The agnosticism stems from an ability of EWS to consider an aggregate systemic condition vis-à-vis the likelihood of systemic stress.[15] SAFE EWS, for example, allows a variety of failure modes through an approach that is less deterministic. SAFE failure modes originate in shocks through return, risk, and liquidity imbalances and act through a variety

14. Thomson (2009).
15. Gramlich et al. (2010); Ergundor and Thomson (2005).

of structural weaknesses (connectivity, concentration, contagion). Thus, the LFM may be complemented by a quantitative framework that, like an EWS, would accommodate a flexible set of propagation mechanisms.

It is worthwhile to detail this point further. Presently, the LFM simulation represents the systemic condition through stability, where stability of the system is the function of the stability of *discrete financial institutions.* However, within an EWS context, the LFM would support the representation of systemic condition through accumulations of systemic stress in *discrete asset classes.* The systemic stress in the EWS context is driven by the aggregated institutional imbalances and structural factors. Stated differently, the flexibility of the LFM may be increased by extending it from the present application in the bottom-up approach to simulate systemic stability from stability of individual institutions to a top-down approach to obtain early warning of stress in the financial system as a whole through accumulated imbalances in asset classes, including their structural characteristics.

Uncertainty: Rational, Irrational, and the Unobservable

Rational and irrational aspects present another interesting avenue of exploration. In the LFM, through the onset of shocks, banks make defensive choices at each quarterly period. The simulated results then serve as inputs for subsequent quarterly iteration. One possible shortcoming of this approach is that in practice failure is uncertain.[16] In the LFM, the failure state is deterministic. The mechanism of shocks and defensive actions by the banks is rational. There is a probability, however, presently not addressed in the LFM, that failure may be stochastic, the result of *random shocks,* or that network interactions become driven by *irrational* events.[17] Even more precariously, these factors may in fact be *rational from the perspective of the system as a whole,*[18] but remain opaque and *unobservable* to the individual institutions. Regardless of the precise nature of these factors—stochastic, irrational, or unobservable—the individual institutions may not anticipate precisely the timing, frequency, and severity of their impacts, but need to sustain them effectively in order to survive. Allowing these uncertain drivers (stochastic, irrational, or unobservable)[19] within a systemic model would enhance its usefulness. Therefore, if the irrational or unobservable drivers are allowed, then the natural question is, "Can they emerge spontaneously in the model?" If yes, then a systemic model will need to assess whether a healthy institution or system can withstand these drivers. Estimation of uncertainty in these driv-

16. For example, a particular source of uncertainty may be a regulatory action or inaction in the face of changing market or institutional conditions.
17. For example, some of these irrational events may be triggered by information asymmetry, perceptions of counterparty risk, or even fears—a whole variety of concerns.
18. For example, the system as whole may be driven by the aggregate market factors, asset-class characteristics, or structural attributes of a specific network.
19. Unobservable from the point of view of individual institutions.

ers then becomes a critical challenge for such a model. This is difficult and perhaps impossible to do well, since the uncertainty, particularly the irrational, are unknowable in the Knightian sense. Nevertheless, in order to deal effectively with this uncertainty, the model must find a way to estimate it.[20]

Suggestions

A number of the deterministic features of the LFM (e.g., BVAR, the defined interbank lending network, mechanics of credit rating migrations) and the lack of explicit stochastic elements and jump factors serve to limit the effective question of the LFM to whether liquidity-induced failure is likely. To the extent that the LFM seeks to expand its application within a systemic risk framework from the "likely" to the "possible," it needs to begin to incorporate some stochastic elements, jump conditions, and mechanisms that represent uncertainty of the market behavior and irrational market drivers.

The chapter already discusses a number of extensions that include similar elements. To this end, I would offer the following additional suggestions:

1. *Fire-sale model.* The LFM generates a relatively minor range in fire-sale haircuts from 2 percent to 5 percent. Recalibration of the fire-sale model factors θ and ε may be suggested.[21] In addition, the LFM can further emphasize the role of the market shock factor ε in the current LFM fire-sale model. Ideally, these model factors would capture a varying risk and some uncertainty.

2. *Asset-price model.* The Bayesian macroeconomic model (BVAR) does not strongly explain sample data on asset price shocks. Further, the LFM's asset price shocks occur in two parts, first from a decline in economic fundamentals and second from institutional liquidity feedback effects. The LFM can further explore the systemic stress condition that may be induced not by institutional effects but by asset-class effects, such as jump reversion to some long-term economic fundamentals (e.g., due to loss of confidence).

3. *PD / LGD correlations.* Discussion in a prior version of the study[22] reveals that PDs have limited and deteriorating power to explain debt in arrears during economic downturns. One possible explanation of this is due to an omitted variable that arises significantly during downturn conditions, for example, correlation between PD and LGD.

---

20. One possible method for dealing with uncertainty may be allowed by the application of the LFM within an EWS approach. In the SAFE EWS, the relative distances between crisis-driven valuations, stress-driven valuations, and normal valuations are monitored each period. Similar to the LFM, the stress and crisis valuations are amplified (Krishnamurthy 2009b) through liquidity feedback and asset fire sales. In SAFE, the crisis valuations are driven by "irrational" valuations in hypothetical immediate fire sales, whereas the stress valuations are driven by longer horizon asset sales, where "irrational" concerns are allowed to progressively subside.

21. See, for example, Board of Governors of the Federal Reserve System (2009); Basel Committee on Banking Supervision (2009); and Krishnamurthy (2009a).

22. Aikman et al. (2009).

Conclusion

In its current state, the LFM is essentially a simulation tool for institutional stability that looks at systemic stability from a particular propagation mechanism of macroeconomically-fed liquidity constraint. In addition, the LFM has limited ability to address uncertainty and asset-class effects. A useful extension of the LFM's application can be considered: from quantification of systemic risk from institutional stability to an EWS objective of monitoring systemic stress. It may therefore be highly desirable to extend the LFM to enable an analytical convergence that would incorporate a robust early warning system and a powerful LFM simulation engine.

References

Aikman, David, Piergiorgio Alessandri, Bruno Eklund, Prasanna Gai, Sujit Kapadia, Elizabeth Martin, Nada Mora, Gabriel Sterne, and Matthew Willison. 2009. "Funding Liquidity Risk in a Quantitative Model of Systemic Stability." Bank of England Working Paper, no. 372, June. London: Bank of England.

Basel Committee on Banking Supervision. 2009. "International Framework for Liquidity Risk Measurement, Standards and Monitoring." Consultative Document, December. Basel: Bank for International Settlements.

Board of Governors of the Federal Reserve System. 2009. "The Supervisory Capital Assessment Program: Overview of Results." White Paper, May 7. Washington, DC: Board of Governors of the Federal Reserve System.

Borio, Claudio, and Mathias Drehmann. 2009. "Assessing the Risk of Banking Crises—Revisited." *Bank for International Settlements Quarterly Review* March: 29–46.

Ergungor, Emre O., and James B. Thomson. 2005. "Systemic Banking Crises." Federal Reserve Bank of Cleveland Policy Discussion Paper no. 2. Cleveland: Federal Reserve Bank of Cleveland.

Gramlich, Dieter, Gavin Miller, Mikhail Oet, and Stephen Ong. 2010. "Early Warning Systems for Systemic Banking Risk: Critical Review and Modeling Implications." *Banks and Bank Systems* 5 (2): 199–211.

Hanschel, Elke, and Pierre Monnin. 2005. "Measuring and Forecasting Stress in the Banking Sector: Evidence from Switzerland." BIS Working Paper no. 22. Basel: Bank for International Settlements.

Illing, Mark, and Ying Liu. 2003. "An Index of Financial Stress for Canada." Bank of Canada Working Paper no. 2003-14, June. Ottawa: Bank of Canada.

———. 2006. "Measuring Financial Stress in a Developed Country: An Application to Canada." *Journal of Financial Stability* 2 (3): 243–65.

Krishnamurthy, Arvind. 2009a. "Amplification Mechanisms in Liquidity Crises." NBER Working Paper no. 15040. Cambridge, MA: National Bureau of Economic Research, June.

———. 2009b. "Amplification Mechanisms in Liquidity Crises." Unpublished Working Paper. Presented at the 45th Annual Conference on Bank Structure and Competition, Federal Reserve Bank of Chicago. Chicago, Illinois, April 16.

Kroszner, Randall. 1996. "The Evolution of Universal Banking and Its Regulation in Twentieth Century America." In *Universal Banking: Financial System Design Reconsidered,* edited by A. Saunders and I. Walter, 70–99. Chicago: Irwin.

Oet, Mikhail V., Ryan Eiben, Timothy Bianco, Dieter Gramlich, Stephen J. Ong, and

Jin Wang. 2011. "SAFE: An Early Warning System for Systemic Banking Risk." Federal Reserve Bank of Cleveland Working Paper, no. 11-29. Cleveland: Federal Reserve Bank of Cleveland.

Thomson, James B. 2009. "On Systemically Important Financial Institutions and Progressive Systemic Mitigation." Federal Reserve Bank of Cleveland Policy Discussion Paper no. 27, August. Cleveland: Federal Reserve Bank of Cleveland.

Endogenous and Systemic Risk

Jon Danielsson, Hyun Song Shin,
and Jean-Pierre Zigrand

2.1 Introduction

Financial crises are often accompanied by sharp price changes. Commentators and journalists delight in attributing such unruly volatility to the herd mentality of the financial market participants, or to the fickleness and irrationality of speculators who seemingly switch between fear and overconfidence in a purely random fashion. Such crisis episodes lead to daily headlines in financial newspapers such as "Risk Aversion Rises" or "Risk Aversion Abates."

Such price swings would be consistent with price efficiency if they were entirely driven by pay-off-relevant fundamental news. A large part of this volatility is, however, due to a number of feedback effects that are hardwired into the system. We labeled this *endogenous risk* in Danielsson and Shin (2003) to emphasize that while the seeds of the volatility are exogenous, a large part of its eventual realized magnitude is due to the amplification of the exogenous news within the system.

Endogenous risk is the additional risk and volatility that the financial system adds on top of the equilibrium risk and volatility as commonly understood. For this reason, in the formal modeling exercise we will assume that financial institutions are risk neutral. This has the advantage that any feedback effects must be due to the system itself, rather than due to the risk-averse behavior of the financial institutions.

Jon Danielsson is a reader in finance at the London School of Economics. Hyun Song Shin is the Hughes-Rogers Professor of Economics at Princeton University and a research associate of the National Bureau of Economic Research. Jean-Pierre Zigrand is a reader in finance at the London School of Economics.

For acknowledgments, sources of research support, and disclosure of the authors' material financial relationships, if any, please see http://www.nber.org/chapters/c12054.ack.

Once the financial system is fully modeled to take account of the hard-wiring of risk feedback, it has the potential to magnify risk considerably. However, by the same token, the system can dampen realized risks "artificially," thereby encouraging the build-up of potential vulnerabilities. Part of our task is to show under which circumstances the magnifications occur. For empirical evidence, see Adrian and Shin (2010), who note that the major market-based financial intermediaries were deleveraging aggressively during the crisis, and that such financial intermediaries could be seen as the marginal investors for the determination of risk premiums.

In our model, endogenous risk and the inherent nonlinearities of the system are associated with fluctuations in the capitalization of the financial sector. As the capital of the financial sector fluctuates, so does realized risks. The balance sheet capacity of the financial sector fluctuates for both reasons. The risk exposure supported by each dollar of capital fluctuates due to shifts in measured risks, and so does the aggregate dollar capital of the financial sector itself.

The mutual dependence of realized risks and the willingness to bear risk means that the risk capacity of the financial system can undergo large changes over the cycle. Occasionally, short and violent bouts of risk shedding sweep the markets during which the financial institutions' apparent willingness to bear risk evaporates. Those are the episodes that are reported on in the news under the headline "risk aversion." It is as if there was a latent risk aversion process that drives financial markets. Of course, the fluctuation in risk aversion is itself endogenous, and in this chapter we sketch the mechanisms that drive the fluctuation.

By conceptualizing the problem in terms of constraints rather than preferences, we can address an apparent puzzle. How can it be that human beings are risk averse one day, in a perfectly coordinated fashion, selling their risky holdings across the board and reinforcing the crisis, only to become contagiously risk-loving not too long thereafter, pushing prices back to the precrisis levels? Surely they do not all together feel compelled to look right and left ten times before crossing the street one day while blindly crossing the next?

We then apply the results from the theoretical model to more practical questions of systemic risk. Empirical studies and financial history have taught us that financial markets go through long periods of tranquility interspersed by short episodes of instability, or even crises. Such behavior can be understood within our framework as periods where leverage growth and asset growth go together, leading financial institutions on a path driven by positive feedback between increasing leverage, purchases of risky assets, and higher prices. During this period, greater willingness to take on risk dampens measured risks and tends to reinforce the dormant volatility. The active trading by financial institutions works to reduce volatility while thickening the tails of the outcome distribution, and increases the magnitude of extreme events.

The amplification of risk over the cycle poses considerable challenges for bank capital regulation. A fundamental tenet of microprudential capital regulation is the idea that if every institution is individually safe, then so is the financial system itself. A surprising and counterintuitive result of analyzing prudential regulations is that the individually prudent behavior by a financial institution causes an overall amplified crisis. This is an illustration of the *fallacy of composition,* as discussed by Danielsson et al. (2001), who criticized the Basel II capital rules on these grounds.

Our results also have implications for financial risk forecasting and recent models of empirical systemic risk forecasting. The vast majority of such models assumes financial risk is exogenous, which may be an innocuous assumption during times when the financial markets are calm, but not during market turmoil. In general, an assumption of exogenous risk is likely to lead to an underestimation of risk when things are calm and an overestimation of risk during crisis. This means that most extant financial risk forecast models and empirical systemic risk models might fail when needed the most; that is, in the accurate forecasting of extreme risk.

There are also implications for regulation of over-the-counter (OTC) derivatives. The impact of moving OTC derivatives to central counterparties (CCPs) is analyzed by Zigrand (2010) in the light of endogenous risk. He notes that CCPs need to protect themselves from counterparty risk, implying institutionalized initial margin and maintenance margin rules based on continuous marking-to-market. Endogenous risk appears in several guises, to be elaborated in the following.

2.2 Endogenous Risk and Price Movements

In the main, price movements have two components—a portion due to the incorporation of fundamentals news, and an endogenous feedback component due to the trading patterns of the market participants over and above the incorporation of fundamentals news.

Large price movements driven by fundamentals news occur often in financial markets, and do not constitute a crisis. Public announcements of important macroeconomic statistics are sometimes marked by large, discrete price changes at the time of announcement. These changes are arguably the signs of a smoothly functioning market that is able to incorporate new information quickly.

In contrast, the distinguishing feature of crisis episodes is that they seem to gather momentum from the endogenous responses of the market participants themselves. This is the second component, the portion associated with *endogenous risk* (see Danielsson and Shin 2003). We can draw an analogy with a tropical storm gathering force over a warm sea or with the wobbly Millennium bridge in London.

A small gust of wind produces a small sway in the Millennium bridge.

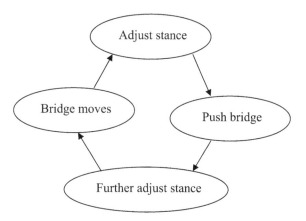

Fig. 2.1   Feedback loop of the Millennium Bridge

Pedestrians crossing the bridge would then adjust their stance slightly as a response, pushing the bridge further in the same direction. Provided sufficiently more pedestrians find themselves in the same situation, they will find themselves coordinating spontaneously and unwittingly to move in lockstep, thereby reinforcing the swaying into something much more violent. Even if the initial gust of wind is long gone, the bridge continues to wobble. Similarly, financial crises appear to gather more energy as they develop. And even if the initial shock is gone, volatility stays high. What would have been almost impossible if individual steps were independent becomes a sure thing given feedback between the movement of the bridge and the adjustment by pedestrians (see figure 2.1).

Analogously, as financial conditions worsen, the willingness of market participants to bear risk seemingly evaporates even in the absence of any further hard news, which in turn worsens financial conditions, closing the loop. Any regulatory interventions might be best aimed at understanding and mitigating those negative spillover effects created purely within the financial system. If one cannot prevent gusts of wind, then at least one can make sure the pedestrians do not act in lockstep and cause the bridge to collapse by critically amplifying the initial swing.

The workings of endogenous risk can be sketched as follows. An initial negative piece of news, leading either to capital losses to the financial institutions (FI) or to an increase in market volatility, must be followed by a risk exposure reduction on behalf of many market participants (or capital raising, which are difficult to do pull off quickly, especially in the midst of a crisis). The reason for contagious behavior lies in the coordinated responses of market participants arising from the fact that market prices are imperatives for action through risk constraints imposed on individual traders or desks (such as value at risk [VaR] constraints[1]), or through the increase in haircuts and the implied curtailment of leverage by credit providers.

To the extent that such rules are applied continuously, the market participants are induced to behave in a short-term manner. It follows that the initial wave of asset sales depresses prices further, increasing the perceived risk as well as reducing capitalization levels further, forcing a further round of fire sales, and so on. The fall in valuation levels is composed of a first chunk attributable to the initial piece of bad news, as well as to a second chunk entirely due to the noninformation related feedback effects of market participants. In formal models of this phenomenon, the feedback effects can be many times larger than the initial seed of bad news.

2.2.1   Leading Model

We illustrate the ideas sketched above through the dynamic model of endogenous risk developed in Daníelsson, Shin, and Zigrand (2011). The model has the advantage that it leads to a rational expectations equilibrium that can be solved in closed form. Here, we give a thumbnail sketch of the workings of the model. The detailed solution and the properties of the model can be found in Daníelsson, Shin, and Zigrand (2011).

Time flows continuously in $[0, \infty)$. Active traders (financial institutions) maximize profit by investing in risky securities as well as the riskless security. The financial institutions are subject to a short-term VaR constraint stipulating that the VaR is no higher than capital (tangible common equity), given by V_t. In order to emphasize the specific contribution of risk constraints to endogenous risk, all other channels are switched off. The short rate of interest r is determined exogenously.

Given rational behavior, prices, quantities and expectations can be shown to be driven in equilibrium by a set of relevant aggregate variables, chiefly the (mark-to-market) capitalization level of the financial sector. The financial institutions are interacting with each other and with passive investors (the non-financial investors, including individual investors, pension funds and so forth).

The risky security has an (instantaneous) expected equilibrium return μ_t and volatility of σ_t. The equilibrium processes μ and σ are endogenous and forward looking in the sense that the beliefs $(\tilde{\mu}_t, \tilde{\sigma}_t)$ about actual moments (μ_t, σ_t) are confirmed in equilibrium. Financial institutions in equilibrium hold diversified portfolios commensurate with those beliefs, scaled down by their effective degree of relative risk aversion γ_t (solved in equilibrium) imposed upon them by the VaR constraints:

---

1. See Danielsson and Zigrand (2008), where a VaR constraint lessens a free-riding externality in financial markets, and Adrian and Shin (2010) for a model whereby a VaR constraint is imposed in order to alleviate a moral hazard problem within a financial institution.

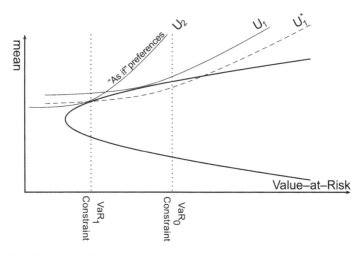

Fig. 2.2   Changing risk appetite

$$(1) \qquad\qquad D_t = \frac{V_t}{\gamma_t}^{-1} \sum_t (\mu_t - r),$$

with D being the monetary value of their holdings.

The model is closed by introducing value investors who supply downward-sloping demand curves for the risky asset. The value investors in aggregate have the exogenous demand schedule for the risky asset y_t where

$$(2) \qquad\qquad y_t = \frac{\delta}{\sigma_t^2}(z_t - \ln P_t),$$

where P_t is the market price for risky asset and where dz_t is a (favorable) Itô demand shock to the demand of the risky asset. Each demand curve can be viewed as a downward sloping demand hit by demand shocks, with δ being a scaling parameter that determines the size of the value investor sector.

Even though the financial institutions are risk neutral, the VaR constraints imply that they are compelled to act "as if" they were risk averse and scale their risky holdings down if VaR is high compared to their capitalization level:[2]

coefficient of effective relative risk aversion

= coeff. of relative risk aversion

+ Lagrange multiplier on the VaR constraint.

Thus, even if the traders were risk-neutral, they would act in a risk-averse way depending on how tightly the risk constraint is binding. Figure 2.2

2. This goes back to Danielsson and Zigrand (2008), first circulated as Danielsson and Zigrand (2001).

illustrates the general intuition as to why risk aversion is effectively fluctuating randomly as a function of the tightness of the VaR constraints of financial institutions. For the purpose of illustration, we draw the indfference curves consistent with some degree of inherent risk aversion. Suppose the FI initially has sufficient capital so that its VaR constraint is nonbinding at VaR_0. In this case, the indifference curve is U_1. Suppose investment opportunities stay constant but capital is reduced, so that the VaR constraint becomes binding at VaR_1. Therefore, the optimal portfolio chosen is no longer a tangency point between the indifference curve (shifted down to U_1^*) and the efficient set. An outside observer might conclude that the VaR constrained portfolio choice actually was the choice of a more risk-averse investor (steeper indifference curve U_2): "as if" risk aversion increased. In the dynamic model, investment opportunities change endogenously as well of course.

In a rational expectations equilibrium, the actual volatility of prices implicit in this equation, σ_t, and the beliefs about the volatility, $\tilde{\sigma}_t$, must coincide. To compute the actual volatility of returns, we resort to Itô's Lemma and get

$$\sigma_t = \eta\sigma_z + \underbrace{\tilde{\sigma}_t \times (\text{diffusion of } V_t}_{\text{vol due to FI's wealth} - \text{VaR effect}} + \underbrace{V_t \times (\text{diffusion of } \tilde{\sigma}_t}_{\text{vol due of hanging beliefs}}$$

$$= \eta\sigma_z + V_t\left[\tilde{\sigma}_t + V_t\frac{\partial\tilde{\sigma}}{\partial V_t}\right].$$

Equilibrium volatility is determined as the fixed point where $\sigma_t = \tilde{\sigma}_t$, which entails solving for the function $\sigma_t(V_t)$ from an ordinary differential equation. Daníelsson, Shin, and Zigrand (2011) show that there is a unique closed-form solution given by

(3)
$$\sigma(V_t) = \eta\sigma_z\frac{\alpha^2\delta}{V_t}\exp\left\{-\frac{\alpha^2\delta}{V_t}\right\} \times Ei\left(\frac{\alpha^2\delta}{V_t}\right),$$

where $Ei(w)$ is the well-known exponential integral function[3]:

(4)
$$Ei(w) \equiv -\int_{-w}^{\infty}\frac{e^{-u}}{u}du.$$

The $Ei(w)$ function is defined provided $w \neq 0$. The expression $\alpha^2\delta/V_t$, which appears prominently in the closed-form solution (3) can be interpreted as the relative scale or size of the value investor sector (parameter δ) compared to the banking sector (total capital V_t normalized by VaR).

The closed-form solution also reveals much about the basic shape of the

---

3. http://mathworld.wolfram.com/ExponentialIntegral.html

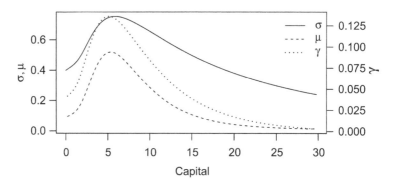

Fig. 2.3   Equilibrium risk premia, volatility, and risk-aversion/Sharpe ratio

volatility function $\sigma(V_t)$. Consider the limiting case when the banking sector is very small, that is, $V_t \to 0$. Then $\alpha^2\delta/V_t$ becomes large, but the exponential term $\exp\{-\alpha^2\delta/V_t\}$ dominates, and the product of the two goes to zero. However, since we have exogenous shocks to the value investor demands, there should still be nonzero volatility at the limit, given by the fundamental volatility $\eta\sigma_z$. The role of the $Ei(w)$ term is to tie down the end point so that the limiting volatility is given by this fundamental volatility.

The endogenous term reduces the fundamental volatility if the FI are sufficiently capitalized (i.e., if V_t is large enough) and dramatically increases the volatility in a nonlinear fashion as V drops, as depicted in figure 2.3, where the properties of our model are illustrated graphically.

The figure plots the equilibrium diffusion σ_t, the drift (expected return) μ_t, and risk-aversion γ_t as a function of the state variable V_t. The parameters chosen for all plots in this chapter are $r = 0.01$, $\delta = 0.5$, $\alpha = 5$, $\sigma_z = 0.4$, $\eta = 1$, and $c = 10$. There is nothing special about this particular parameter constellation, almost any other combination of parameters would generate the same shapes of the plots and hence the same results. For this reason, the choice of parameters is not very important for understanding the basic intuition as a model. However, different parameters generate different magnitudes, and for this reason, we roughly calibrated the parameters so the outcome would correspond to daily returns for relatively high-risk stocks. In future work we are planning to estimate the model; that is, make the parameters data-driven.

The equilibrium volatility is σ and γ_t is the endogenous effective risk aversion. Higher levels of capital represent a well-capitalized banking sector, where volatility is below the fundamental annual volatility of 40 percent. As capital is depleted, volatilities, risk premia, and Sharpe ratios increase.

In the extreme case where capital gets fully depleted to zero, the economy has no financial institutions, and so volatility is equal to the fundamental volatility. With a well-capitalized financial sector, variance is low as the financial sector absorbs risk.

In the leading model, volatility, risk premia, as well as generalized Sharpe

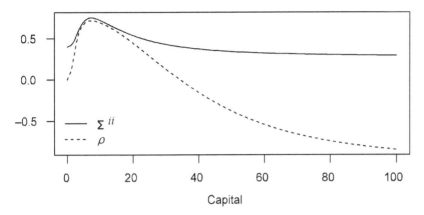

Fig. 2.4   Equilibrium correlations

ratios are all countercyclical, rising dramatically in a downturn, providing ex ante compensation for the risks taken, as illustrated in figure 2.3. These features align our model with available empirical evidence. As can be seen from the graphs, market volatility is a function of the state variable V_t and so the model generates stochastic volatility.

Volatility is lower than fundamental news-induced volatility in times when the financial sector is well-capitalized, when financial institutions play the role of a buffer that absorbs risks and thereby reduces the equilibrium volatility of financial markets. The FI are able to perform this function because by having a sufficient capital level, their VaR constraints are binding less hard, allowing them to act as risk absorbers. However, as their capital is depleted due to negative shocks, their risk constraints bind harder, inducing them to shed risk and amplify market distress.

A similar picture emerges in a multivariate version of the model when there is more than one risky security. The added dimension allows us to address the emergence of endogenous correlation in the returns of risky assets whose fundamentals are unrelated. We illustrate the properties of the bivariate case in figure 2.4. Here, Σ^{ii} is the variance of the returns on security i and ρ^{ij} is the correlation coefficient between the returns on securities i and j, where securities i and j are intrinsically uncorrelated.

2.3   Feedback Effects and Empirical Predictions

Some features of the model of endogenous risk can be presented under several subheadings. We begin with the role of constraints in propagating feedback.

2.3.1   Constraints and Feedback

The main driver of the results in the leading model are feedback effects, which increase in strength along with the homogeneity in behavior and

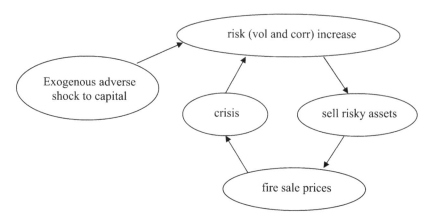

Fig. 2.5   Feedback in leading model

beliefs among financial institutions, especially during crises. Just as in the example of the Millennium Bridge where an initial gust of wind eventually causes the pedestrians to react *identically* and *at the same time,* constraints on financial institutions together with marking-to-market can lead to synchronized institutional behavior in response to an external shock. The ultimate effect is to synchronize the behavior of all financial institutions, dampening risks in the up-turn and amplifying risks in the downturn.

For a well-capitalized financial sector, correlations between the various securities are reduced since the financial institutions have ample capacity to absorb risk. For low levels of capital, however, volatility increases, as shown in figure 2.4. This gives rise to an adverse feedback loop. When capital falls, financial institutions need to shed their risky exposures, reducing prices and raising volatility across all securities. This in turn forces financial institutions to engage in another round of fire sales, and so forth. This is illustrated in figure 2.3. These effects are summarized in figure 2.5, where an initial adverse shock to capital leads to an adverse feedback loop.

Within the leading model, the feedback effects can be understood in terms of the slope of the demand functions of the financial institutions. When the financial sector is undercapitalized, an adverse shock prompts the financial institutions to shed risky securities because risk constraints bind harder and because the price drop leads to a capital loss. So a lower price prompts a sale rather than a purchase. This sale in turn prompts a further fall in price and the loop closes.

This is demonstrated in figure 2.6 which plots supply and demand responses. Note that figure 2.6 charts total demand response, taking account of changes in V and volatility in equilibrium, not the demand curve in a partial equilibrium sense at a given V for different prices. In other words, figure 2.6 shows the continually evolving demand response as the FI continues

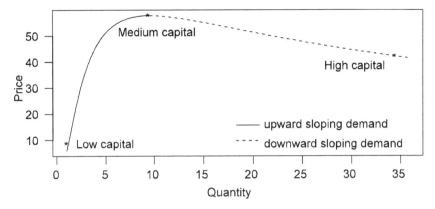

Fig. 2.6   The demand function
Note: Same parameters. Low capital is $V = 4$, medium capital $V = 19$, and high capital $V = 34$.

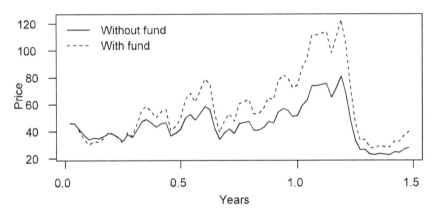

Fig. 2.7   Simulation of price paths
Note: Start at $V = 12$. In the first case σ and μ are constants, since the FI exerts no price impact when not present in the market.

buying or selling. The reduced-form demand function is upward sloping[4] for low levels of capital. As prices increase so does demand. This phenomenon is what gives rise to the amplification effects in the Monte Carlo simulations in figures 2.7 and 2.8. As the FI becomes better capitalized, its equilibrium demand function assumes the typical downward shape. Instead, for small V, the FI increases endogenous risk, while for larger capital levels it decreases endogenous risk.

4. An early example of an endogenous risk-type result with an upward sloping demand function comes from Gennotte and Leland (1990). In their model of portfolio insurance, delta hedging of a synthetic put option requires the delta-hedger to sell a security into a falling market, magnifying the volatility.

We further demonstrate this feature by means of simulations of price paths. Figure 2.7 shows a typical path with a year and a half worth of prices in a univariate model in the absence of risk-constrained traders (and hence where prices follow a geometric Brownian motion). The prices in the absence of risk constraints (P_a for autarchy) rise slowly (at a mean rate of return equal to the risk-free rate), followed by a crash in the beginning of the second year. For the same sequence of fundamental shocks the prices when (there are risk-constrained FIs(P_{FI})) show a much bigger rise followed by a bigger crash.

2.3.2   Endogenous Risk and Comovements

Correlations (or more generally dependence, linear or nonlinear) between risky assets are of key importance in characterizing market returns. In the absence of correlations in the fundamentals, diversification can enable the mitigation of risk. However, endogenous risk and the associated risk constraints imply that assets whose fundamentals are unrelated may still give rise to correlations in market prices due to the fluctuations in risk constraints of the FIs. Since risk constraints give rise to "as if" risk aversion, the correlation in return is associated with fluctuations in the degree of "as if" risk aversion. The sudden increase in correlations during the crisis is well documented and has repeatedly wrong-footed sophisticated proprietary trading desks in many banks that have attempted to exploit historical patterns in asset returns.[5] In crises, volatilities and implied volatilities shoot up at the same time, whether it be the implied volatility of S&P 500 options or of interest rate swaptions. Again, all those spikes in comovements are driven by the same unifying heightened effective risk aversion factor, itself driven by the capitalization level in the financial sector.

We illustrate this by simulating price paths for the bivariate model, shown in figure 2.8. The correlations initially decline slowly, the price of the second asset increases sharply, while the price of the first asset is steady. Then in year 4, an averse shock to its price leads to a sharp increase in correlations, causing the price of the first asset to fall as well.

As we see from figure 2.4, variances move together, and so do variances with correlations. This feature is consistent with the empirical evidence in Andersen et al. (2001) who show that

> [T]here is a systematic tendency for the variances to move together, and for the correlations among the different stocks to be high/low when the variances for the underlying stocks are high/low, and when the correlations among the other stocks are also high/low. (46)

They conjecture that these comovements occur in a manner broadly consistent with a latent factor structure. A good candidate for such a latent

---

5. This occurs in equilibrium in our model, with the FI portfolio that gives rise to the described offloading itself chosen in equilibrium.

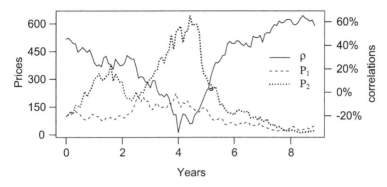

Fig. 2.8   Simulation of prices and correlations

factor would be the tightness of the risk constraint implied by FI's capitalization, discussed earlier.

2.3.3   Endogenous Risk and the Implied Volatility Skew

Options markets offer a direct window displaying endogenous risk in simple graphical terms. Equity index options markets have, at least since 1987, consistently displayed a skew that is fanning-out over longer maturities. Out-of-the-money puts have much higher implied volatilities than out-of-the-money calls. Shorter dated options have a more pronounced skew compared to longer dated options. The fear in the market that drives such features in the options market seems to be of a latent violent downturn (against which the expensive out-of-the money puts are designed to protect), while strings of positive news over the longer term are expected to lead to less volatile returns over longer horizons, the great moderation. The sharp downturn is not expected to be permanent, hence the mean-reverting fanning-out of the skew. We find this result in our model (see figure 2.9).

Our discussion of the way in which endogenous risk plays out in the market is a promising way to address the stylized empirical features in the option market. Endogenous risk embeds an asymmetry between the downside and the upside. Depletion of capital and endogenously increasing risks generate sharply higher volatility, while no such corresponding effects operate on the upside. The widely accepted version of the events of the stock market crash of October 1987 (see, for instance, the formulation of Gennotte and Leland 1990) places at the center of the explanation the feedback effects from synthetic delta-hedged puts embedded in portfolio insurance mandates. The "flash crash" of May 6, 2010 almost certainly has more complex underpinnings, but it would be a reasonable conjecture that the program trades executed by algorithmic high frequency traders conspired in some way to create the amplifying feedback loop of the kind seen in October 1987.

As well as the omnipresent implied volatility skew at any given moment

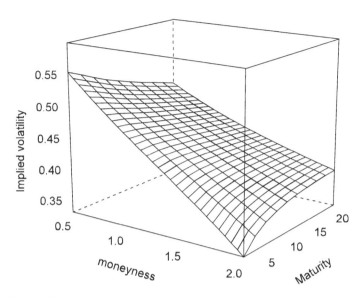

Fig. 2.9   **Implied volatility surface**

in time, our model also predicts that implied volatilities move together in a crisis, which has indeed occurred, across securities as well as across asset classes.

2.4   Implications for Financial Regulation

As we have seen, the financial system can go through long periods of relative tranquility, but once endogenous risk breaks out, it grips the entire financial market. This happens because the balance sheets of large financial institutions link all securities. Our results hold important implications for financial regulation. Regulators will need to be prepared for the prospect that once a storm hits, it has a significant probability of being a "perfect storm," where everything goes wrong at the same time. In the presence of endogenous risk, the focus of regulatory policy should be more toward the system, rather than individual institutions. Even if the economy starts out stable, continued prosperity makes way for an unstable system. An apposite comment is given in Crockett (2000):

> The received wisdom is that risk increases in recessions and falls in booms. In contrast, it may be more helpful to think of risk as increasing during upswings, as financial imbalances build up, and materialising in recessions.

This reasoning is also consistent with Minsky's financial instability hypothesis. Stability can sow the seeds of future instability because financial institutions have a tendency to react to the tranquility by building up their risky asset holdings that increase the thickness of the left tail of the future outcome distribution, which ultimately undermines stability. At some point, a negative shock arrives, and markets go through an abrupt correction. The longer the period is of dormant volatility, the more abrupt and violent is the correction when it arrives.

While our model of endogenous risk has a single-state variable (the FI capital level V), it would be possible to develop more complex versions where the history of the financial system affects future crisis dynamics. One way of doing so would be to posit market participants who extrapolate from last market outcomes in the manner recommended by standard risk management systems that use time series methods in forecasting volatility. One popular version of belief updating is the exponentially-weighted moving average (EWMA) method that forecasts future volatility as a function of last return realizations.

To the extent that volatility is simply dormant during upturns rather than being absent, there is a rationale for countercyclical tools that lean against the build-up of vulnerabilities during upturns.

Our model of endogenous risk is consistent with leveraging and deleveraging of financial intermediaries as discussed by Adrian and Shin (2010) and Danielsson, Shin, and Zigrand (2011). Credit increases rapidly during the boom but increases less rapidly (or even decreases) during the downturn, driven partly by shifts in the banks' willingness to take on risky positions over the cycle. The evidence that banks' willingness to take on risky exposures fluctuates over the cycle is especially clear for financial intermediaries that operate in the capital market.

Deleveraging causes risk aversion to curtail credit in the economy, leading to a downturn in economic activity. The role of a liquidity and capital provider of last resort can be important in dampening financial distress. While financial institutions may be overly leveraged going into a crisis, the endogenous feedback effects may lead to excessive deleveraging relative to the fundamentals of the economy, prompting institutions to curtail lending to the real economy.

2.4.1   Forecasting Risk

Our model of endogenous risk has direct implications for empirical risk forecasting. Almost every model used in practice for forecasting risk assumes financial risk is exogenous. In other words, the financial institutions are price takers, where their trading decisions do not affect price dynamics. So long as individual trading portfolios represent a relatively small part of overall market capitalization and financial institutions are different, an assumption of exogenous risk is relatively innocuous. This is likely to be the situation most of the time, perhaps 99.9 percent of all trading days.

It is, however, the other 0.1 percent that matter most for financial stability.

This is when market turmoil becomes extreme, constraints become especially binding, and financial institutions start acting in harmony, shedding the same risky assets and buying the same safe assets. At that time, financial risk becomes highly endogenous, implying that financial risk forecast models based on an assumption of exogeneity of risk are likely to fail.

The underlying reason is the dual role of market prices. On the one hand, market prices reflect the current value of an asset, but on the other, they also reflect the constraints on financial institutions, and hence are an imperative to act. Constraints may not be binding tightly during calm times but may become highly restrictive during crisis, leading to adverse feedback between increasingly tight constraints and falling asset prices.

This suggests that market prices during periods of calm may be a poor input into forecast models, since any reliable empirical systemic risk model needs to address the transition from noncrisis to crisis. Market prices during calm times may not be informative about the distribution of prices that follow after a crisis is triggered. In addition, price dynamics during one crisis may be quite different in the next, limiting the ability to draw inference from crisis events.

Consequently, risk models are likely to underestimate risk during calm times and overestimate risk during crisis—they get it wrong in all states of the world.

2.4.2   Empirically Modeling Systemic Risk

The tendency of risk models to fail during crisis, as discussed earlier, has particular implications for the the burgeoning field of empirical systemic risk modeling. Here, the question of interest is not the risk of financial institutions failing, but rather the risk of cascading failures. Consequently, the challenge for a reliable systemic risk model is to capture the risk of each systematically important institution, as well as their interactions. These models generally attempt to use observed market variables to provide an indication of the risk of some future systemic event. The current crop of systemic risk models is examined empirically by Danielsson et al. (2011), who find that because of high model risk, such models are highly unreliable.

Systemic risk is concerned with events that happen during crisis conditions, looking far into the tails of distributions. This makes the paucity of relevant data a major concern. Over the last fifty or so years we have observed less than a dozen episodes of extreme international market turmoil. Each of these events is essentially unique, driven by different underlying causes. We should therefore expect that models that are fed with inputs from calm periods will perform much less well during periods of stress.

As a consequence, we feel that the current crop of systemic risk forecast models is unlikely to perform as expected. Instead, such models would need to incorporate endogenous risk explicitly if they are to capture the underestimation of systemic risk prior to a crisis event, as well as the overestimation of systemic risk during the crisis event, both of which are damaging.

2.4.3   Leverage and Capital

Endogenous risk implies *nonlinearities* due to the feedbacks that conspire to make the regulator's problem very difficult. Capital held by the FI is proportional to the risk-tolerance of the nonfinancial sector times the square of the tightness of the VaR constraint.[6] Leverage in the leading model is

$$\frac{\text{assets}}{\text{capital}} = \frac{1}{\text{VaR}_t},$$

where VaR_t is proportional to volatility over short periods. In other words, the growth rate of the capital ratio is equal to the growth rate of volatility. Leverage is procyclical and builds up in quiet booms where VaR is low and unwinds in the crisis. In practice, deleveraging is exacerbated by increased haircuts, reinforcing the feedback loops further through this second channel of forced delevering (see Xiong 2001; Gromb and Vayanos 2002; Geanakoplos 2010; Adrian and Shin 2010; and Brunnermeier and Pedersen 2009). Of course, if capital requirements are not risk-based, for example by using the leverage ratio, procyclicality is not increased by the capital requirements.

Financial crises and strong destabilizing feedback effects naturally occur when capital levels are too low, as can be seen in the previous figures. When capitalization is adequate, financial institutions allow absorption and diffusion of risk, resulting in calmer and more liquid markets to prevail. But endogenous risk raises the fundamental level of volatility in the economy during periods of low capitalization and diminishes the fundamental level of volatility otherwise.

Low capitalization therefore go hand-in-hand with low liquidity.[7] The first effects of the recent crisis became visible through a liquidity crisis in the summer of 2007, where central bank interventions were crucial, but then the crisis quickly turned into a solvency crisis. The liquidity crisis was the harbinger of the later solvency crisis. The two must be linked in any account of the recent crisis.

Countercyclical measures that reduce the feedback loops can be one way to mitigate the boom-bust cycle. Capital adequacy therefore has a major role to play. Since the strength of the adverse feedbacks is very sensitive to the procyclicality of capital adequacy rules, a sufficient capital buffer needs to be imposed in conjunction with countercyclical rules that lean against

---

6. In Basel II, the level of tightness of the VaR constraints for market risk is three times the relevant quantile.

7. Recall the earlier discussion on the critical level of capital that would allow the financial system to perform its socially useful role.

the build-up of vulnerabilities during the boom. A large capital buffer that either cannot be used, or that imposes positive feedback loops, is counterproductive exactly in those situations where it would be needed most. This is aptly demonstrated by Goodhart's metaphor of the weary traveler and the lone cab driver (Goodhart 2009, ch. 8). A weary traveler arrives late at night by train to an unknown town. One taxi is waiting and the traveler goes to it, requesting to be taken to his hotel. The taxi driver refuses and points to a sign on the wall that says "local regulations stipulate that a taxi must be present at the taxi stand at all times." In addition, excessive bank capital tied up in government bonds is socially costly because it hampers the socially productive activities of banks to transform maturities and to take on risks by lending.

Risk builds up during the good times when perceived risk is low and imprudent leverage and complex financial networks build up quietly, perhaps aided by moral hazard (Altunbas, Gambacorta, and Marques-Ibanez 2010). It is only in a crisis that this risk materializes and becomes plainly visible. A promising avenue to think about capital adequacy, based on an idea in chapters 10 and 11 in Goodhart (2009), that deserves further thought would be to require financial institutions to set aside an initial capital buffer, plus an additional variation capital buffer that is a function of the *growth rate* of various assets (both on and off balance sheet) as well as of the maturity mismatch (and of the probable liquidity in a crisis) imposed by those asset classes.

The variation buffer can then be naturally and countercyclically depleted in a downturn, provided the financial institutions do not feel compelled to take large amounts of hidden toxic assets back onto their balance sheets during the downturn. As far as we know, this idea has yet to be formally analyzed.

Note, however, that while countercyclical regulatory capital requirements are a step forward,[8] they are not sufficient to stem all procyclical forces in the markets. For instance, financial institutions will still allocate capital to traders according to a VaR type formula, forcing them to unwind risky positions if risk shoots up. Haircuts will always go up in a downturn. Central clearing houses will impose daily settlement and contribute to procyclicality. Net derivative positions will still be at least partly delta hedged, implying reinforcing feedback effects (on top of the VaR-induced feedback effects) if delta hedgers are net short gamma.

In summary, the omnipresence and inevitability of adverse procyclical spillover effects in financial markets reinforces the need for countercyclical *regulatory* capital rules.

---

8. Whereas regulators relaxed capital adequacy requirements during the S&L crisis, no such formal countercyclical regulatory forbearance seems to have been applied in this crisis.

2.4.4   Endogenous Risk and Central Clearing Counterparties (CCPs)

The volume of OTC derivatives exceeds the global annual GDP by some margin and such derivatives have been widely blamed for their contribution to systemic risk. In particular, the opaque nature of the OTC market, coupled with counterparty risk, have been singled out as especially dangerous. Consequently, there are ongoing discussions about moving a nonnegligible fraction of the OTC trade onto central counterparties (CCPs), with the expectation that the most dangerous systematic impacts of OTC would be mitigated if they were forced to be centrally cleared.

This directly related to the very recent development of credit value adjustment (CVA) desks in financial institutions, which now are some of the largest desks in financial institutions.

The impact of moving OTC derivatives to CCPs are analyzed by Zigrand (2010) in the context of endogenous risk. He notes that CCPs need to protect themselves from counterparty risk, implying institutionalized initial margin and maintenance margin rules based on frequent marking-to-market. We have observed earlier that such margin calls bear the hidden risk of exasperating downward spirals. Endogenous risk appears in at least five guises.

First, an important question to ask is to what extent the current OTC markets resemble CCPs; that is, how many feedback rules are embedded already in OTC? Daily collateral exchanges in the OTC market play the role of daily margin calls, and up-front collateral ("independent amount") plays the role of the initial margin. So some of the mechanisms to reduce counterparty risk are also applied in the OTC market. Still, it seems that a sufficiently large part of the OTC exposures have not been dealt with in this way. The International Swaps and Derivatives Association (ISDA) states that 70 percent of OTC derivatives trades are collateralized, while a survey by the European Central Bank (ECB 2009) estimated that EU bank exposures may be collateralized well below this. Singh (2010) estimates undercollateralization is about 2 trillion dollars for residual derivative payables. This justifies our working hypothesis that should trade move onto CCPs, it is conceivable that feedback effects become stronger than they currently are.

The second appearance of endogenous risk is the fallacy of composition. It is not true that if all products are cleared, and therefore appear to be safe, that the system overall is safe. Indeed, it probably is safer to only require clearing of products that are mature and well understood, for the risk of CCP failure imposed by an immature contract is very costly.

The third aspect of endogenous risk arises in the way the *guarantee fund* of the CCP is replenished. The CCPs provide very little guidance on how exactly they expect to manage the replenishment by member firms. It would appear natural to presume that the CCP would replenish through risk-sensitive (e.g., VaR) rules whereby in periods of higher risk or past capital losses, the CCP will ask for new capitalizations. Member firms being broker dealers, they may be forced to sell risky assets or increase haircuts to their debtors to raise the required capital, thereby contributing to procyclicality in the marketplace. Even the original move from OTC to CCP will require such a sale as currently, there is simply not enough collateral (Singh 2010).

The fourth aspect of endogenous risk has to do with the number of CCPs. Assume that one FI (call it FI1) currently trades with another one, FI2, in the OTC markets. Assume also, as occurs commonly, that the two financial institutions have two open exposures to each other that roughly net out. If both exposures were cleared by the same CCP, then a deterioration in the markets would have no effects on the variation margin calls (but may have an effect on the initial margin, which we ignore for simplicity), and therefore will not create any feedback loops. If, however, both positions were cleared on two separate CCPs with no links between the two CCPs, or one position on one CCP and the other one stays bilaterally cleared, then an increase in volatility will lead, regardless of the direction of the markets, to margin calls and the selling of risk. Again, if capital is fixed in the short run, the individually prudent course of action is to shed risks. This affects prices, which in turn affects the mark-to-market capital and VaR of *all* financial institutions, not just of the two engaged in the original trades. All financial institutions start to act in lock step, and the bridge wobbles. The fallacy of composition appears again in the sense that even if every exposure is centrally cleared, the overall exposure is not centrally cleared when there are multiple CCPs. Cross-margining would mitigate this, as occurs, for instance, for options through the Options Clearing Corporation (OCC) hub between ICE Clear US and the CME Group.

The fifth endogenous risk feedback effect again has its origin in mark-to-market. Financial institutions mostly know when a contract is not liquid, and some financial institutions spend enormous amounts of resources on trying to properly value a derivatives position. If such a contract was centrally cleared and the price made available to the market, this mark may give the appearance of "officially correct audited market prices."[9] But it is unavoidable that relatively illiquid products will get marks that will force all financial institutions, even the ones that have not traded that day and the ones whose accurate internal models predict better marks, to mark their books to these new CCP marks. Since by assumption this market is illiquid, the demand is inelastic and a big sale on one day will move prices and generate strong feedbacks through forced selling, leading to a quick drying-up of liquidity.

---

9. The CCPs do have mitigating procedures put in place to try to make sure that the marks are actually prices at which clearing members would be willing to trade.

2.5   Conclusion

Each financial crisis has its own special features, but there are also some universal themes. In this chapter, we have focused on the role of endogenous risk that propagates through increasingly tight risk constraints, reduction in risk-bearing capacity, and increased volatility. Deleveraging and the shedding of risk imply that asset price movements increase manifold through the feedback effects that are hardwired into the financial system itself. This chapter has aimed at spelling out the precise mechanism through which endogenous risk manifests itself and has suggested ways of mitigating it.

References

Adrian, T., and H. S. Shin. 2010. "Liquidity and Leverage." *Journal of Financial Intermediation* 19:418–37.

Altunbas, Y., L. Gambacorta, and D. Marques-Ibanez. 2010. "Does Monetary Policy Affect Bank Risk-Taking?" Discussion Paper, Bank for International Settlements (BIS), Working Paper 298.

Andersen, T., T. Bollerslev, F. Diebold, and H. Ebens. 2001. "The Distribution of Realized Stock Return Volatility." *Journal of Financial Economics* 61:43–76.

Brunnermeier, M., and L. H. Pedersen. 2009. "Market Liquidity and Funding Liquidity." *Review of Financial Studies* 22:2201–38.

Crockett, A. 2000. "Marrying the Micro- and Macro-Prudential Dimensions of Financial Stability." The General Manager of the Bank for International Settlements. http://www.bis.org/review/rr000921b.pdf.

Danielsson, J., P. Embrechts, C. Goodhart, C. Keating, F. Muennich, O. Renault, and H. S. Shin. 2001. "An Academic Response to Basel II." *The New Basel Capital Accord: Comments Received on the Second Consultative Package.* http://www.bis.org/bcbs/ca/fmg.pdf.

Danielsson, J., K. James, M. Valenzuela, and I. Zer. 2011. "Dealing with Systemic Risk When We Measure Systemic Risk Badly." Working Paper, London School of Economics. www.RiskResearch.org.

Danielsson, J., and H. S. Shin. 2003. "Endogenous Risk." In *Modern Risk Management—A History,* edited by Peter Field, 297–314. London: Risk Books.

Danielsson, J., H. S. Shin, and J.-P. Zigrand. 2011. "Balance Sheet Capacity and Endogenous Risk." http://www.princeton.edu/~hsshin/www/balancesheet capacity.pdf.

Danielsson, J., and J.-P. Zigrand. 2001. "What Happens When You Regulate Risk? Evidence from a Simple Equilibrium Model." Working Paper, London School of Economics (LSE), www.RiskResearch.org.

———. 2008. "Equilibrium Asset Pricing with Systemic Risk." *Economic Theory* 35:293–319.

European Central Bank (ECB). 2009. *Credit Default Swaps and Counterparty Risk.* Frankfurt, Ger.: ECB.

Geanakoplos, J. 2010. "The Leverage Cycle." In *NBER Macroeconomics Annual 2009,* edited by Daron Acemoglu, Kenneth Rogoff, and Michael Woodford, 1–65. Chicago: University of Chicago Press.

Gennotte, G., and H. Leland. 1990. "Market Liquidity, Hedging, and Crashes." *American Economic Review* 80 (5): 999–1021.

Goodhart, C. 2009. *The Regulatory Response to the Financial Crisis.* Cheltenham, UK: Edward Elgar.

Gromb, D., and D. Vayanos. 2002. "Equilibrium and Welfare in Markets with Financially Constrained Arbitrageurs." *Journal of Financial Economics* 66:361–407.

Singh, M. 2010. "Collateral, Netting and Systemic Risk in the OTC Derivatives Market." Discussion Paper WP/10/99, IMF. Washington, DC: International Monetary Fund.

Xiong, W. 2001. "Convergence Trading with Wealth Effects: An Amplification Mechanism in Financial Markets." *Journal of Financial Economics* 62:247–92.

Zigrand, J.-P. 2010. "What Do Network Theory and Endogenous Risk Theory Have to Say About the Effects of CCPs on Systemic Stability?" Financial Stability Review, 14, Banque de France [Central Bank of France].

Comment   Bruce Mizrach

Introduction

US financial markets began to stabilize in the spring of 2009. Fiscal stimulus, capital injections to banks through the Trouble Asset Relief Program (TARP), near zero short-term interest rates, and quantitative easing by the Federal Reserve have all combined to rally the equity and corporate bond markets and restore positive GDP growth. Even as this process was ongoing, a series of papers in macroeconomics and asset pricing have begun to explore the causes of the crisis and provide a road map to a more stable financial system.

Hyun Shin of Princeton has joined with a series of coauthors, Adrian and Shin (2008, 2010) and Adrian, Moench, and Shin (2010), to explore the role of leverage and risk-based capital requirements. A key message has been the procyclicality of leverage and value at risk (VaR) measures that might encourage excessive risk taking.

The chapter in this volume by Danielsson, Shin, and Zigrand (DSZ) belongs to a second set of papers that explore the asset pricing implications of changing risk appetite. This chapter looks at assets more broadly and builds upon earlier papers by these authors: Danielsson, Shin, and Zigrand (2004) and Danielsson and Zigrand (2008). Related work on other assets includes Adrian, Etula, and Shin (2009), who focus on exchange rates.

The Model

The implicit microfoundation for the VaR criteria is from Adrian and Shin (2008). They show that firms with exponential loss functions will use VaR

Bruce Mizrach is professor of economics at Rutgers University.

I would like to thank Tobias Adrian and Jean-Pierre Zigrand for helpful comments. For acknowledgments, sources of research support, and disclosure of the author's material financial relationships, if any, please see http://www.nber.org/chapters/c12055.ack.

to evaluate their risk exposure. More formally, for every optimal contract, the intermediary maintains just enough capital to keep VaR where the probability of default is a constant.[1]

In a companion paper (DSZ 2011), the authors model risk-neutral traders who choose a dollar investment D_t in the risky equities V_t, with endogenous expected mean and standard deviation (u_t, σ_t) subject to a value at risk constraint,

$$\max r V_t + D_t^T + \alpha \sqrt{D_t^T \sigma_t \sigma_t^T D_t}\,.$$

Variable r is the risk-free rate, and α is a normalizing constant. The Lagrange multiplier for the VaR constraint,

$$\gamma_t = \frac{\sqrt{(\mu_t - r)^T (\sigma_t \sigma_t^T)^{-1}(\mu_t - r)}}{\alpha},$$

is proportional to the generalized Sharpe ratio. This makes the risk-neutral traders act *as if* they were risk averse with a coefficient of relative risk aversion $\alpha^2 \gamma_t$.

In this chapter, DSZ study asset demand functions

$$D_t = \frac{V_t}{\gamma_t} \sum_t^{-1}(\mu - r).$$

The authors obtain, in the single asset case, a closed-form rational expectations equilibrium[2] for the volatility and drift of the risky asset price process,

$$\frac{(\mu_t - r)}{\sigma_t} = \frac{1}{2\alpha\eta\sigma_z}\left\{2\alpha(r^* - r) + \alpha\sigma_t^2 - \eta\sigma_z + (\sigma_t - \eta\sigma_z)[2\alpha^2 r + \frac{\alpha^2\delta}{V_t} - 2]\right\}.$$

Volatility and drift can be expressed as a function of the state variable V_t, which is the author's graph in their figure 2.3 for the parameterization $r = 0.01$, $\alpha = 5$, $\sigma_z = 0.4$, and $c = 10$, where $\eta = 1$ and $\delta = 0.5$ are scaling parameters for the demand functions.

Asset Pricing Implications

The key result is that volatility is nonmonotonic, with a range in which volatility increases in the risky asset holdings. At this intermediate value, there is a positive feedback effect in which rising stock prices lead the trader to hold even more equity. In the multivariate case, they show that return correlation can also rise over the same range. The attractive feature of this model is the endogenous rise in volatility and asset correlations.

My first comment concerns the need to calibrate the model to the mag-

---

1. While not modeled, one could also motivate the chapter with a regulatory regime like Basel II where capital requirements are risk-based.
2. The equilibrium is unique up to a constant of integration c.

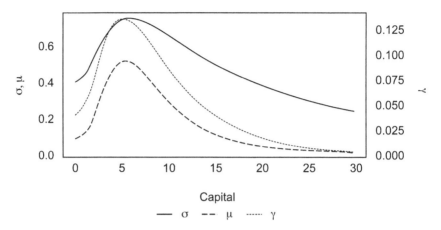

Fig. 2C.1   Mean, volatility, and risk aversion in equilibrium

Note: The figure, from Danielsson, Shin, and Zigrand, graphs the model's equilibrium mean, volatility, and risk aversion for the parameters: $r = 0.01$, $\delta = 0.5$, $\alpha = 5$, $\sigma_z = 0.4$, $\eta = 1$, and $c = 10$.

nitude of the crisis. Is the change from the low volatility to high volatility regime large enough to explain the events of 2007 to 2009?

Policy Implications

Aggregating from a representative firm, the model has important policy implications. Indeed, these market-wide implications are an appealing part of the model. I focus on the case where the economy is on the downward sloping portion of figure 2C.1. If all firms add to their risky asset positions following a positive shock, volatility in this region is actually falling. This loosens the VaR constraint, and leads banks to take on even more leverage. This mechanism for procyclical leverage has been cited by the Committee on the Global Financial System (CFGS 2009) of the Bank for International Settlements as an important source of instability.

In the model's version of a crisis, the firm starts to climb back up the hill in figure 2C.1 as V_t falls. A negative shock leads to rising volatility and can set off a sequence of deleveraging. By most accounts this process is still ongoing.

As I continue with my discussion, I now turn to whether there is evidence in the data for this very appealing model.

Evidence from the US Financial Sector

I begin with a broad view of the US financial sector, looking at both commercial and investment banks. I then develop a case study comparison of two investment banks, Bear Stearns and Goldman Sachs, the first to collapse and the institution that has emerged as perhaps the strongest.

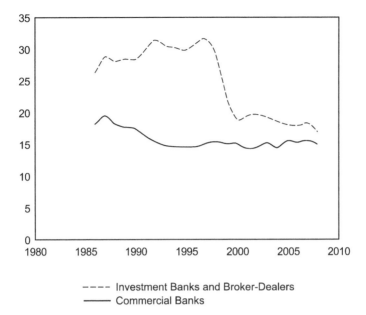

---- Investment Banks and Broker-Dealers
—— Commercial Banks

Fig. 2C.2   Leverage in the banking sector
Notes: The data are from Compustat. Leverage is computed as the ratio of assets to share-holder equity (ATQ/SEQQ). The first group is Standard Industrial Classification (SIC) code 6211, which includes investment banks, broker dealers, and flotation companies. The second group is SIC code 6020, which includes commercial banks but not savings institutions. I limit both groups to a minimum of $5 billion in assets and $1 billion in shareholder equity.

Leverage in Commercial and Investment Banks

I graph in figure 2C.2 the leverage ratios, measured as the ratio of assets to shareholder equity, for US investment banks and brokerage firms and commercial banks from 1985 to 2008. If there is any trend in leverage leading into the crisis, it is negative. Indeed, leverage was higher in the 1980s than the 2000s.

Adrian and Shin (2008) have emphasized that risk may have become more concentrated at the large institutions. If I limit the analysis to the five largest firms in each category, there is an upward trend in leverage among the investment banks after 2004.[3] (See fig. 2C.3.)

I do not have any comprehensive data on value at risk, but the CFGS notes that VaR was stable or declining into mid-2006 for the largest banks in the United States, Europe, and Japan.

3. On April 28, 2004, the SEC made amendments to Rule 15c3-1, which established net capital requirements for investment banks. The five largest institutions were allowed to become Consolidated Supervisory Entities, which allowed them to use VaR models for setting capital requirements.

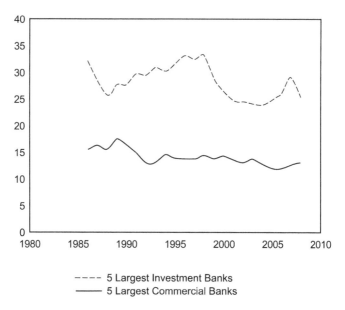

Fig. 2C.3   Leverage at the largest institutions

Notes: The data are from Compustat. Leverage is computed as the ratio of assets to share-holder equity (ATQ/SEQQ). The five investment banks are Bear Stearns, Goldman Sachs, Lehman Brothers, Merrill Lynch, and Morgan Stanley. The five commercial banks are Bank of America, Citigroup, JP Morgan Chase, Wachovia, and Wells Fargo.

The remainder of this section is a case study of Bear and Goldman. I discuss the commercial banks in a related paper, Mizrach (2011).

Bear Stearns versus Goldman Sachs

Between 1999 and 2004, leverage, graphed in figure 2C.4, was higher at Bear than Goldman, but Goldman closed the gap after 2004. Bear's leverage was falling and dropped below thirty in 2006, the year before their implosion.

There is no trend in value at risk, graphed in figure 2C.5 for the two firms, until the crisis is well under way. Goldman has a slightly higher VaR.

These data are consistent with the model. It seems that the VaR constraint was never binding until Bear Stearns began to shed assets in the summer of 2007. It seems as though I need to go beyond VaR and leverage to understand why Bear Stearns failed.

(Off) Balance Sheets

I will emphasize three things in my discussion: (1) the role of special purpose entities, (2) Level 3 asset valuation, and (3) interruptions in funding liquidity. All three require a careful consideration of balance sheets and regulatory filings.

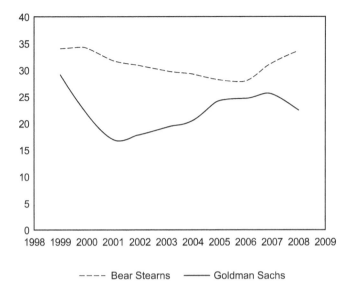

Fig. 2C.4 Leverage at Bear Stearns versus Goldman Sachs
Notes: The data are from Compustat. Leverage is computed as the ratio of assets to share-holder equity (ATQ/SEQQ). I restrict the period here to 1999 to 2008, a time span in which both firms were publicly traded.

Special Purpose Entities

The vulnerability of a securities firm to a panic depends upon the structure of their assets and liabilities. The firms that failed (including Bear) had relatively large off-balance sheet exposures. Many of these were organized in the form of special purpose entities (SPEs). There is an academic literature on the purpose of the SPEs, but the impact was nonetheless to make the firm's balance sheet more opaque.

The accounting treatment of securitizations was governed by the Financial Accounting Standard Board (FASB) Statement 140 originally issued in September 2000. The standard defined a Qualifying Special Purpose Entity (QSPE). To determine whether the exposures went off-balance sheet, the asset structure had to be a "true sale" that limited the recourse with respect to the parent. Financial Interpretation No. (FIN) 46, revised substantially in December 2003, defines a related structure called a Variable Interest Entity (VIE).

Figure 2C.6 shows that Bear Stearns relied on these structures to a much larger extent than Goldman.[4] Their exposures nearly triple between February 2005 and May 2007, rising from 3.46 percent to 11.32 percent of assets. Goldman never allowed their exposure to exceed 2 percent. Perhaps more importantly, they began to reduce their exposure in February 2006.

---

4. As Mizrach (2011) notes, off-balance sheet activity was even more substantial at the large commercial banks where Tier 1 capital was closely monitored.

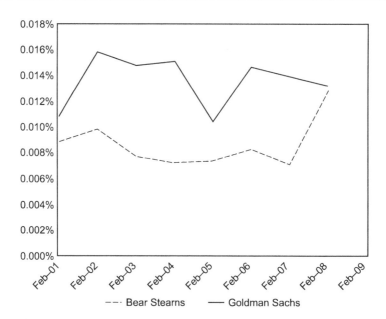

Fig. 2C.5   Daily value at risk at Bear Stearns versus Goldman Sachs

Notes: The data are from the first quarter SEC 10-Q filings of both banks for each year. The value at risk is a one-day 95 percent loss coverage calculation expressed in dollars, which I have converted into a percentage by dividing by total assets.

Illiquid Assets

The most overused word in the crisis has been liquidity. It has many meanings. In the context of asset valuation, it refers to the ability to produce accurate, real time fair market values for a bank's positions. A related point captured by the DSZ model is the potential for losses from having to make a fire sale of these illiquid positions.

In September 2006, the FASB issued Statement 157 on Fair Value Measurements. The standard considers a hierarchy of transparency ranging from Level 1 assets, which have publicly quoted prices, and Level 3 assets, which may often be priced using internal models.

Bear Stearns first reported its Level 3 assets in the first quarter of 2007 Securities and Exchange Commission (SEC) filings. Their exposure was similar to Goldman Sachs, with both firms at around 5 percent of total assets. I compare these levels in quarterly snapshots in table 2C.1.

As the crisis unfolded, it appears that Goldman was able to reduce or limit their exposure while Bear Stearn's kept rising right up until their collapse. In determining the fate of the two companies, it appears that the type of Level 3 assets held matters more than the level. In the case of Bear Stearns, there has been more (eventual) disclosure; a portion of their illiquid assets wound up in a special purpose entity created by the Federal Reserve Bank of New

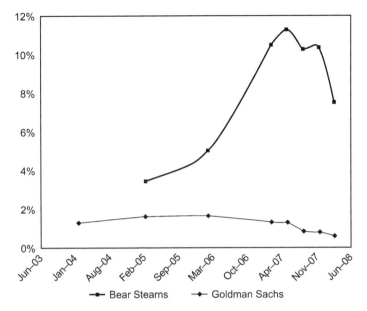

Fig. 2C.6   Special purpose and variable interest entities as a percent of total assets

Notes: The data are from the SEC 10-Q and 10-K filings of both banks for each year. I report the consolidated assets of the Qualified Special Purpose Entities (QSPEs) and Variable Interest Entities (VIEs) of both firms as a percentage of total assets.

Table 2C.1   Bear Stearns versus Goldman Sachs Level 3 assets

Date	Bear		Goldman	
	$bn	% of assets	$bn	% of assets
2-1-2007	19.0	4.81	47.6	5.22
5-1-2007	18.0	4.26	54.1	5.74
8-3-2007	20.3	5.10	72.0	6.89
11-1-2007	23.9	6.05	54.7	4.89
2-28-2008	37.4	9.36	82.3	6.92

Note: The data are from the SEC 10-Q and 10-K filings of both banks for each year.

York called Maiden Lane 1. Using the Maiden Lane financial statement,[5] I estimate that 56 percent of the portfolio was in commercial (48 percent) and residential (8 percent) mortgage-backed securities. Maiden Lane had an unrealized capital loss of more than $4 billion on the Level 3 portfolio in the eight months after its acquisition.

The type of assets also mattered a great deal once their counterparties began to demand more collateral.

5. http://www.newyorkfed.org/aboutthefed/annual/annual08/MaidenLanefinstmt2009.pdf

Bear's Collapse

Bear Stearns operated two hedge funds with leveraged exposure to the subprime mortgage market,[6] largely through collateralized debt obligations (CDOs). High Grade Structured Credit Strategies Fund (SCSF) had $925 million in capital employed at six times leverage. It was three years old and had forty straight months without a loss, producing a cumulative 50 percent return. High Grade Structured Credit Enhanced Leverage Fund (SELF) was started in August 2006. It invested $638 million in investor capital at ten times leverage.

The SCSF reported its first ever loss in March 2007. In late April, Goldman, as a counterparty to some of the trades, marked down subprime assets to $0.55. When Bear questioned the marks, which ranged between $0.80 to $0.98 from other parties, Goldman offered to sell their own subprime assets to Bear at their mark. Bear did not bite.

Bear posted a –19 percent decline in SCSF for April. Redemptions followed, Merrill Lynch pulled collateral in June, and both funds collapsed at the end of July 2007. Bear took the remaining assets in both funds and put them on their own balance sheet.

As subprime assets continued to deteriorate,[7] Bear's SPEs are marked down. In their final quarterly financial statement, February 29, 2008, the value of the special purpose entities falls by –32.5 percent to $26.74 billion.

Turn Off the Lights: Funding Liquidity

Gorton and Metrick (2009) have emphasized that in the final stages of the investment bank's collapse, there was a modern version of a bank panic that they call the "run on the repo." Repo refers to the lending of securities as a source of day-to-day funding liquidity, a mechanism that has also been emphasized by Brunnermeier and Pedersen (2009). As Bear's positions soured, they prudently began to raise cash, which rises from 3.8 to 8.9 percent of the balance sheet, shown in table 2C.2, between February 2007 and February 2008.

They sold off and/or wrote down financial instruments and the structured entities on the balance sheet. They were squeezed (perhaps rationally) by their counterparties, however: securities pledged as collateral rose to 5.7 percent of assets, and it also appears that firms were slow to pledge collateral in return, as this fell to less than 4 percent of assets.

---

6. Despite claiming only 6 percent exposure to subprime, the funds' exposures were actually closer to 60 percent.

7. Marklt's ABX index of subprime CDS is a reasonable proxy (see, e.g., Gorton 2008 or Mizrach 2012).

Table 2C.2   Bear Stearns consolidated assets

Assets $mn	2-28-2007	%	5-31-2007	%	8-31-2007	%	11-30-2007	%	2-29-2008	%
Cash	5,891	1.5	11,178	2.6	18,143	4.6	21,406	5.4	20,786	5.2
Cash segregated	9,126	2.3	4,653	1.1	13,460	3.4	12,890	3.3	14,910	3.7
Securities revd. as collateral	21,227	5.4	18,948	4.5	18,301	4.6	15,599	4.0	15,371	3.9
Securities to resell	37,248	9.4	42,272	10.0	32,144	8.1	27,878	7.1	26,888	6.7
Securities borrowed	84,015	21.3	92,050	21.8	80,039	20.2	82,245	20.8	87,143	21.8
Receivables	40,730	10.3	46,984	11.1	43,320	10.9	53,522	13.5	53,332	13.4
Financial instruments	134,410	34.1	136,411	32.2	126,870	32.0	122,518	31.0	118,201	29.6
Pledged as collateral	12,754	3.2	12,265	2.9	15,004	3.8	15,724	4.0	22,903	5.7
Assets of VIEs and QSPEs	41,483	10.5	49,985	11.8	41,045	10.3	33,553	8.5	29,991	7.5
Property and equipment	508	0.1	547	0.1	586	0.2	605	0.2	608	0.2
Other	7,119	1.8	8,011	1.9	8,180	2.1	9,422	2.4	8,862	2.2
Total	394,512		423,304		397,091		395,362		398,995	

Note: The data are from the SEC 10-Q and 10-K filings.

The $18 billion in cash that Bear Stearns possessed[8] on Monday, March 17, 2008, only managed to last until the weekend's emergency merger with JP Morgan Chase.

Conclusion

Leverage can be a problematic measure, but it seems as though leverage was not excessive compared to prior noncrisis episodes. The VaR was held relatively constant, and the level does not have much predictive value in the crisis.

Back in the superficially calm days of January 2007, with the Chicago Board Options Exchange (CBOE) volatility index below 10, the markets may have been in the right-hand side of DSZ's figure 2.1. As firms like Bear sold assets, volatility rose and asset prices fell, leading to additional selling. What the model and many economists are still struggling to explain is why the hill was so steep given the relatively small size of the subprime sector.

My discussion tries to sketch out a more comprehensive theory. The components of this model would have to incorporate: (1) balance sheet transparency (SPE, VIEs, etc.); (2) the complexity of assets in the portfolio (Level 3 assets like synthetic CDOs); (3) how crowded the trades are—Adrian and Brunnermeier's (2009) concept of a distressed bank's value at risk, called CoVar, may prove useful here; and (4) seizures in funding liquidity.

This chapter is still an important first step, and it will be on my syllabus next semester.

References

Adrian, Tobias, and Markus Brunnermeier. 2009. "CoVar." Working Paper. Princeton University.

Adrian, Tobias, Erkko Etula, and Hyun Shin. 2009. "Risk Appetite and Exchange Rates." Federal Reserve Bank of New York Staff Report no. 361. New York: Federal Reserve Bank of New York.

Adrian, Tobias, Emanuel Moench, and Hyun Shin. 2010. "Financial Intermediation, Asset Prices and Macroeconomic Dynamics." Federal Reserve Bank of New York Staff Report no. 422. New York: Federal Reserve Bank of New York.

Adrian, Tobias, and Hyun Shin. 2008. "Financial Intermediary Leverage and Value at Risk." Federal Reserve Bank of New York Staff Report no. 338. New York: Federal Reserve Bank of New York.

———. 2010. "Liquidity and Leverage." *Journal of Financial Intermediation* 19: 418–37.

Brunnermeier, Markus, and Lasse Pedersen. 2009. "Market Liquidity and Funding Liquidity." *Review of Financial Studies* 22:2201–38.

8. Kelly (2009) reports that the cash cushion was cut in half in just three days. Bear Stearns needed a short-term loan from the Federal Reserve, via JP Morgan, on Friday, March 21, 2008, just to make it to the weekend.

Committee on the Global Financial System. 2009. "The Role of Valuation and Leverage in Procyclicality." CGFS Papers no 34.

Danielsson, Jon, Hyun Shin, and Jean-Pierre Zigrand. 2004. "The Impact of Risk Regulation on Price Dynamics." *Journal of Banking and Finance* 28:1069–87.

Danielsson, Jon, and Jean-Pierre Zigrand. 2008. "Equilibrium Asset Pricing with Systemic Risk." *Economic Theory* 35:293–319.

Danielsson, Jon, Hyun Shin, and Jean-Pierre Zigrand. 2011. "Balance Sheet Capacity and Endogenous Risk." http://www.riskresearch.org.

Gorton, Gary. 2008. "The Panic of 2007." Working Paper. Yale University.

Gorton, Gary, and Andrew Metrick. 2009. "Securitized Banking and the Run on Repo." Working Paper. Yale University.

Kelly, Kate. 2009. *Street Fighters.* New York: Penguin.

Mizrach, Bruce. 2011. "Accounting for the Crisis." Working Paper. Rutgers University. http://papers.ssrn.com/sol3/papers.cfm?abstract_id=1894805.

———. 2012. "Jump and Cojump Risk in Subprime Home Equity Derivatives." *Journal of Portfolio Management* 38:136–46.

Comment   Terence C. Burnham

Introduction: Consilience and Economics

> He who understands baboon would do more towards metaphysics than Locke.
>
> —Charles Darwin (1838) *The M Notebook*

Economists should pay more attention to baboons and less to mathematics. The chapter by Danielsson, Shin, and Zigrand (hereafter, DSZ) explores "anomalous" behavior in financial markets. An anomaly is actual human behavior that differs from behavior predicted by standard neoclassical theory.

Economic efforts to reconcile neoclassical theory with anomalies involve relaxing one of more of the standard assumptions and showing that some stylized features of actual behavior are consistent with the modified assumptions. This approach is now common in many behavioral papers on topics such as other-regarding preferences (Bolton 1991) and intertemporal decisions (Laibson 1997).

E. O. Wilson advocates a radically different approach in his book *Consilience* (Wilson 1998). He has long advocated that social scientists ground their work in the natural sciences (Wilson 1978). Consilience is the "jumping

Terence C. Burnham is associate professor in the George L. Argyros School of Business and Economics at Chapman University.

For acknowledgments, sources of research support, and disclosure of the author's material financial relationships, if any, please see http://www.nber.org/chapters/c12056.ack.

together" of fields. In practice, Wilson's advice suggests that social scientists should leave their hermeneutic departments and work with biologists, primatologists, archeologists, neurologists, and scientists from a host of other fields.

The eventual result of a consilient approach to economic behavior will, Wilson argues, be a richer and more accurate field. The result need not be inconsistent with mathematical models, but mathematical models without natural science knowledge will remain the "limited descriptors of surface phenomena."

The rest of this comment describes the economic and consilient approaches to understanding behavioral anomalies. It then describes some pioneering work using natural science approaches to understanding risk, the anomalous behavior that is the focus of DSZ's chapter.

Two Approaches to Anomalies

Economic Approach

The anomalies literature has documented a wide variety of divergences between actual human behavior and that predicted by standard economic theory. The behavioral school has become so well-known that citations are not required; most practitioners know to look at the work of Daniel Kahneman, Amos Tversky, and Richard Thaler.

The early phase of the behavioral approach focused on documenting failures of the standard model. These are labeled "anomalies" in the lexicon taken from Thomas Kuhn's *The Structure of Scientific Revolutions.*

A second phase of the behavioral approach attempts to build models of the anomalous behavior. These models tend to relax a small number of assumptions in the standard framework and end up with a model that mimics the most significant stylized facts in actual human behavior.

Consider, for example, behavior in the "ultimatum" game (Guth, Schmittberger, and Schwarze 1982). In the ultimatum game, one person proposes a division of a fixed amount of money. The second person faces an ultimatum; either accept their proposed share or receive nothing. Standard economic theory predicts that people will accept all positive amounts of money, even offers that are low or a small percentage of the total. Actual people, however, tend to reject small offers, choosing to leave with nothing instead of something.

How do we reconcile ultimatum game rejections with a theory that predicts no rejections? The answer, contained in many behavioral economic papers, is to retain all of the standard assumptions of economics except one. Rather than assume that people only care about themselves, these behavioral papers argue that ultimatum game rejections are the product of rational maximization of "other-regarding" preferences.

These other-regarding preference structures, when made sufficiently complex, can be made consistent with some significant percentage of the experimental results. It is not clear, however, that any of these other-regarding preference structures extends our understanding of the phenomena beyond the evidence.

DSZ's chapter follows exactly this formula. The anomaly, discovered again in the financial crises of 2008, is that people's willingness to bear risk goes down as asset markets decline. This produces the paradoxical result that investors loved owning equities when the Dow Jones Industrial Average was at 14,000, they became scared when the Dow hit 10,000, and sold in a panic at Dow 6,500. The chapter describes the puzzle: "as financial conditions worsen, the willingness of market participants to bear risk seemingly evaporates even in the absence of any further hard news, which in turn worsens financial conditions."

Using the standard view that people are rational maximizers, how can we make sense of buying stocks when the Dow is at 14,000, and selling them at less than half the price? The chapter relaxes a few assumptions, and is able to build a model that has some of the features of reality. In particular, DSZ's chapter relaxes the standard setup by allowing some traders to be forced to curtail risk because of VaR (value at risk) rules. The chapter then applies standard tools of rational expectations and fixed-point equilibrium.

Does the model work? It is consistent with some of the stylized facts that we knew before the model was written. Specifically, the authors write, "As well as the omnipresent implied volatility skew at any given moment in time, our model also predicts that implied volatilities move together in a crisis, which has indeed occurred, across securities as well as across asset classes."

Consilience Approach

E. O. Wilson suggests we look to natural science to understand human attitudes toward risk. In the natural sciences, Nobel Laureate Nikolaas Tinbergen (his brother Jan won the Nobel Prize in economics) provides a framework for examining behavior (Mayr 1961; Tinbergen 1963, 1968).

Tinbergen argues that behavior should be examined from four perspectives.

1. Ultimate cause: How does the behavior lead to increased evolutionary success? This is the domain of maximizing models in evolutionary biology.

2. Proximate cause: What machinery in the brain and body produces the behavior? Proximate explanations include hormonal influence, neuroscience work on brain function, and cognitive studies of how the brain stores and uses information.

3. Ontogeny: How does the behavior develop over the lifetime of an organism? When do children develop these traits and what influences their manifestations?

4. Phylogeny: Looking across species, what can we learn about how and why the trait developed over evolutionary time?

These are early days in consilient economics, but the number of studies is expanding rapidly. There is quite a significant field on neuroeconomics, some significant work on hormones and economic behavior, a handful of studies on nonhuman primates and economic behavior, and a few twin studies.

The next section describes four studies on risk that I label as "consilient." These are new approaches and they are not as well-developed as areas that have been under persistent study for decades.

Consilience and Risk: Pioneering Natural Science Work on Risk

Dopamine Receptor Structure and Risk Taking

Dopamine is a central reward pathway in human brains. The dopamine receptor D_4 (*DRD4*) gene is hypothesized to be involved in modulation of a variety of behaviors. Individuals vary in the genetic structure of the *DRD4* receptor. One variant, 7R+, has been shown to be associated with a "blunted" response to dopamine. Some studies argue that people with the 7R+ allele are more risk seeking because higher levels of risk are needed to generate a dopamine-based positive feeling.

One study reports that the 7R+ allele is correlated with risk-seeking behavior in an economic experiment (Dreber et al. 2009). Subjects had their *DRD4* alleles genotyped, and, for this analysis, were divided into those with 7R+ allele and those with other alleles (7R−). The subjects were asked to allocate $250 between a safe and risky investment. The safe investment returned 100 percent of the money invested with certainty. The risky investment had two outcomes—0 or 250 percent of the money invested. Thus, the investment was risky, but had higher expected value than the safe option.

The study correlated the amount invested in the risky investment with the dopamine allele. It reports that subjects with the 7R+ allele took more risks than 7R− subjects. Specifically, the 7R+ subjects invested an average of $175 in the risky asset versus $136 for the 7R− subjects (p-value = 0.023).

Genes and Portfolio Choice

One study used twins to observe risky behavior in laboratory games, and concluded that risk attitudes are heritable (Cesarini et al. 2009). The partial privatization of Swedish pensions allowed examination of the genetic role in portfolio choice beyond the laboratory.

In 2001, Sweden altered its pension system to allow individuals to choose their portfolio allocation with part of their forced retirement savings (Cronqvist and Thaler 2004). The participants could choose to remain in a default allocation, or choose to allocate among approximately 500 different funds. Each of the funds was ranked for level of risk (based on the prior thirty-six months of monthly returns). The risk level was assigned to one of five categories ranging from very safe (low standard deviation of historical monthly returns) to very risky.

Twin studies separate the effects of gene and environment by comparing behavioral correlations between identical or monozygotic twins (MZ) versus fraternal or dizygotic twins (DZ). The MZ twins start with identical genetic material while DZ twins are as closely related as siblings born in separate pregnancies. Traits that are heritable will be more similar in MZ twins than in DZ twins. At an extreme, a trait like eye color will be the same in almost all monozygotic twins (not 100 percent, as mutations can occur during cell division). Nonheritable traits, such as the color of one's car, will be no more correlated between MZ twins than between DZ twins (actually, color preference might be heritable).

The study of the genetic influence on portfolio choice uses the Swedish pension reform in a classic twin study (Cesarini et al. 2010). The study uses only twins, and examines the overall risk level of the portfolio. The methodology allows an estimate of the genetic contribution to portfolio choice. The direction of the analysis is that the greater the genetic contribution, the higher the relative correlation of portfolio risk between MZ twins as compared to DZ twins.

The paper reports significantly higher correlations for MZ twins than for DZ twins: "In women, the correlations are 0.27 and 0.16. In men, they are 0.29 and 0.13." The authors state that 30 percent of the variation of portfolio risk is explained by shared genes and environment. The exact proportion that is genetic is not identifiable, as it is possible that MZ twins have a more common environment than DZ twins. Parents may treat MZ twins more similarly than DZ twins, and they may be part of the reason that MZ twins' portfolios are more correlated. That said, it is also possible that parents treat MZ twins more similarly because MZ twins are more alike genetically.

Testosterone and Risk Taking

Testosterone is associated with a variety of behaviors in men and males of a wide variety of species (Wingfield et al. 1990). In men, high testosterone is correlated with dominance-seeking behavior (Mazur and Booth 1998). When dominance is mediated by aggression, testosterone also appears to facilitate this process. A meta-analysis summarizing the results of forty-five human studies found a consistent, positive relationship between aggression and testosterone (Book, Starzyk, and Quinsey 2001). Testosterone is hypothesized to mediate status and hierarchy in an adaptive manner (Mazur 1973, 1983, 1985; Kemper 1990). Testosterone modulates a variety of behaviors that are risky.

Subjects in a study of testosterone and risk taking (Apicella et al. 2008) had their testosterone levels assayed using saliva samples. They participated in the same experimental assessment of risk as the study of the *DRD4* allele. Specifically, they allocated $250 between a safe asset and a risky asset. The study reports that a one standard deviation increase in testosterone is associated with 12 percent higher contribution ($30) to the risky asset.

Nonhuman Apes and Risk Taking

Chimpanzees (*Pan troglodytes*) and bonobos (*Pan paniscus*) are the closest living relatives to humans. In the wild, chimpanzees depend on riskier food sources than do bonobos. The authors of a study of the phylogeny of risk attitudes hypothesize that if risk preferences are shaped by the environment over evolutionary time periods then chimpanzees should exhibit riskier behavior than bonobos (Heilbronner et al. 2008).

Chimpanzees and bonobos made a risky choice in a laboratory setting. The animals selected one of two upside-down bowls. The safe bowl always contained four grape pieces. The risky bowl contained either one grape piece or seven with equal chance. (Note that the risky option had the same expected value as the safe option.) Chimpanzees selected the risky option 64 percent of the time, versus 28 percent for the bonobos ($p = 0.003$). Thus the hypothesis that chimpanzees are built to be more risk seeking than bonobos is consistent with the findings.

Concluding Comments

The chapter by DSZ begins with a puzzle about human nature. When asset markets decline, people seek safety and sell their risky assets. What have we learned about risk from the four studies just described?

In summary, the studies suggest that biology and evolution play a role in our risky behaviors. Chimpanzees and bonobos in the wild live in different environments, and these environments are hypothesized to connect to their risk attitudes in experiments. If the "natural" environment shaped bonobo and chimpanzee risk preferences, then we might learn a lot about human risk preferences by learning more about humans "in the wild." Some important scholars argue that the wild environment for humans ended 10,000 years ago with the invention of agriculture (Tooby and Cosmides 1990; Cosmides and Tooby 1994). If we are, as these scholars argue, "Pleistocene hunter-gatherers," then economists will have to learn from archeologists and anthropologists.

Our shared human environment might explain average levels of risk taking but what about variation between people? The early twin studies suggest that different genes in different people influence behavior. Our genes may have profound influences on our choices, ranging from laboratory gambles to asset allocation. If this is true, economists have much to learn from geneticists and evolutionary biologists.

How do genes alter risky choices? We have two studies that suggest roles for dopamine and testosterone. Those with particular brain structures, particularly the 7R+ allele of dopamine, may be more risk seeking. In addition, those with high testosterone may be more likely to take risky economic decisions. If these are important for a wide range of economic behaviors, the lesson is that economists should learn from the related natural science fields.

The consilient approach to economic behavior is a growing part of the literature. For it to become more fully integrated, scholars in both social and natural sciences will have to spend more time together, and learn from each other.

References

Apicella, C. L., A. Dreber, B. Campbell, P. B. Gray, M. Hoffman, and A. C. Little. 2008. "Testosterone and Financial Risk Preferences." *Evolution and Human Behavior* 29:384–90.

Bolton, G. 1991. "A Comparative Model of Bargaining: Theory and Evidence." *American Economic Review* 81 (5): 1096–136.

Book, A. S., K. B. Starzyk, and V. L. Quinsey. 2001. "The Relationship between Testosterone and Aggression: A Meta-Analysis." *Aggression & Violent Behavior* 6 (6): 579–99.

Cesarini, D., C. T. Dawes, M. Johannesson, P. Lichtenstein, and B. Wallace. 2009. "Genetic Variation in Preferences for Giving and Risk Taking." *Quarterly Journal of Economics* 124:809–42.

Cesarini, D., M. Johannesson, P. Lichtenstein, Ö. Sandewall, and B. Wallace. 2010. "Genetic Variation in Financial Decision-Making." *Journal of Finance* 65 (5): 1725–54.

Cosmides, L., and J. Tooby. 1994. "Better than Rational: Evolutionary Psychology and the Invisible Hand." *American Economic Review* 84 (2): 327–32.

Cronqvist, H., and R. H. Thaler. 2004. "Design Choices in Privatized Social-Security Systems: Learning from the Swedish Experience." *American Economic Review* 94 (2): 424–48.

Dreber, A., C. L. Apicella, D. T. A. Eisenberg, J. R. Garcia, R. S. Zamore, J. K. Lum, and B. Campbell. 2009. "The 7R Polymorphism in the Dopamine Receptor D$_4$ Gene (*DRD4*) is Associated with Financial Risk Taking in Men." *Evolution and Human Behavior* 30 (2): 85–92.

Guth, W., R. Schmittberger, and B. Schwarze. 1982. "An Experimental Analysis of Ultimatum Bargaining." *Journal of Economic Behavior and Organization* 3 (4): 367–88.

Heilbronner, S. R., A. G. Rosati, J. R. Stevens, B. Hare, and M. D. Hauser. 2008. "A Fruit in the Hand or Two in the Bush? Divergent Risk Preferences in Chimpanzees and Bonobos." *Biology Letters* 4 (3): 246–49.

Kemper, T. D. 1990. *Social Structure and Testosterone: Explorations of the Socio-Bio-Social Chain.* New Brunswick, NJ: Rutgers University Press.

Laibson, D. 1997. "Golden Eggs and Hyperbolic Discounting." *The Quarterly Journal of Economics* 112 (2): 443–78.

Mayr, E. 1961. "Cause and Effect in Biology." *Science* 134:1501–06.

Mazur, A. 1973. "A Cross-Species Comparison of Status in Small Established Groups." *American Sociological Review* 38:513–30.

———. 1983. "Hormones, Aggression and Dominance in Humans." In *Hormones and Aggressive Behavior,* edited by B. Svare, 563–76. New York: Plenum.

———. 1985. "A Biosocial Model of Status in Face-to-Face Primate Groups." *Social Forces* 64 (2): 377–402.

Mazur, A., and A. Booth. 1998. "Testosterone and Dominance in Men." *Behavioral and Brain Sciences* 21:353–63.

Tinbergen, N. 1963. "On Aims and Methods in Ethology." *Zeitschrift für Tierpsychologie* 20:410–33.

———. 1968. "On War and Peace in Animals and Man. An Ethologist's Approach to the Biology of Aggression." *Science* 160:1411–18.

Tooby, J., and L. Cosmides. 1990. "The Past Explains the Present: Emotional Adaptations and the Structure of Ancestral Environments." *Ethology and Sociobiology* 11:375–424.

Wilson, E. O. 1978. *On Human Nature.* Cambridge, MA: Harvard University Press.

———. 1998. *Consilience.* New York: Knopf.

Wingfield, J. C., R. E. Hegner, A. M. Dufty Jr., and G. F. Ball. 1990. "The 'Challenge Hypothesis': Theoretical Implications for Patterns of Testosterone Secretion, Mating Systems, and Breeding Strategies." *American Naturalist* 136:829–46.

Systemic Risks and the Macroeconomy

Gianni De Nicolò and Marcella Lucchetta

3.1 Introduction

The recent financial crisis has underscored the need for a deeper understanding of the key drivers of systemic financial risk and its two-way relationship with real activity. We believe that to accomplish these goals, at least two requirements need to be met. First, measures of systemic risk need to be associated with the potential for undesirable welfare consequences, such as extreme adverse real effects. Second, the interplay between real and financial activity needs to be assessed through the implications of some theoretical model, and correspondingly quantified. Importantly, detecting macrofinancial linkages through a consistent and tractable framework may make it feasible to design risk monitoring tools implementable in real time. Contributing to accomplishing these goals is the main objective of this chapter.

We design a modeling framework that aims at tracking and quantifying the impact and transmission of structurally identifiable shocks within/between the macroeconomy, financial markets, and intermediaries, as well as their "tail" realizations. In terms of figure 3.1, the proposed framework aims at identifying which sectors of the economy are most affected by a shock at

Gianni De Nicolò is a senior economist in the Research Department of the International Monetary Fund. Marcella Lucchetta is assistant professor of economics at the University of Venice Ca' Foscari.

We thank without implications Fabio Canova, David Romer, Ken West, Hao Zhou, Harry Mamaysky, and seminar participants at the IMF and at the November 2009 NBER-Federal Reserve Bank of Cleveland Research Conference on Quantifying Systemic Risk for comments and suggestions. The views expressed in this chapter are those of the authors and do not necessarily represent the views of the International Monetary Fund. For acknowledgments, sources of research support, and disclosure of the authors' material financial relationships, if any, please see http://www.nber.org/chapters/c12051.ack.

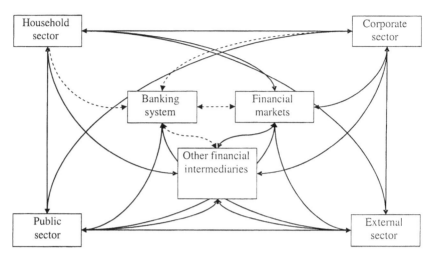

Fig. 3.1   **Financial exposures (stocks and flows) between sectors**

impact, to gauge size and persistence of shocks' propagation within and between sectors, and forecast their systemic real and financial outcomes.

Ideally, a computable general equilibrium model specified at a suitable level of disaggregation would allow us to identify the sources of shocks as well as the linkages through which they are propagated. In practice, formulating and implementing such a model is a formidable theoretical and computational task. At present, an increasing number of research resources are devoted to develop macroeconomic models with meaningful interaction between financial and real sectors. However, work in this direction is still in its infancy, since workhorse dynamic stochastic general equilibrium (DSGE) models do not yet embed essential financial structure or sectors, being their modeling of financial markets and institutions highly stylized.[1]

As a result, the available modeling technologies are still relatively underdeveloped. Some models analyzing the impact of macroeconomic shocks on segments of the financial sector have been developed recently in some central banks and international organizations. Yet, the feedback effects of financial vulnerabilities on the macroeconomy have been usually left unmodeled, since the output of these models is used mainly for financial supervisory purposes.[2]

Our modeling framework delivers joint forecasts of indicators of systemic

1. However, a rapidly growing literature, briefly reviewed by Walsh (2009), explores the implications of specific financial frictions in the co   yntext of extensions of the "financial accelerator" model of Bernanke, Gertler, and Gilchrist (1999), with work by Christiano, Motto, and Rostagno (2010) at the forefront of this effort.
2. See Sorge (2004) for a review of stress testing, and Huang, Zhou, and Zhu (2009a, 2009b) for recent contributions.

real risk and systemic financial risk, as well as stress tests of these indicators as impulse responses to structurally identifiable shocks. This framework is novel in two respects. First, it uses a dynamic factor model with structural identification based on theory. This permits us to extract information on common sources of shocks contained in a large set of time series, and to characterize their economic content. Second, it integrates the dynamic factor model with quantile regressions techniques, which allow us to estimate and forecast the size of tail realizations of systemic risks. We make a distinction between systemic real risk and systemic financial risk based on the notion that real effects are what concerns policymakers most since they are likely to entail welfare consequences. Our systemic real risk indicator is GDP at risk (GDPaR), defined as the worst predicted realization of quarterly growth in real GDP at 5 percent probability over a predetermined forecasting horizon.[3] Our indicator of systemic financial risk (FSaR) is defined as the worst predicted realization of a system-wide financial risk indicator at 5 percent probability over a predetermined forecasting horizon.

The underlying joint dynamics of GDP growth and the system-wide financial risk indicator is modeled through a factor-augmented vector autoregression (FAVAR) model, following variants of the methodology detailed in Stock and Watson (2002, 2005). Estimates of GDPaR and FSaR indicators are obtained through quantile regressions.

Forecasts of GDPaR and FSaR indicators are obtained by inputting the predicted values of factors obtained from the companion factor-augmented VAR into the relevant quantile regressions. Identification of structural shocks is accomplished with an expanded version of the sign restriction methodology introduced by Canova and De Nicolò (2002), where shocks are identified based on standard macroeconomic *and* banking theory. Stress tests of both systemic risk measures are obtained by inputting impulse responses to shocks identified in the FAVAR model into the relevant quantile regressions.

We implement this framework using a large set of quarterly time series of financial and real activity for the G-7 economies during the 1980Q1 to 2009Q3 period. We obtain two main results. First, we find evidence of out-of-sample forecasting power of the model for tail risk realizations of real activity for several countries. This suggests the usefulness of the model as a risk monitoring tool. Second, in all countries we identify aggregate demand shocks as the main drivers of the real cycle, and bank credit demand shocks are the main drivers of the bank lending cycle. This result is consistent with the hypothesis that shocks to the real economy are the main drivers of both real and financial risks. Importantly, this finding challenges the common

---

3. In this chapter we focus on real GDP growth, but several other indicators can be considered in our framework. In addition to GDP growth, De Nicolò and Lucchetta (2011) consider unemployment.

wisdom that constraints in the aggregate supply of credit have been a key driver of the sharp downturn in real activity experienced by the G-7 economies in 2008Q4 to 2009Q1.

The remainder of the chapter is composed of four sections. Section 3.2 defines systemic risks and describes indicators consistent with these definitions. Section 3.3 outlines the model setup, estimation and forecasting, and the procedure used to identify structural shocks. Section 3.4 describes the implementation of the modeling framework on data for the G-7 countries and the relevant results. Section 3.5 concludes.

3.2   Systemic Risks

3.2.1   Definitions

Following Group of Ten (2001) and De Nicolò and Kwast (2002), we adopt the following definitions:

Systemic financial risk is the risk that a shock will trigger a loss of economic value or confidence in the financial system.

Systemic real risk is the risk that a shock will trigger a significant decline in real activity.

We adopt these definitions for two reasons. First, distinguishing systemic financial risk from systemic real risk allows us to better assess the extent to which a realization of a financial shock is just amplifying a shock in the real sector, or originates in the financial system. Second, financial events that carry significant adverse real effects, such as sharp reductions in output and increases in unemployment, are the ultimate concern of policymakers. The financial shocks following the prick of the dot-com bubble in the United States in 2001, as well as those experienced in several other G-7 countries documented following, appear to have induced no significant real effects. According to our definitions, these shocks may be viewed as realizations of systemic financial risks, but not of systemic real risk.

3.2.2   Measurement

To control risk in financial institutions, risk managers track value at risk (VaR). Value at risk measures the worst possible portfolio loss over a given time horizon at a given probability. To control risk in the economy, policymakers may wish to track measures of worst possible real macroeconomic outcomes. One such a measure is GDPaR, defined here as the worst predicted realization of quarterly growth in real GDP at 5 percent probability.

To control risk in the financial system, policy makers may also wish to track measures of worst possible system-wide financial outcomes. One such a measure is financial system at risk (FSaR), defined as the worst predicted realization of the market-adjusted return of a large portfolios of financial firms at 5 percent probability. Following Campbell, Lo, and MacKinlay (1997), this market-adjusted return is the return of a portfolio of financial firms less the return on the market. We chose this measure for simplicity, treating the portfolio of the financial firms as a composite asset. However, other indicators can be adapted to our framework, such as those based on distance-to-default measures as in De Nicolò, Hayward, and Bathia (2004), those based on CDS spreads, as in Huang, Zhou, and Zhu (2009a, 2009b), as well those based on expected shortfalls constructed on the basis of individual firm returns, such as those in Acharya et al. (2010) and De Nicolò and Lucchetta (2012).

3.3   A Dynamic Factor Model of Systemic Risks

Denote real GDP growth with $GDPG_t$, and the indicator of system-wide financial risk with FS_t. The joint dynamics of $GDPG_t$ and FS_t is modeled by a version of the dynamic factor model (DFM) detailed in Stock and Watson (2002, 2005).

The model is described by the following equations:

$$(1) \qquad GDPG_t = \lambda^R(L)f_t + \gamma_{11}(L)GDPG_{t-1} + \gamma_{12}(L)FS_{t-1} + u_t^1$$

$$(2) \qquad FS_t = \lambda^F(L)f_t + \gamma_{21}(L)GDPG_{t-1} + \gamma_{22}(L)FS_{t-1} + u_t^2$$

$$(3) \qquad X_{it} = \lambda_i(L)f_t + \delta_i X_{it-1} + v_{it}$$

$$(4) \qquad f_t = \Gamma(L)f_{t-1} + \eta_t.$$

Equations (1) and (2) describe a VAR in $GDPG_t$ and FS_t augmented with a factor structure. The dynamics of a (large) vector of series (predictors) X_t indexed by $i \in N$ is represented by the factor model (3), where f_t is a set of *dynamic* factors.[4] Equation (4) describes the dynamics of these factors through a VAR.

As in Stock and Watson (2005), factors and idiosyncratic errors, u_t^1, u_t^2, and v_{it} are assumed to be uncorrelated at all leads and lags. Assuming finite lags up to p, and defining the vector of *static* factors with $F_t \equiv [f_t', f_{t-1}', \ldots, f_{t-p}']$, one obtains the *static form* representation of the DFM:

$$(5) \qquad GDPG_t = \Lambda^{R'}F_t + \gamma_{11}(L)GDPG_{t-1} + \gamma_{12}(L)FS_{t-1} + u_t^1$$

$$(6) \qquad FS_t = \Lambda^{F'}F_t + \gamma_{21}(L)GDPG_{t-1} + \gamma_{22}(L)FS_{t-1} + u_t^2$$

$$(7) \qquad X_{it} = \Lambda_i'F_t + \delta_i X_{it-1} + v_{it}$$

$$(8) \qquad F_t = \Phi(L)F_{t-1} + G\eta_t.$$

---

4. Following Stock and Watson (2006), we do not include GDP growth and the FS indicator in the vector X_t of predictors.

Note that $\Phi(L)$ includes $\Gamma(L)$ and 0's, while G is a matrix of coefficients of dimension $r x q$, where r is the number of static factors and q that of dynamic factors. If $r = q$, then $\Phi(L) = \Gamma(L)$ and $G = I$; that is, (8) is equivalent to (4).

Substituting (8) in (5) and (6), we obtain a FAVAR representation of the DFM, akin to that adopted by Bernanke, Boivin, and Eliasz (2005):

$$(9) \qquad F_t = \Phi(L)F_{t-1} + G\eta_t$$

$$(10) \quad GDPG_t = \Lambda^{R\prime}\Phi(L)F_{t-1} + \gamma_{11}(L)GDPG_{t-1} + \gamma_{12}(L)FS_{t-1} + u_t^1$$

$$(11) \qquad FS_t = \Lambda^{F\prime}\Phi(L)F_{t-1} + \gamma_{21}(L)GDPG_{t-1} + \gamma_{22}(L)FS_{t-1} + u_t^2.$$

3.3.1   Systemic Risk Measures

Using estimates of the static factors F_t, the systemic risk indicators GDPaR and FSaR are obtained by estimating the following quantile regressions:

$$(12) \quad GDPG_t = \alpha_1^q + \Lambda_q^{R\prime}F_t + \gamma_{11}^q(L)GDPG_{t-1} + \gamma_{12}^q(L)FS_{t-1} + u_t^{1q}$$

$$(13) \qquad FS_t = \alpha_2^q + \Lambda_q^{F\prime}F_t + \gamma_{12}^q(L)GDPG_{t-1} + \gamma_{22}^q(L)FS_{t-1} + u_t^{2q}.$$

Denoting the estimated coefficients of (12) and (13) with a "hat," GDPaR$_t$ and FSaR$_t$ are the fitted values of the quantile regressions (12) and (13) with $q = 0.05$:

$$(14) \qquad GDPaR_t = \hat{\alpha}_1^q + \hat{\Lambda}_q^{R\prime}F_t + \hat{\gamma}_{11}^q(L)GDPG_{t-1} + \hat{\gamma}_{12}^q(L)FS_{t-1}$$

$$(15) \qquad FSaR_t = \hat{\alpha}_2^q + \hat{\Lambda}_q^{F\prime}F_t + \hat{\gamma}_{12}^q(L)FS_{t-1} + \hat{\gamma}_{22}^q(L)GDPG_{t-1}.$$

3.3.2   Measures of Systemic Risk Spillovers

It can be useful and informative to compute measures of systemic risk spillovers from real activity to the financial sector (and vice versa) that are net of the impact of common factors on GDPaR and FSaR measures. These can be obtained by using the CoVar measures introduced by Adrian and Brunnermeier (2008). Estimates of Co(GDPaR$_t$) and Co(FSaR$_t$) are given by:

$$(16) \quad Co(GDPaR_t) = \hat{\alpha}_1^q + \hat{\beta}_1^q F_t + \hat{\gamma}_{11}^q(L)GDPaR_{t-1} + \hat{\gamma}_{12}^q(L)FSaR_{t-1}$$

$$(17) \qquad Co(FSaR_t) = \hat{\alpha}_2^q + \hat{\beta}_2^q F_t + \hat{\gamma}_{12}^q(L)GDPaR_{t-1} + \hat{\gamma}_{22}^q(L)FSaR_{t-1}.$$

The existence of systemic risk spillovers can be gauged comparing Co(GDPaR)$_t$ with GDPaR$_t$, and Co(FSaR)$_t$ with FSaR$_t$. For example, if Co(GDPaR)$_t$ < GDPaR$_t$, then negative risk spillovers in the real sector arise from negative risk spillovers either in the real sector, or in the financial sector, or both. However, positive risk spillovers cannot be ruled out, since improvements in real activity, or a reduction in system-wide financial risk, can have positive feedback effects on either sectors. This is apparent noting that the differences between the CoVar and the systemic risk measures are given by:

$$(18) \quad \text{Co(GDPaR)}_t - \text{GDPaR}_t = \hat{\gamma}^q_{11}(L)(\text{GDPaR}_{t-1} - \text{GDPG}_{t-1})$$
$$+ \hat{\gamma}^q_{12}(L)(\text{FSaR}_{t-1} - \text{FS}_{t-1})$$
$$(19) \quad \quad \text{Co(FSaR)}_t - \text{FSaR}_t = \hat{\gamma}^q_{12}(L)(\text{GDPaR}_{t-1} - \text{GDPG}_{t-1})$$
$$+ \hat{\gamma}^q_{22}(L)(\text{FSaR}_{t-1} - \text{FS}_{t-1}).$$

3.4   Estimation and Forecasting

The first estimation step is to compute static factors and choose their number. Since our focus is on forecasts of systemic risk indicators, we adopt the following forecasting criterion to select both number of static factors and lags of the FAVAR (10) and (11).

First, we use principal components to extract all factors with eigenvalues greater than 1, in number R. Second, we order factors according to their explanatory power of the variance of the data, and construct $\tilde{F} = \{(F_{r=1}), (F_1, F_{r=2}), \ldots, (F_1, F_2, \ldots, F_{r=R})\}$. Lastly, we choose the number of lags L and the number of static factors $r \in \tilde{F}$ that maximize $\text{FPE}(L, r) + \text{AIC}(L, r)$, where FPE is the Final Prediction Error Criterion and AIC is the Akaike Information Criterion. As detailed following, our forecasting criterion turns out to yield an optimal number of static factors close to the number of dynamic factors obtained by applying the statistical criterions based on Bai and Ng (2002).

In the second estimation step, we use the optimal number of lags L^* and number of static factors r^* obtained in the previous step to estimate quantile regressions (12) and (13) Note that these quantile regressions can be viewed as forecasting equations of systemic risk indicators. Using the VAR of static factors described by equation (9), we compute dynamic forecasts of static factors k quarters ahead. Then, these forecasts are used to obtain recursive forecasts of indicators of systemic risk using estimated coefficients of regressions (12) and (13). In sum, the foregoing procedure yield forecasts of GDPaR, FSaR, Co(GDPaR), and Co(FSaR) indicators k quarters ahead.[5]

3.5   Identification and Stress Tests

We would like to know how systemic risk indicators respond to structural shocks in the economy. To this end, we can use impulse responses to identified structural shocks through the FAVAR. These impulse responses can be viewed as stress tests of systemic risk indicators to these structural shocks.

---

5. Differing from Stock and Watson (2002), we obtain multistep-forecasts using the FAVAR rather than k-step projections. Assessing the relative merit of these procedures in terms of their out-of-sample forecasting ability is a worthwhile enterprise in future applications.

At a given date, the size of these responses provides a gauge of the sensitivity of systemic risk indicators to shocks of a given (standardized) size. Between dates, changes in the size of impulse responses of the systemic risk indicators to a given shock can provide a measure of changes in the resilience of an economy to a given shock.

3.5.1 Orthogonalization

We can obtain impulse responses of "factors" to their orthogonalized innovations, and translate them into impulse responses of indicators of systemic risk in (14) and (15) via the estimated coefficients of the quantile regressions. Yet, orthogonal innovations extracted from the FAVAR estimation do not have any "economic" interpretation, although they have the useful property of being contemporaneously and serially uncorrelated. Their economic interpretation can be obtained through identification based on some underlying theoretical model, as detailed next.

Under the assumption that the factor VAR of equation (9) is covariance-stationary, we can invert (9) obtaining the moving average (MA) form of the factor VAR:

$$\text{(9a)} \qquad\qquad F_t = A(L)\eta_t,$$

where $A(L) = (I - \Phi(L)L)^{-1} G$. Substituting (9a) in (10) and (11), we obtain:

$$\text{(10a)} \quad \text{GDPG}_t = \Lambda^{R'}A(L)\eta_t + \gamma_{11}(L)\text{GDPG}_{t-1} + \gamma_{12}(L)\text{FS}_{t-1} + u_t^1$$

$$\text{(11a)} \quad \text{FS}_t = \Lambda^{F'}A(L)\eta_t + \gamma_{21}(L)\text{GDPG}_{t-1} + \gamma_{22}(L)\text{FS}_{t-1} + u_t^2.$$

For the sole purpose of identification, we make the simplifying assumption that the dynamic impact of FS on GDPG, and of GDPG on FS, is entirely captured by the dynamics of factors. This amounts to posit $\gamma_{12}(L) = \gamma_{21}(L) = 0$, and converts our forecasting model into the standard factor VAR detailed in Stock and Watson (2005). Under this assumption, inverting (10a) and (11a) yields the MA representation of the FAVAR:

$$\text{(10b)} \qquad\qquad \text{GDPG}_t = B^R(L)\eta_t + w_t^1$$

$$\text{(11b)} \qquad\qquad \text{FS}_t = B^F(L)\eta_t + w_t^2,$$

where $B^R(L) = (1 - \gamma_{11}(L)L)^{-1} \Lambda^{R'}A(L)$, $B^F(L) = (1 - \gamma_{22}(L)L)^{-1} \Lambda^{F'}A(L)$, $w_t^1 = (1 - \gamma_{11}(L)L)^{-1}u_t^1$, and $w_t^2 = (1 - \gamma_{22}(L)L)^{-1}u_t^2$. Likewise, the MA representation of the systemic risk indicators is:

$$\text{(14a)} \qquad\qquad \text{GDPaR}_t = B_q^R(L)\eta_t + v_t^{1q}$$

$$\text{(15a)} \qquad\qquad \text{FSaR}_t = B_q^R(L)\eta_t + v_t^{2q}.$$

where $B_q^R(L) = (1 - \gamma_{11}^q(L)L)^{-1}\Lambda_q^{R'}A(L)$, $B_q^F(L) = (1 - \gamma_{22}^q(L)L)^{-1}\Lambda_q^{F'}A(L), = (1 - \gamma_{11}^q(L)L)^{-1}u_t^{1q}$, and $v_t^{q2} = (1 - \gamma_{22}^q(L)L)^{-1}u_t^{2q}$.

3.5.2   Theory-Based Identification

Extending the identification procedure introduced in Canova and De Nicolò (2002), we identify a chosen set of orthogonal innovations as *structural* shocks if they satisfy certain sign restrictions on key variables derived from aggregate dynamic macroeconomic theory *and* a simple banking model.

Specifically, the theoretical restrictions on the responses of key aggregates to structural shocks implied by an aggregate macroeconomic model are as follows. If a positive *temporary* orthogonal innovation represents a positive transitory aggregate supply shock, then it should generate transitory weakly positive output responses and weakly negative transitory responses in inflation, depending on capacity utilization. On the other hand, if it is a real aggregate demand shock, it should generate weakly positive transitory responses in output and inflation. Canova and De Nicolò (2002) show that these sign restrictions can be derived from a wide class of general equilibrium monetary macroeconomic models with different micro-foundations.

What are the implications of these theoretical responses for the demand and supply of bank credit? To answer this question, we use the implications of textbook partial equilibrium banking models, as, for example, described in chapter 3 of Freixas and Rochet (2008), or the simple model in Boyd, De Nicolò, and Loukoianova (2009). In these models, aggregate shocks can have an impact on both the demand for credit and the supply of funding for intermediaries.

Specifically, the theoretical restrictions on the responses of bank credit growth and changes in loan rates implied by these banking models are as follows. If there is a positive transitory shock to the demand for bank credit (e.g., because of a positive technology shock to firms generating an increase in demand for investment, or an increase in the quality of investment prospects), then we should observe a transitory increase in bank credit growth and an increase in loan rates. We call a shock generating these responses a positive credit demand shock. Conversely, if there is a positive transitory shock to the supply of bank credit (e.g., the supply of bank liabilities increases or banks expand by raising capital), then we should observe a transitory increase in bank credit growth but a decline in loan rates. We call a shock generating these responses a positive credit supply shock. Of course, negative shocks have all the signs of these responses reversed.

Note that real aggregate demand or supply shocks can affect the underlying drivers of the supply and demand for bank credit simultaneously. For example, a negative aggregate demand shock can induce firms and households to decrease their demand for bank credit, shifting the demand for bank credit to the left: this would result in a decline in loan rates ceteris paribus. At the same time, the adverse wealth effects of a negative aggregate demand shock may induce investors to reduce their supply of loanable

Table 3.1   Theoretical responses of key variables to positive shocks

Macroeconomic model	Aggregate supply	Aggregate demand
GDP growth	Positive	Positive
Inflation	Negative	Positive
Banking model	Bank credit demand	Bank credit supply
Bank credit growth	Positive	Positive
Change in lending rates	Positive	Negative

funds to banks, or banks could reduce their supply of credit as they may become increasingly capital constrained or risk averse: this would result in a leftward shift in the supply of credit ceteris paribus. Which effect dominates on net will be reflected in movements in loan rates and bank credit growth. If negative credit demand shocks dominate, then loan rates and bank credit growth should decline, while the converse would be true if negative credit supply shocks dominate.

Table 3.1 summarizes the responses of GDP growth, inflation, bank lending growth, and changes in loan rates in response to positive structural shocks implied by standard aggregate macroeconomic models and partial equilibrium banking models.

Identification of structural shocks will be conducted by checking whether a subset of orthogonal innovations of the FAVAR produces responses of the four variables considered that match the signs of the responses implied by theory.

3.6   Implementation

Our modeling procedure is implemented using quarterly macroeconomic and financial series for the G-7 economies for the period 1980:Q1 to 2009:Q3. All series are taken from Datastream.

For each country, the vector of quarterly series X_t in equation (3) includes about 95 series, which are detailed in the appendix. They can be classified into three main groups. The first group comprises equity markets data, including prices, price/earnings ratios, and dividend yields for the entire market and by sector. The inclusion of all sectors spanning from manufacturing to services allows us to gauge the differential impact of shocks on different sectors of the economy, as well as to capture the impact of specific sectors on systemic risks. The second group includes financial, monetary, and banking variables related to credit conditions, namely, interest rates for different maturities, monetary policy rates, bank prime rates and interbank rates, bank lending, and monetary aggregates. The third and last group includes price and quantity indicators of real activity. This set of variables includes net exports, capacity utilization, firms' investment, consumer confidence, unemployment, consumption and saving for firms, government and household, a consumer price index, industrial production, house prices, and manufacturing orders.

In the reminder of this section, we first report some descriptive statistics, then we detail the results of the forecasting model of systemic risks, and lastly, we carry out a benchmark identification of structural shocks, examining the responses of the systemic risk indicators to these shocks.

3.6.1   Descriptive Statistics

Table 3.2 reports basic statistics for GDP growth (GDPG) and our system-wide indicator of financial risk (FS). Three facts are worth noticing. First, ranges as well as volatilities of GDPG and FS appear to differ markedly across countries, suggesting differential sensitivities of these indicators to underlying shocks. Second, means of FS are generally small and not different from 0 according to simple t-statistics tests: this is expected, as in the long run the evolution of bank stock returns tracks that of the market. Third, the contemporaneous correlation between GDPG and FS appears relatively small, with no significant correlation for the United States, Canada, Japan, and Italy, and a positive and significant—albeit small—correlation for the United Kingdom, France, and Germany.

As shown in figure 3.2, however, the comovement between GDPG and FS appears to be the most pronounced during recessions and the latest "crisis" period in all countries. This suggests either an increase in the sensitivities of both indicators to common shocks, or a significant increase in risk spillovers between real and financial activity, or a combination of both. Furthermore, in several instances the indicators of systemic financial risk worsen with no

Table 3.2		Descriptive statistics of real GDP growth (GDPG) and the system-wide financial risk indicator (FS)				
		Mean	Std. dev.	Min	Max	Correlation
United States	GDPG	1.41	0.84	−1.38	4.57	0.08
	FS	−0.19	8.58	−33.5	38.34	
Canada	GDPG	0.53	1.06	−3.16	3.09	0.16
	FS	−0.31	10.27	−29.09	56.07	
Japan	GDPG	0.53	1.07	−3.43	3.09	0.15
	FS	−0.17	10.19	−29.09	56.07	
United Kingdom	GDPG	0.54	0.71	−2.52	2.17	**0.20**
	FS	−0.06	8.61	−38.68	19.52	
France	GDPG	0.46	0.51	−1.52	1.48	**0.15**
	FS	0.46	9.81	−41.3	29.16	
Germany	GDPG	0.32	0.75	−3.6	1.8	**0.38**
	FS	−0.69	6.85	−34.26	19.66	
Italy	GDPG	0.36	0.67	−2.76	2.19	0.03
	FS	−0.2	7.71	−17.69	29.26	

Note: Bold values indicate an estimate significantly different from zero at a 5 percent confidence level.

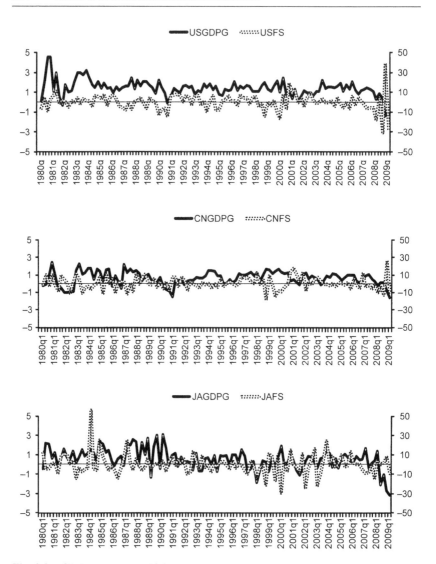

Fig. 3.2   GDP growth and FS indicators

detectable adverse effect on the indicators of systemic real risk, supporting the usefulness of our distinction between the systemic real and financial risks.

Assessing to what extent movements in real activity and the financial risk indicator are primarily driven by common shocks or primarily by spillovers is especially important during periods of both real and financial instability. Whether the recent crisis has been one in which the sharp contraction in real activity registered at end of 2008 and beginning of 2009 has been caused by

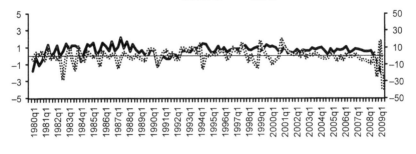

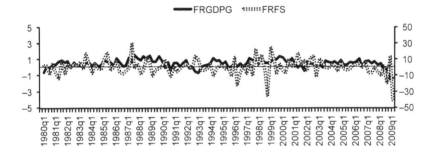

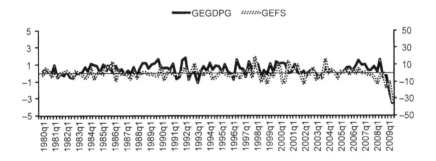

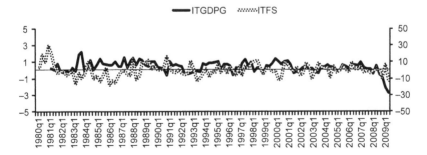

Fig. 3.2   (cont.)

sharp declines in the aggregate supply of bank credit, or alternatively, sharp declines in real activity are the main drivers of the reduction in the demand for bank credit, is still an open issue. Indeed, the conventional wisdom has been one in which the credit crunch has prompted banking systems to curtail lending, and banks' increasingly binding capital constraints have forced banks to de-leverage, with the attendant contraction of their asset size and further constraints in their lending capacity. Yet, bank loan growth in the United States and the Euro area, for example, has been buoyant since the start of the crisis, although it has decelerated since September 2008. This may suggest that the contraction in bank lending growth reflects primarily the sharp decline in the demand for credit resulting from the severe contraction in consumption growth and investment.[6]

Identification is essential to address these issues, and this is exactly what we do. Capturing the main drivers of the demand and supply of credit, and assessing whether shifts in the demand or supply of bank credit dominate on net requires identification of structural shocks.

3.6.2   Estimation and Forecasting

We estimated static factors and autoregressive coefficients of each variable by principal components according to the iterative procedure described in Stock and Watson (2005), and chose their number and the lags of equations (12) and (13) according to the forecasting criterion described previously. Notably, for all data sets of the seven countries our forecasting criterion selected the same number of static factors and lags: five factors and one lag. As a cross-check, we also estimated the number of static factors chosen according to the Bai and Ng's IC_{p1} and IC_{p2} criterions, obtaining eleven static factors for the United States—consistent with Stock and Watson (2005) results—and between nine and twelve static factors for the other countries. We also estimated the number of dynamic factors as principal components of the residuals of each variable in equations (10) and (11), obtaining six dynamic factors for the United States, and between four and six dynamic factors for the other countries. In light of these results, and because our focus is on forecasting and on identification with restrictions dictated by theory, we acted conservatively by treating the five estimated static factors equal to the number of dynamic factors, essentially assuming $F_t = f_t$, so that in equation (8) $G = I$.

We used these five estimated factors as independent variables of quantile regressions (14) and (15) specified with one lag. The resulting GDPaR and FSaR estimates were also used to compute CoVar measures (16) and (17).

As detailed in the previous section, forecasts of GDPaR and FSaR eight

---

6. For the United States, Chari, Christiano, and Kehoe (2008) made assertions at variance with the common wisdom, which were countered by Cohen-Cole et al. (2008) and Ivashina and Sharfstein (2008), to whom the former authors further replied.

quarters ahead were obtained projecting forward the factors through the VAR of equation (8) and using the estimated quantile coefficients to project forward GDPaR and FSaR values. Forecasts were undertaken with all data available as of September 25, 2009, that is, at end of 2009Q3. Note, however, that at that time actual real GDP was available only up to 2009Q2, so that the first effective forecast date for GDPaR is 2009Q3 and the estimated 2009Q3 GDP growth is a "nowcast."

Figure 3.3 reports estimated GDPaR and FSaR series, together with their forecasts eight quarters ahead of 2009Q3. Table 3.3 reports basic descriptive statistics of the systemic risk indicators, as well as the difference between CoVar and at-risk measures. As noted, the latter measure is useful to gauge risk spillovers in excess of those implied by the dependence of both measures on common factors.

We point out two main findings. First, means of FSaR estimates are very similar across countries, but their standard deviations vary significantly across countries. The converse is true for GDPaR, whose measures exhibit marked cross-country variations, while their standard deviations do not

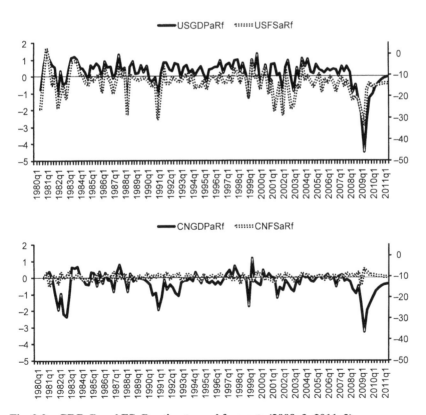

Fig. 3.3   **GDPaR and FSaR estimates and forecasts (2009q3–2011q2)**

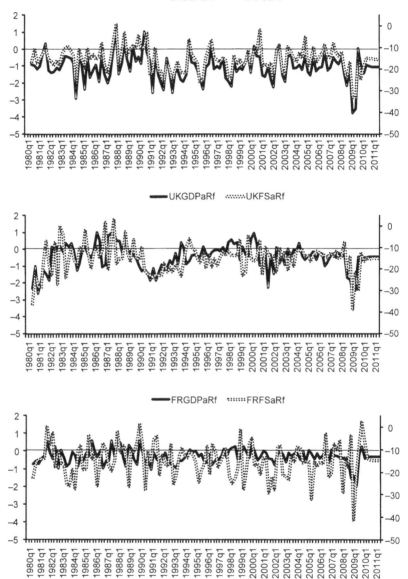

Fig. 3.3 (cont.)

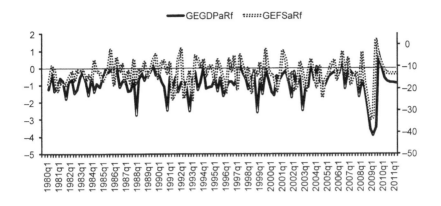

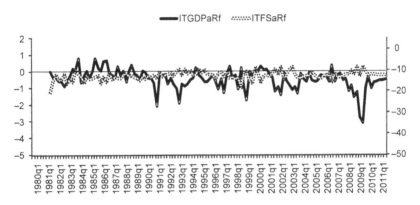

Fig. 3.3   (cont.)

appear to vary markedly. Second, risk spillovers are present for GDPaR measures, as table 3.3 exhibits negative values for all countries, while spillovers for FSaR measures are on average small and not significantly different from zero. Overall, common factors appear to be the dominant drivers of systemic risk indicators, whereas risk spillovers (net of common factors) seem relatively small in all countries.

Turning to GDPaR and FSaR forecasts, figure 3.3 indicates for all countries a V-shaped pattern of systemic risk indicators, with forecasts pointing at a return of these systemic risk indicators to their historical mean by mid-2010. This means that the model predicts a significant decline in the size of real and financial losses associated with tail risk events.

One intuitive—albeit informal—way of judging the forecasting ability of the model is to assess whether out-of-sample forecasts of the systemic risk indicator GDPaR move in the same direction of subsequent actual values of GDP growth. A full formal evaluation of the forecasting performance

Table 3.3   Descriptive statistics of systemic risk indicators

		Mean	Std. dev.	Min	Max
United States	GDPaR	0.24	0.81	−4.51	1.46
	FSaR	−13.6	5.95	−33.5	2.32
	dcoGDPaR	−0.73	0.56	−3.43	0.6
	dcoFSaR	−2.97	2.78	−13.98	3.63
Canada	GDPaR	−0.46	0.59	−2.74	1.16
	FSaR	−10.35	3.17	−18.78	2.75
	dcoGDPaR	−0.34	0.29	−1.45	0.33
	dcoFSaR	2.08	1.03	−0.41	5.46
Japan	GDPaR	−0.99	0.8	−3.67	1.17
	FSaR	−15.47	6.12	−33.63	1.06
	dcoGDPaR	0.08	0.24	−0.61	1.06
	dcoFSaR	1.32	4.03	−10.44	18.04
United Kingdom	GDPaR	−0.46	0.77	−2.61	0.97
	FSaR	−15.16	6.81	−38.68	3.18
	dcoGDPaR	0.13	0.39	−1.1	1.17
	dcoFSaR	−2.92	4.46	−15.93	8.01
France	GDPaR	−0.31	0.42	−1.94	0.67
	FSaR	−14.94	7.65	−41.3	2.26
	dcoGDPaR	−0.52	0.31	−1.42	0.07
	dcoFSaR	3.46	8.37	−20.79	32.87
Germany	GDPaR	−0.88	0.78	−3.95	0.89
	FSaR	−13.2	6.3	−34.26	1.87
	dcoGDPaR	−0.62	0.35	−2.07	0.03
	dcoFSaR	−12.62	8.92	−45.29	1.6
Italy	GDPaR	−0.46	0.62	−3.1	0.8
	FSaR	−12.83	1.96	−20.64	−8.62
	dcoGDPaR	−0.15	0.35	−1.17	0.72
	dcoFSaR	0.11	1.06	−2.83	2.79

Notes: GDPaR is GDP at risk; FSaR is the financial-system at risk indicator; dcoGDPaR = co(GdPaR) – GDPaR, where co(GDPaR) is the CoVaR version of the systemic real risk indicator; dcoFSaR = co(FSaR) – FSaR, where co(FSaR) is the CoVaR version of the systemic financial risk indicator.

of the model is outside the scope of this chapter. However, here we report perhaps the most demanding assessment of the model's forecasting ability. Namely, we assess if the model signals a decline in GDPaR prior to one of the largest historical declines in real activity: that experienced in 2008Q4 to 2009Q1 in all G-7 countries.

Figure 3.4 reports the results of this comparison: the blue line is the out-of-sample GDPaR forecasts made in 2008Q3, while the red line is actual GDP growth. Predicted changes in GDPaR and actual GDP growth go in the same direction for at least one quarter ahead within a three quarters' horizon (up to 2009Q1) in all countries. Although informal, we view this evidence as notable. The out-of-sample consistency of GDPaR forecasts with the future evolution of actual GDP growth for the most unpredictable

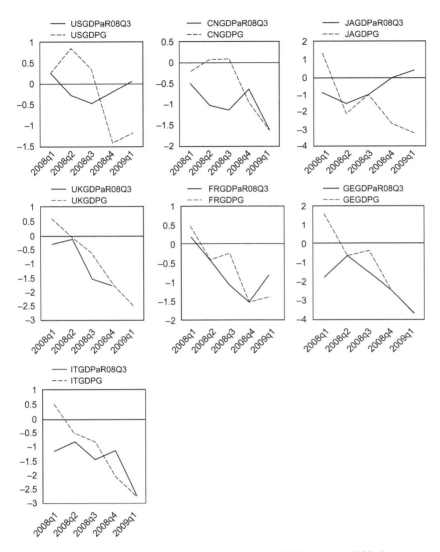

Fig. 3.4   GDPaR out-of-sample forecasts and actual GDP growth (2008q3–2009q1)

event in decades suggests the potential usefulness of our model as a real-time risk-monitoring tool.

3.6.3   Identification of Structural Shocks

We implemented the identification procedure outlined previously by following three steps. First, we selected an orthogonal decomposition of the MA representation (9a). Second, we computed impulse responses of FAVARs for GDP growth, inflation, bank lending growth, and first differences in loan rates for each country. Third, we checked whether the joint signs of the responses of these variables conformed to the signs predicted for different shocks by the basic macro and banking models summarized in table 3.1.

As a benchmark orthogonalization, we chose a Choleski decomposition with factors ordered according to their explanatory power of the common variations in the data, with factor 1 ordered first, factor 2 second, and so on, and with GDPG, inflation, bank lending growth, and first differences in loan rates ordered last in each FAVAR equation. The simple assumption underlying this choice is that the casual ordering implied by this decomposition reflects the relative importance of factors in explaining variations in the data, and each idiosyncratic component of the observable variables does not affect any of the factors at impact.

To check robustness, however, we examined alternative decompositions with inverted ordering of the variables, obtaining similar signs of the responses of each of the observable variables to shock to orthogonalized innovations. We also examined the covariance matrix of innovations of the VAR of each country, and such matrices appeared approximately diagonal in all cases, indicating that the ordering of variables in the VAR was not likely to change results under the casual ordering selected. Furthermore, the approximate diagonality of these covariance matrices also suggests that our results may be robust to alternative orthogonal decompositions—not necessarily recursive—that can be extracted applying the systematic statistical search implemented by Canova and De Nicolò (2002).

Figure 3.5 reports impulse responses of GDP growth, inflation, bank lending growth, and changes in lending rates for each of the G-7 countries. Strikingly, the response of all variables to all shocks at impact or for at least up to two quarters after impact is either strictly positive (in most cases) or nonnegative (in few cases).[7] Hence, according to table 3.1, *under the assumed benchmark orthogonalization, all structural shocks in these economies can be identified as aggregate demand shocks associated with bank credit demand shocks.* The finding of aggregate demand shock as the predominant drivers of real cycles in the G-7 economies is matching the findings by Canova and De Nicolò (2003), who used only a small dimension VAR for the G-7 countries, but implemented a full search for shocks interpretable according to aggregate macroeconomic theory in the entire space of nonrecursive orthogonalizations of the VAR of each country. This finding is also consistent with recent work by Arouba and Diebold (2010), who find demand shocks as the dominant source of aggregate fluctuations in the United States.

The finding that aggregate bank demand shocks are the predominant drivers of cycles in bank credit growth is consistent with their being prompted

---

7. The only exception is the shock associated with the third factor for Canada, whose responses do not satisfy any of the sign restrictions in table 3.1, and thus the results are unidentified.

United States

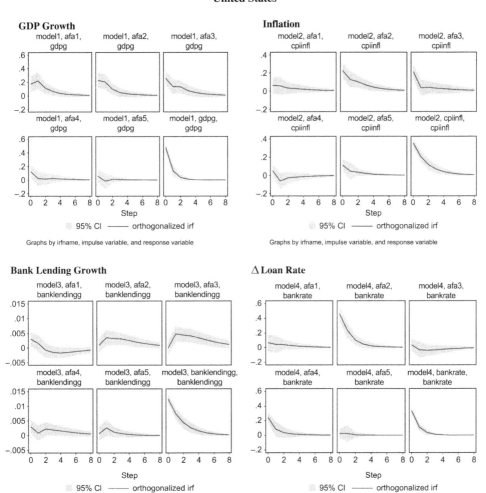

Fig. 3.5 Impulse responses of GDP growth, inflation, bank lending growth, and change in lending rate to shocks to factors and own shock

Canada

GDP Growth

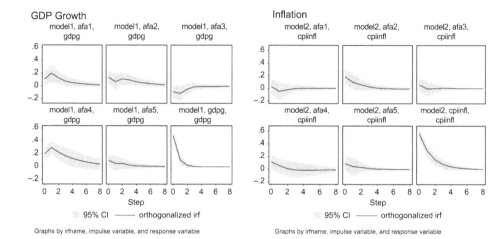

Inflation

Bank Lending Growth

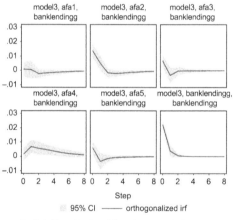

Δ Loan Rate

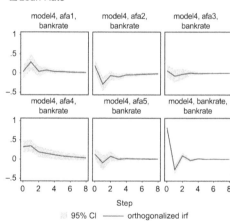

Fig. 3.5   (cont.)

Japan

GDP Growth

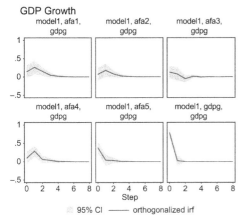

Inflation

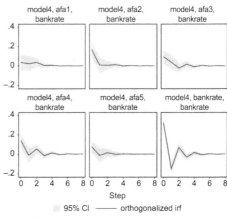

Bank Lending Growth

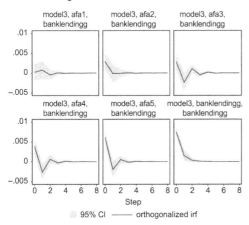

Δ Loan Rate

Fig. 3.5   (cont.)

United Kingdom

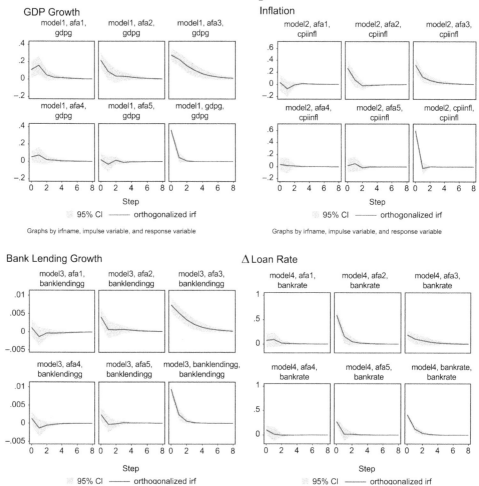

Fig. 3.5 (cont.)

France

GDP Growth

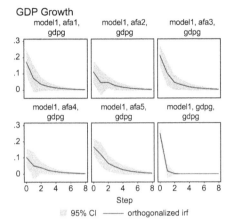

Graphs by irfname, impulse variable, and response variable

Inflation

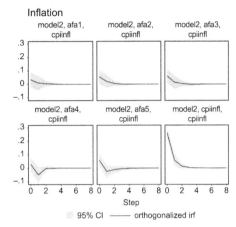

Graphs by irfname, impulse variable, and response variable

Bank Lending Growth

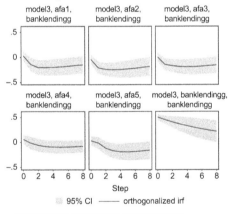

Graphs by irfname, impulse variable, and response variable

Δ Loan Rate

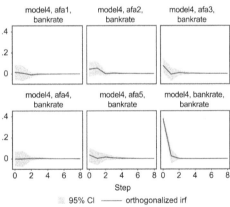

Graphs by irfname, impulse variable, and response variable

Fig. 3.5   (cont.)

Germany

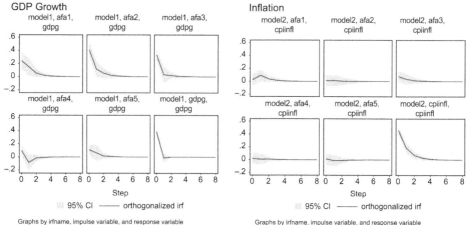

GDP Growth

model1, afa1, gdpg · model1, afa2, gdpg · model1, afa3, gdpg
model1, afa4, gdpg · model1, afa5, gdpg · model1, gdpg, gdpg

Inflation

model2, afa1, cpiinfl · model2, afa2, cpiinfl · model2, afa3, cpiinfl
model2, afa4, cpiinfl · model2, afa5, cpiinfl · model2, cpiinfl, cpiinfl

95% CI —— orthogonalized irf

Graphs by irfname, impulse variable, and response variable

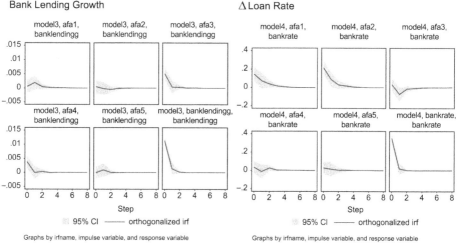

Bank Lending Growth

model3, afa1, banklendingg · model3, afa2, banklendingg · model3, afa3, banklendingg
model3, afa4, banklendingg · model3, afa5, banklendingg · model3, banklendingg, banklendingg

△ Loan Rate

model4, afa1, bankrate · model4, afa2, bankrate · model4, afa3, bankrate
model4, afa4, bankrate · model4, afa5, bankrate · model4, bankrate, bankrate

95% CI —— orthogonalized irf

Graphs by irfname, impulse variable, and response variable

Fig. 3.5   (cont.)

Italy

GDP Growth

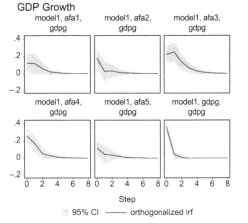

Graphs by irfname, impulse variable, and response variable

Inflation

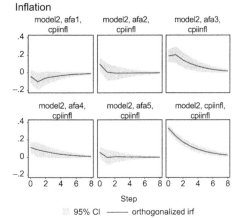

Graphs by irfname, impulse variable, and response variable

Bank Lending Growth

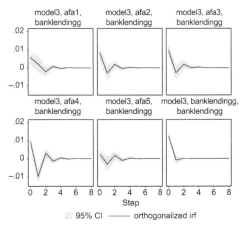

Graphs by irfname, impulse variable, and response variable

Δ Loan Rate

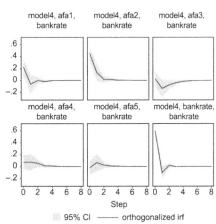

Graphs by irfname, impulse variable, and response variable

Fig. 3.5   (cont.)

by aggregate demand shocks. This result also supports the conjecture that slowdowns in aggregate bank credit growth are primarily the result of downturns in real activity, as they reflect declines in the aggregate demand for bank credit by households and firms, rather than a reduction in the aggregate supply of bank credit. Recent evidence by Berrospide and Edge (2010) and Kahle and Stulz (2010) for the United States is also consistent with our results.

Notably, the five identified aggregate demand and bank credit demand shocks are not all the same, as they have a differential impact on GDP growth, inflation, bank lending growth, and changes in loan rates within as well as between countries. This suggests that the sectors of the economy where they originate are different. As shown in table 3.4, the variance decompositions of the four variables VAR in each country show that the variance explained by each shock varies across both variables and countries, with most shocks resulting relevant in each country.[8]

Similar results are obtained when we look at the impulse responses and variance decompositions of GDPaR and FSaR measures. As shown in figure 3.6, the sign of the impact of each shock on GDPaR is essentially the same in each country, although magnitude and persistence of these shocks widely differ. As shown in table 3.5, the relevant variance decompositions indicate the importance of each of the identified shocks for the systemic risk indicators in each country.

In sum, all identified structural shocks are aggregate demand shocks associated with bank credit demand shocks, this identification is the same for all countries considered, and it appears robust to alternative orthogonalizations of the innovations in the FAVAR.

3.7 Conclusion

This chapter has developed a modeling framework that delivers forecasts of indicators of systemic real and financial risks that can be updated in real time. In addition, the proposed identification procedure allows gauging the sensitivity of these indicators to structural shocks identified by theory, giving economic content to stress tests. The implementation of such framework appears promising as a risk-monitoring tool.

We view this framework as a first building block for an analysis of the determinants of systemic risks. As it can be inferred from our discussion, refinements and extensions of our framework are aplenty, since we have exploited the rich information provided by the factor model only in a limited way.

There remain deeper questions that need yet to be answered: Where do

---

8. The results echo the findings of an increased impact of sectoral shocks on aggregate industrial production indexes documented recently by Foerster, Sarte, and Watson (2008).

Table 3.4   Variance decomposition of GDP growth, inflation, bank lending growth, and changes in loan rates to identified aggregate demand and bank credit demand shocks

	Shock 1	Shock 2	Shock 3	Shock 4	Shock 5	Shock sum	Idiosyncratic
United States							
GDP growth	**0.17**	**0.18**	**0.19**	0.03	0.01	0.58	0.42
Inflation	0.03	**0.24**	**0.14**	0.02	0.05	0.48	0.52
Bank credit growth	0.05	**0.11**	**0.20**	0.06	0.02	0.44	0.56
Loan rate	0.02	**0.58**	0.01	**0.14**	0.00	0.75	0.25
Canada							
GDP growth	**0.12**	0.09	0.09	**0.30**	0.01	0.61	0.39
Inflation	0.01	0.08	0.00	0.03	0.02	0.14	0.86
Bank credit growth	0.01	**0.21**	0.06	**0.13**	0.05	0.46	0.54
Loan rate	0.07	0.10	0.02	**0.22**	0.03	0.44	0.56
Japan							
GDP growth	**0.10**	0.03	0.01	0.09	**0.11**	0.34	0.66
Inflation	0.03	0.02	0.04	**0.15**	**0.23**	0.47	0.53
Bank credit growth	0.02	0.01	0.05	**0.17**	**0.29**	0.54	0.46
Loan rate	0.02	**0.14**	**0.08**	**0.10**	0.01	0.35	0.65
United Kingdom							
GDP growth	0.09	**0.14**	**0.42**	0.02	0.00	0.67	0.33
Inflation	0.01	**0.14**	**0.22**	0.00	0.01	0.38	0.62
Bank credit growth	0.02	0.08	**0.44**	0.02	0.03	0.59	0.41
Loan rate	0.02	**0.53**	0.08	0.01	0.10	0.74	0.26
France							
GDP growth	0.15	0.07	**0.25**	0.06	**0.20**	0.73	0.27
Inflation	0.01	0.04	0.05	0.04	0.05	0.19	0.81
Bank credit growth	**0.11**	**0.17**	**0.10**	0.02	0.08	0.48	0.52
Loan rate	0.00	0.03	0.04	0.00	0.01	0.08	0.92
German							
GDP growth	**0.15**	**0.33**	**0.20**	0.03	0.03	0.74	0.26
Inflation	0.04	0.00	0.03	0.00	0.00	0.07	0.93
Bank credit growth	0.02	0.00	**0.15**	0.08	0.00	0.25	0.75
Loan rate	**0.13**	**0.25**	0.03	0.01	0.00	0.42	0.58
Italy							
GDP growth	0.07	0.08	**0.30**	**0.22**	0.04	0.71	0.29
Inflation	0.05	0.02	**0.29**	0.07	0.01	0.44	0.56
Bank credit growth	0.07	**0.14**	**0.17**	**0.33**	0.03	0.74	0.26
Loan rate	0.08	**0.33**	0.04	0.02	0.01	0.48	0.52

Note: Boldfaced values denote estimates significantly different from zero at 5 percent confidence levels.

these structural shocks originate? To which other sectors are they transmitted? In terms of figure 3.1 of the introduction, answering these questions amounts to identifying in which box shocks originate, and disentangles the linkages between the originating box and other boxes in the picture; that is, the web of linkages implied by the transmission mechanism of these shocks.

Answering these questions amounts to exploit further the rich information structure provided by the factor model. We believe that such an explora-

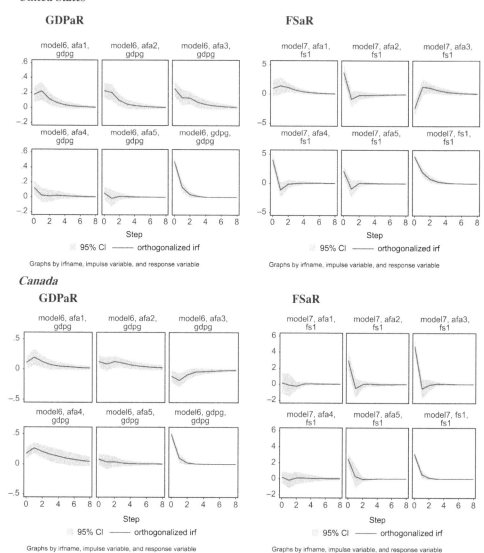

Fig. 3.6 Impulse responses of GDPaR and FSaR to identified aggregate demand and bank credit demand shocks and own shock

Japan

GDPaR

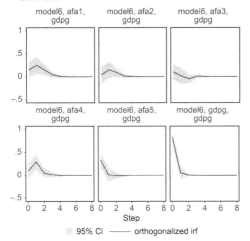

95% CI ——— orthogonalized irf

Graphs by irfname, impulse variable, and response variable

FSaR

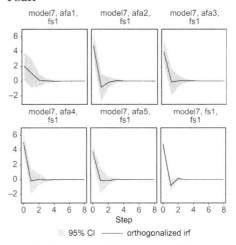

95% CI ——— orthogonalized irf

Graphs by irfname, impulse variable, and response variable

United Kingdom

GDPaR

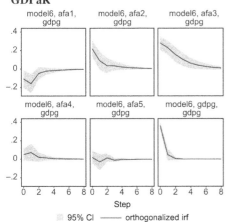

95% CI ——— orthogonalized irf

Graphs by irfname, impulse variable, and response variable

FSaR

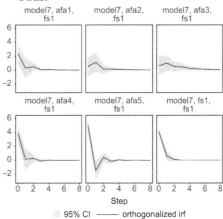

95% CI ——— orthogonalized irf

Graphs by irfname, impulse variable, and response variable

Fig. 3.6   (cont.)

France

GDPaR

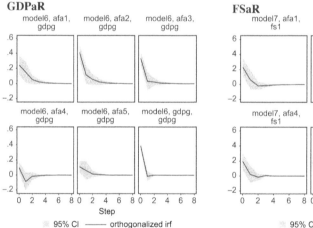

FSaR

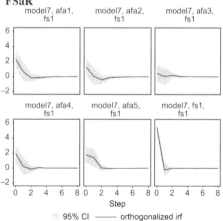

Germany

GDPaR

FSaR

Fig. 3.6   (cont.)

tion is likely to yield increasing returns. It can guide a more effective integration of financial frictions into current macroeconomic modeling, encourage the development of more disaggregated versions of such macroeconomic modeling by incorporating the insights of models of financial intermediation, and can be a powerful monitoring tool available to policymakers. Carrying out some of these extensions is already part of our research agenda.

Italy

GDPaR

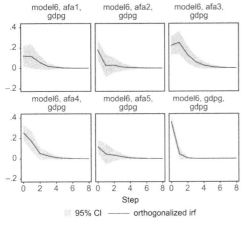

FSaR

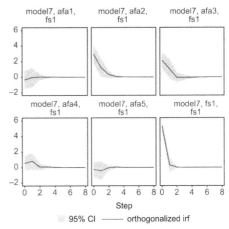

Fig. 3.6 (cont.)

Table 3.5   **Variance decomposition of GDPaR and FSaR to identified aggregate demand and bank credit demand shocks**

	Shock 1	Shock 2	Shock 3	Shock 4	Shock 5	Shock sum	Idiosyncratic
United States							
GDPaR	**0.12**	0.09	0.09	**0.30**	0.01	0.61	0.39
FSaR	0.06	**0.19**	0.12	**0.22**	0.07	0.67	0.33
Canada							
GDPaR	**0.15**	0.02	0.08	**0.17**	0.06	0.48	0.52
FSaR	0.00	**0.18**	**0.47**	0.00	**0.13**	0.79	0.21
Japan							
GDPaR	**0.10**	0.03	0.01	0.09	**0.11**	0.34	0.66
FSaR	0.05	**0.22**	**0.14**	**0.24**	**0.13**	0.78	0.22
United Kingdom							
GDPaR	0.09	**0.14**	**0.42**	0.02	0.00	0.67	0.33
FSaR	0.09	0.02	0.03	**0.22**	**0.40**	0.76	0.24
France							
GDPaR	**0.15**	0.07	**0.25**	0.06	**0.21**	0.74	0.26
FSaR	**0.13**	0.04	**0.05**	**0.45**	0.01	0.68	0.32
Germany							
GDPaR	**0.15**	**0.33**	**0.20**	0.03	0.03	0.74	0.26
FSaR	**0.12**	0.04	0.01	0.08	**0.11**	0.36	0.64
Italy							
GDPaR	0.07	0.08	**0.30**	0.22	0.04	0.71	0.29
FSaR	0.00	0.22	**0.13**	0.02	0.01	0.38	0.62

Note: Boldfaced values denote estimates significantly different from zero at 5 percent confidence levels.

Appendix

Equity markets	Transformations
Equity indices, price earnings ratios, and dividend yields total and by sector	
Market	Δln
Oil and gas	Δln
Chemicals	Δln
Basic resources	Δln
Construction and materials	Δln
Industrial goods and services	Δln
Auto and parts	Δln
Food and beverages	Δln
Personal and household goods	Δln
Health care	Δln
Retail	Δln
Media	Δln
Travel and leisure	Δln
Telecom	Δln
Utilities	Δln
Banks	Δln
Insurance	Δln
Financial services	Δln
Technology	Δln
Credit conditions	
3-month money rate	Δlevels
Treasury bonds	
2 YR	Δlevels
3 YR	Δlevels
5 YR	Δlevels
7 YR	Δlevels
10 YR	Δlevels
30 YR	Δlevels
Financial variables	
Money base	Δln
Money supply M1	Δln
Interbank rate	Δlevels
Prime rate charged by banks (month AVG)	Δlevels
Bank lending	Δln
Real sector variables	
GDP	Δln
Personal consumption expenditure	Δln
Government consumption and investment	Δln
Private domestic fixed investment	Δln
Export of goods on balance of payments basis	Δln
Import of goods on balance of payments basis	Δln
Net export or capital and financial account balance	Δln
Consumer confidence index	Δlevels
Personal income	Δln

Table A3.1   (continued)

Equity markets	Transformations
Personal savings as percent of disposal income	Δlevels
Unemployment rate	Δlevels
Output per hour of all persons	Δln
Industrial production-total index	Δln
CPI all items	Δln
New orders manufacturing	Δln
Capacity utilization	Δlevels
Housing market index	Δlevels

Notes: All variables are extracted for each country in the G-7 group during the 1980Q1–2009Q3 period. The frequency of all series is quarterly. Data transformations are implemented to make all series stationary. Δln = log level difference; Δlevels = level difference. CPI = consumer price index.

References

Acharya, Viral, Lasse Pedersen, Thomas Philippon, and Matthew Richardson. 2010. "Measuring Systemic Risk." Unpublished Manuscript. New York University Stern School of Business, May.

Adrian, Tobias, and Markus K. Brunnermeier. 2008. "CoVar." Federal Reserve Bank of New York Staff Report no. 348. September.

Aruoba, S. Boragan, and Francis X. Diebold. 2010. "Real-Time Macroeconomic Monitoring: Real Activity, Inflation, and Interactions." *American Economic Review* 100:20–24.

Bai, Jushan, and Serena Ng. 2002. "Determining the Number of Factors in Approximate Factor Models." *Econometrica* 70 (1): 191–221.

Bernanke, Ben, Jean Boivin, and Piotr Eliasz. 2005. "Measuring the Effects of Monetary Policy: A Factor-Augmented Vector Autoregressive (FAVAR) Approach." *Quarterly Journal of Economics* 120:387–422.

Bernanke, Ben, Mark Gertler, and Simon Gilchrist. 1999. "The Financial Accelerator in a Quantitative Business Cycle Framework." In *Handbook of Macroeconomics,* edited by John Taylor and Michael Woodford, 1341–393. Amsterdam: North Holland.

Berrospide, Jose, and Rochelle Edge. 2010. "The Effects of Bank Capital on Lending: What Do We Know? What Does it Mean?" *International Journal of Central Banking* December:5–54.

Boyd, John, Gianni De Nicolò, and Elena Loukoianova. 2009. "Banking Crises and Crisis Dating: Theory and Evidence." IMF Working Paper no. 09/141. Washington, DC: International Monetary Fund.

Campbell, John Y., Andrew W. Lo, and A. Craig MacKinley. 1997. *The Econometrics of Financial Markets.* Princeton, NJ: Princeton University Press.

Canova, Fabio, and Gianni De Nicolò. 2002. "Monetary Disturbances Matter for Business Cycle Fluctuations in the G-7." *Journal of Monetary Economics* 49 (6): 1121–159.

———. 2003. "On the Sources of Business Cycles in the G-7." *Journal of International Economics* 59 (1): 77–100.

Chari, V. V., Lawrence Christiano, and Patrick J. Kehoe. 2008. "Facts and Myths About the Financial Crisis of 2008." Federal Reserve Bank of Minneapolis Working Paper 666, October.

Christiano, Lawrence, Roberto Motto, and Massimo Rostagno. 2010. "Financial Factors in Economic Fluctuations." ECB Working Paper no. 1192. Frankfurt: European Central Bank.

Cohen-Cole, Ethan, Burcu Duygan-Bump, José Fillat, and Judit Montoriol-Garriga. 2008. "Looking Behind the Aggregates: A Reply to Facts and Myths about the Financial Crisis of 2008." Federal Reserve Bank of Boston, Working Paper no. QAU08-5.

De Nicolò, Gianni, Peter Hayward, and Ashok Bathia. 2004. "US Large Complex Banking Groups: Business Strategies, Risks and Surveillance Issues." Special Issue Paper, IMF Country Report no. 04/228, July. Washington, DC: International Monetary Fund.

De Nicolò, Gianni, and Myron Kwast. 2002. "Systemic Risk and Financial Consolidation: Are They Related?" *Journal of Banking and Finance* 26 (5): 861–80.

De Nicolò, Gianni, and Marcella Lucchetta. 2012. "Systemic Real and Financial Risks: Measurement, Forecasting and Stress Testing." IMF Working Paper no. 12/58, February. Washington, DC: International Monetary Fund.

Foerster, Andrew T., Pierre-Daniel G. Sarte, and Mark W. Watson. 2008. "Sectoral vs. Aggregate Shocks: A Structural Factor Analysis of Industrial Production." NBER Working Paper no. 14389. Cambridge, MA: National Bureau of Economic Research, October.

Freixas, Xavier, and Jean-Charles Rochet. 2008. *Microeconomics of Banking,* 2nd ed. Cambridge, MA: MIT Press.

Group of Ten. 2001. *Report on Consolidation in the Financial Sector.* Basel: Bank for International Settlements. http://www.bis.org/publ/gten05.pdf.

Huang, Xin, Hao Zhou, and Hai Zhu. 2009a. "A Framework for Assessing the Systemic Risk of Financial Institutions." BIS Working Paper no. 281, April. Basel: Bank for International Settlements.

———. 2009b. "Assessing the Systemic Risk of a Heterogeneous Portfolio of Banks during the Recent Financial Crisis." FEDS Working Paper 2009-44. Washington, DC: Board of Governors of the Federal Reserve System.

Ivashina, Victoria, and David Scharfstein. 2008. "Bank Lending during the Financial Crisis of 2008." Working Paper. Harvard Business School.

Kahle, Kathreen, and Rene Stulz. 2010. "Financial Policies and the Financial Crisis: Impaired Credit Channel or Diminished Demand for Capital?" Unpublished Manuscript, October.

Stock, James, and Mark Watson. 2002. "Macroeconomic Forecasting Using Diffusion Indexes." *Journal of Business Economics and Statistics* April:147–62.

———. 2005. "Implications of Dynamic Factor Models for VAR Analysis." NBER Working Paper no. 11467. Cambridge, MA: National Bureau of Economic Research, July.

———. 2006. "Forecasting with Many Predictors." In *Handbook of Economic Forecasting,* edited by Graham Elliott, Clive W. J. Granger, and Allan Timmermann, 516–54. Amsterdam: North Holland.

Sorge, Marco. 2004. "Stress Testing Financial Systems: An Overview of Current Methodologies." BIS Working Paper no. 165. Basel: Bank for International Settlements.

Walsh, Carl. 2009. "Using Monetary Policy to Stabilize Real Activity." Unpublished Manuscript, September.

Comment   Hao Zhou

There are two approaches to understanding the issue of systemic risk and macroprudential regulation—one is empirical macroeconomics based, and the other is financial market based. These two approaches have different methodologies, emphases, and purposes. De Nicolò and Lucchetta's chapter belongs to the macro-centric approach. It helps us to better understand the fundamental linkage between the real economy and the financial sector, especially in the long run. However, unlike a financial-centric approach, the chapter is silent on the interaction among large banks, the nonlinear feedback effect, and the identification of individual institutions that are systemically important.

Two Approaches to Systemic Risk

There is a long tradition in the empirical macroeconomics literature (see, e.g., Bernanke, Gertler, and Gilchrist 1998) that introduces the financial sector as a market imperfection into a real business cycle framework. Such an add-on approach typically labels the financial sector as an accelerator, multiplier, or amplifier, in that shocks into the economy come from the real side and are magnified by the financial sector. The recent financial crisis and deep recession have also prompted more research along this direction.[1]

This chapter follows De Nicolò and Kwast (2002) in defining systemic risk as the risk that either a real or a financial shock will trigger a significant decline in real activity. The systemic financial risk is measured as the value at risk (VaR) for the market-adjusted return of a large portfolio of financial firms at the 5 percent level, and the systemic real risk is measured by the similar GDP 5 percentile. The empirical implementation builds on the dynamic factor model of Stock and Watson (2005) with quarterly data. For estimating systemic risks, GDP and financial VaRs are estimated via quantile regressions, and can be explicitly related to the conditional VaR (CoVaR) framework advocated by Adrian and Brunnermeier (2009). Empirical estimation consists of two steps: first, a standard dynamic factor approach is adopted to estimate the VaR parameters and to filter out the latent factors; then, the standard quantile regression is applied to the GDP and financial and impulse-response or stress testing is conducted.

Hao Zhou is a senior economist in the Risk Analysis Section, Divison of Research and Statistics, at the Board of Governors of the Federal Reserve System.

The views presented here are solely those of the author and do not necessarily represent those of the Federal Reserve Board or its staff. For acknowledgments, sources of research support, and disclosure of the author's material financial relationships, if any, please see http://www .nber.org/chapters/c12052.ack.

1. One example is the Federal Reserve and JMCB (*Journal of Money, Credit, and Banking*) Conference on Financial Market and Monetary Policy held in June 2009, which emphasizes the linkage between financial market and macroeconomy and the implications for monetary policy.

An alternative approach is to focus on the microeconomic structure of the financial industry, while treating macroeconomy only as a background. The CoVaR measure (Adrian and Brunnermeier 2009) looks at the VaR of one portfolio conditional on the VaR of another portfolio, which focuses on the spillover effect from one bank's failure to the safety of another bank or the whole banking system. The "Shapley Value" decomposition approach (Tarashev, Borio, and Tsatsaronis 2009) constructed in the game theory used by Tarashev, Borio, and Tsatsaronis (2009) allocates the systemic risk to individual banks by defining the contribution of each bank as a weighted average of its add-on effect to each subsystem of that bank. Huang, Zhou, and Zhu (2010) consider bank's systemic importance as its marginal contribution to a hypothetical insurance premium of distress loss that a banking system may suffer. Such an intuitive method has advantages of being both subadditive, as opposed to the CoVaR measure, and simple to implement, as opposed to the Shapley value approach.

Advantages and Disadvantages

For the impulse-response analysis in empirical macroeconomics, typically the shocks to factors are extracted through othogonalization but without meaningful economic interpretations. This chapter uses economic theory implied sign restrictions to help identify whether the real or financial shocks are coming from supply side or demand side. A large class of general equilibrium monetary macroeconomic models can identify aggregate demand shock if both GDP and inflation responses are positive and identify aggregate supply shock if GDP response is positive, while inflation response is negative (Canova and De Nicolò, 2002). On the other hand, partial equilibrium banking models (see, e.g., Boyd, De Nicolò, and Loukoianova 2009) can identify credit demand shock from positive responses in both bank credit growth and lending rate change and identify credit supply shock from positive response of bank credit growth and negative response of lending rate change.

Such an identification scheme for shocks to the system generates meaningful empirical findings about systemic risk and stress testing. For example, a common misunderstanding of the 2007 to 2009 economic crisis is that it was caused by the credit crunch and de-leveraging, rather than the sharp declines in real activity since December 2007. With a rigorous identification scheme, this chapter finds that in the long run it is (always) the real shocks in final demand that ultimately determine the investment fluctuations, in association with the indirect credit demand channel. And bank credit growth slowdowns are primarily the results of the declines in aggregate real demand, not the other way around. It is the most important finding in the chapter, which also has implications for the financial-centric approach in systemic risk. For a financial crisis to have enduring effect on the business cycle, the crisis must be originated from the real economy.

What is missing in such a macro-centric approach for systemic risk monitoring? One obvious problem is that by treating all the financial firms in one sector, the approach overlooks the interaction among large institutions, which is a main cause for this and previous financial crises. Also, by adopting the empirical macroeconomic VaR, the chapter cannot address the nonlinear feedback effect that is instrumental in spreading fear during the recent financial turmoil. Last, but not least, the macro-centric method cannot identify individual institutions that are deemed too-big-to-fail or systemically important.

Alternative Financial-Centric Approach

An alternative approach to systemic risk is a micro-based financial-centric one, with attention to individual firms' asset correlations, leverage ratios, and liability sizes (Huang, Zhou, and Zhu 2009). Such a systemic risk indicator, a hypothetical insurance premium against catastrophic losses in a banking system, is constructed from real-time financial market data using the portfolio credit risk technique. The two key default risk factors, the probability of default (PD) of individual banks and the asset return correlations among banks, are estimated from credit default swap (CDS) spreads and equity price comovements, respectively. Together with the banks' liability sizes, these inputs effectively capture the three main ingredients missed by the macro-centric approach—interconnectedness, leverage, and too-big-to-fail—for large complex financial institutions.

For the purpose of macroprudential regulation, it is important not only to monitor the level of systemic risk, but also to understand the sources of risks in a financial system. One perspective is to decompose the credit risk of the portfolio into the risk contributions associated with individual subportfolios (either a bank or a group of banks). As demonstrated by Huang, Zhou, and Zhu (2010), the total risk can be usefully decomposed into a sum of marginal risk contributions. Each marginal risk contribution is the conditional expected loss from that subportfolio or a bank, conditional on a large loss for the full portfolio. It is important that the marginal contribution of each subgroup or bank adds up to the aggregate systemic risk. This additivity property is desirable from an operational perspective, because it allows the macroprudential regulation to be implemented at individual bank level.

Huang, Zhou, and Zhu (2010, figure 3) shows that such a systemic risk indicator for twenty-two Asia-Pacific banks was very low at the beginning of the global crisis. The indicator then moved up significantly, reaching the first peak when Bear Stearns was acquired by JP Morgan on March 16, 2008. Things changed dramatically in September 2008 with the failure of Lehman

Brothers. The distress insurance premium hiked up and hovered in the range of 150 and 200 basis points (or 50 to 70 billion USD). The situation did not improve until late March 2009. Since the G20 Summit in early April 2009, the distress insurance premium has come down quickly and returned to pre-Lehman levels in May 2009.

Huang, Zhou, and Zhu (2010, figure 8) further divide banks into six groups: Australian banks, Hong Kong banks, Indian banks, Korean banks, Singapore banks, and banks from Indonesia, Malaysia, and Thailand. In relative terms, the marginal contribution of each group of banks was quite stable before mid-2008. Australian banks were obviously the most important ones and contributed the most to the systemic vulnerability. However, since September 2008, the relative contribution of Australian banks decreased substantially, whereas banks from Hong Kong and Singapore became more important from a systemic perspective.

Summary

To conclude, the macro-centric approach to financial systemic risk, as in De Nicolò and Lucchetta's chapter, among others, can help us better understand why the business cycle is ultimately driven by the shocks from the real side of the economy, especially in the long run. However, such an approach lacks attention to details—asset correlation, leverage ratio, and too-big-to-fail—for identifying individual institutions that are systemically important. A micro-centric approach, as in Huang, Zhou, and Zhu (2009, 2010), among others, captures these missing ingredients critical in systemic risk regulation and is potentially more operational in practice than a macro-centric approach.

References

Adrian, Tobias, and Markus Brunnermeier. 2009. "CoVaR." Federal Reserve Bank of New York Staff Reports.
Bernanke, Ben S., Mark Gertler, and Simon Gilchrist. 1998. "The Financial Accelerator in a Quantitative Business Cycle Framework." NBER Working Paper no. 6455. Cambridge, MA: National Bureau of Economic Research, March.
Boyd, John, Gianni De Nicolò, and Elena Loukoianova. 2009. "Banking Crises and Crisis Dating: Theory and Evidence." IMF Working Paper no. 09/141. Washington, DC: International Monetary Fund.
Canova, Fabio, and Gianni De Nicolò. 2002. "Monetary Disturbances Matter for Business Cycle Fluctuations in the G-7." *Journal of Monetary Economics* 49: 1121–59.
De Nicolò, Gianni, and Myron Kwast. (2002). "Systemic Risk and Financial Consolidation: Are They Related?" *Journal of Banking and Finance* 26:861–80.
Huang, Xin, Hao Zhou, and Haibin Zhu. 2009. "A Framework for Assessing the Systemic Risk of Major Financial Institutions." *Journal of Banking and Finance* 33:2036–49.

————. 2010. "Assessing the Systemic Risk of a Heterogeneous Portfolio of Banks during the Recent Financial Crisis." FEDS 2009-44, Federal Reserve Board.

Stock, James, and Mark Watson. 2005. "Implications of Dynamic Factor Models for VAR Analysis." NBER Working Paper no. 11467. Cambridge, MA: National Bureau of Economic Research, July.

Tarashev, Nikola, Claudio Borio, and Kostas Tsatsaronis. 2009. "Allocating Systemic Risk to Individual Institutions: Methodology and Policy Applications." Bank for International Settlements Working Paper. Basel: BIS.

4

Hedge Fund Tail Risk

Tobias Adrian, Markus K. Brunnermeier,
and Hoai-Luu Q. Nguyen

4.1   Introduction

Our financial architecture has undergone dramatic changes in recent years as market-based financial institutions have gained ever more importance in the allocation of capital and credit. The hedge fund sector has become one of the key parts of the market-based financial system, supporting liquidity provision and price discovery across financial markets. While hedge funds are liquidity providers in usual times, during times of market crisis, they can be forced to delever, potentially contributing to market volatility. The extent to which various hedge fund strategies are exposed to the tail risk that occurs during market turmoil is important to understand for risk management and financial stability purposes. This chapter provides a framework for understanding the tail risk exposures of hedge fund strategies in more detail.

The recent global financial crisis provides several examples of large hedge fund failures. The beginning of the crisis in June 2007 was marked by the failure of two highly levered structured credit hedge funds owned by Bear

Tobias Adrian is vice president of the Capital Markets Function at the Federal Reserve Bank of New York. Markus K. Brunnermeier is the Edwards S. Sanford Professor of Economics at Princeton University and a research associate of the National Bureau of Economic Research. Hoai-Luu Q. Nguyen is a PhD candidate in economics at the Massachusetts Institute of Technology.

The authors would like to thank René Carmona, Xavier Gabaix, Beverly Hirtle, John Kambhu, Burton Malkiel, Maureen O'Hara, Matt Pritsker, José Scheinkman, Kevin Stiroh, and seminar participants at Columbia University, Princeton University, Cornell University, Rutgers University, and the Federal Reserve Bank of New York for helpful comments. Brunnermeier acknowledges financial support from the Alfred P. Sloan Foundation. For acknowledgments, sources of research support, and disclosure of the authors' material financial relationships, if any, please see http://www.nber.org/chapters/c12057.ack.

The views expressed in this chapter are those of the authors and do not necessarily represent those of the Federal Reserve Bank of New York or the Federal Reserve System.

Stearns. Subsequently, in March 2008—less than two weeks prior to Bear Stearns' failure—the Carlyle Capital Corporation, another highly levered fixed income hedge fund, declared bankruptcy due to margin calls. In addition, the hedge fund sector as a whole experienced severe losses following the failure of Lehman Brothers in September 2008.

During the financial crisis, distress spread across institutions due to liquidity spirals. In a liquidity spiral, initial losses in some asset classes force levered investors to reduce their positions, which leads to additional mark-to-market losses and potential spillovers to other asset classes. Importantly, margins and haircuts widen at the same time, forcing levered investors to reduce their leverage ratio (Brunnermeier and Pedersen 2009). As such, banks and prime brokers with large credit risk exposures to hedge funds may suffer potentially large losses if many hedge funds experience distress at the same time. From a financial stability point of view, it is therefore important to understand the degree to which different hedge fund strategies tend to experience simultaneous large losses.

In this chapter, we use quantile regressions to empirically study the interdependencies between different hedge fund styles in times of crisis. We find that tail sensitivities between different strategies are higher in times of distress, suggesting the potential for simultaneous losses across many hedge funds. Furthermore, we identify seven risk factors that are related to these tail dependencies and show that offloading this risk significantly reduces the sensitivities where we define offloaded returns as the residuals obtained from regressing the raw returns on the seven risk factors. However—consistent with existing literature—we also find that these factors explain a large part of hedge funds' expected returns, and we provide some evidence suggesting that capital flows across strategies and over time reward those that load more heavily on the tail risk factors. Consequently, while offloading would be beneficial for a fund manager in the sense that it would reduce his exposure to tail risk, managers face strong incentives to load on tail risk factors as they tend to increase both the incentive fee (calculated as a percentage of the fund's profit) as well as their management fee (calculated as a percentage of total assets under management).

4.1.1   Related Literature

Our chapter contributes to the growing literature that sheds light on the link between hedge funds and the risk of a systemic crisis. Boyson, Stahel, and Stulz (2008) document contagion across hedge fund styles using logit regressions on daily and monthly returns. However, they do not find evidence of contagion between hedge fund returns and equity, fixed income, and foreign exchange returns. In contrast, we show that our pricing factors explain the increase in comovement among hedge fund strategies in times of stress. Chan et al. (2006) document an increase in correlation across hedge funds, especially prior to the Long-Term Capital Management (LTCM) crisis and after 2003. Adrian (2007) points out that this increase in correlation since 2003 is due to a reduction in volatility—a phenomenon that occurred across many financial assets—rather than to an increase in covariance. Dudley and Nimalendran (2010) present an empirical analysis of the liquidity spiral associated with margin increases in futures exchanges. The methods used in this chapter to analyze the tail risk exposures of hedge funds to risk factors have also been used in Adrian and Brunnermeier (2009). However, while Adrian and Brunnermeier (2009) focus on the quantification of systemic risk of each financial institution, this chapter focuses on the hedging of tail risk, not quantifying systemic risk.

Asness, Krail, and Liew (2001) and Agarwal and Naik (2004b) document that hedge funds load on tail risk in order to boost their performance according to the capital asset pricing model (CAPM-α). Agarwal and Naik (2004b) capture the tail exposure of equity hedge funds with nonlinear market factors that take the shape of out-of-the-money put options. Patton (2009) develops several "neutrality tests" including a test for tail and value at risk (VaR) neutrality and finds that many so-called market neutral funds are, in fact, not market neutral. Bali, Gokcan, and Liang (2007) and Liang and Park (2007) find that hedge funds that take on high left-tail risk outperform funds with less risk exposure. In addition, a large and growing number of papers explain average returns of hedge funds using asset pricing factors (see, e.g., Fung and Hsieh 2001, 2002, 2003; Hasandhodzic and Lo 2007). Our approach is different in the sense that we study factors that explain the codependence across the tails of different hedge fund styles.

In section 4.2, we study the tail dependencies between hedge fund strategies in normal times and during crises. In section 4.3, we estimate a risk factor model for the hedge fund returns and show that tail risk factors explain a large part of the dependencies between the strategies. We also study the incentives hedge funds face in taking on tail risk. Finally, section 4.4 concludes.

4.2 q-Sensitivities

In this section, we examine the pairwise dependence of returns between hedge fund styles. We find that these dependencies are significantly higher in times of stress. We call these dependencies among hedge funds in times of stress "q-sensitivities," because we use quantile regressions to estimate them. The q stands for the tail quantile for which the dependence is estimated.

4.2.1   Hedge Fund Return Data

As private investment partnerships that are largely unregulated, hedge funds are more challenging to analyze and monitor than other financial institutions such as mutual funds, banks, or insurance companies. Only very limited data on hedge funds are made available through regulatory filings and, consequently, most studies rely on self-reported data. We follow this approach and use the hedge fund style indices compiled by Credit Suisse/Tremont.[1]

Several papers have compared the self-reported returns of different vendors (e.g., Agarwal and Naik 2004a), and some research compares the return characteristics of hedge fund indices with the returns of individual funds (Malkiel and Saha 2005). The literature also investigates biases such as survivorship bias (Brown, Goetzmann, and Ibbotson 1999; Liang 2000), termination and self-selection bias (Ackermann, McEnally, and Ravenscraft 1999), backfilling bias, and illiquidity bias (Asness, Krail, and Liew 2001; Getmansky, Lo, and Makarov 2004). We take from this literature that, while hedge fund return indices are certainly not ideal, they are still the best data available and their study is useful. Moreover, Malkiel and Saha (2005) provide evidence that the Credit Suisse/Tremont indices appear to be the least affected by various biases.

Table 4.1 displays summary statistics of monthly excess returns for the ten hedge fund style indices included in the Credit Suisse/Tremont data over the period January 1994 to November 2009. These styles have been extensively described in the literature (see Agarwal and Naik 2004a for a survey), and characterizations can also be found on the Credit Suisse/Tremont website (www.hedgeindex.com). We report the hedge fund returns in order of their average weights in the overall index, calculated over the entire sample period. These weights are determined by the proportion of total assets under management in the hedge fund sector dedicated to each strategy, and the average values are reported in the last column of table 4.1. We also report summary statistics of monthly excess returns for the overall hedge fund index, as well as for the Center for Research in Security Prices (CRSP) equity market excess return, which we sometimes interpret as a proxy for a well-diversified mutual fund. The cumulative returns to the overall hedge fund index and the market are shown in figure 4.1.

Table 4.1 shows that, while there is a wide disparity of Sharpe ratios across different strategies, the Sharpe ratio of the overall hedge fund index (0.21) is more than twice the Sharpe ratio of the market (0.09). Since hedge funds invest part of their wealth in highly illiquid instruments with stale or managed prices, they are able to smooth their returns and manipulate Sharpe ratios (see, e.g., Asness, Krail, and Liew 2001; Getmansky, Lo, and Makarov 2004). The summary statistics also show that the hedge fund index has less negative skewness than the market return (–0.27 vs. –0.86) and higher kurtosis (5.26 vs. 4.43). With the exception of Managed Futures, normality is rejected on the basis of either skewness or kurtosis for all hedge fund styles. Thus, consistent with previous findings, the returns to hedge funds have both skewed and fat-tailed returns relative to normality.

---

1. A notable exception is a study by Brunnermeier and Nagel (2004), who use quarterly 13F filings to the Securities and Exchange Commission (SEC) and show that hedge funds were riding the tech-bubble rather than acting as a price-correcting force.

Table 4.1   Summary statistics of monthly excess returns

| | | | | | | | | Tests for normality | | |
	Sharpe	Mean	Std Dev	Skew	Kurt	Min	Obs	Pr(Skew) (%)	Pr(Kurt) (%)	Average weight (%)
Hedge fund strategies										
Long/short equity	0.19	0.56	2.89	−0.06	6.44	−11.85	191	74	0	29
Global macro	0.25	0.73	2.96	−0.11	6.15	−11.89	191	51	0	25
Event driven	0.30	0.52	1.74	−2.61	17.78	−12.19	191	0	0	19
Fixed income arbitrage	0.06	0.11	1.75	−4.00	28.69	−14.10	191	0	0	6
Multistrategy	0.23	0.36	1.58	−1.69	8.71	−7.45	191	0	0	5
Emerging markets	0.10	0.44	4.51	−0.79	7.61	−23.45	191	0	0	5
Equity market neutral	0.07	0.22	3.11	−11.87	155.83	−40.47	191	0	0	4
Managed futures	0.09	0.29	3.40	0.03	3.09	−9.80	191	86	61	4
Convertible arbitrage	0.16	0.33	2.07	−2.56	17.81	−12.65	191	0	0	4
Dedicated short bias	−0.08	−0.37	4.88	0.73	4.54	−9.58	191	0	0	1
Weighted average	**0.20**	**0.51**								
Hedge fund index	0.21	0.47	2.24	−0.27	5.26	−7.97	191	12	0	
Market	0.09	0.44	4.65	−0.86	4.43	−18.55	192	0	0	

Notes: This table reports summary statistics for the ten Credit Suisse/Tremont hedge fund style returns. All returns are in excess of the three-month Treasury bill rate. The Sharpe ratio is the ratio of mean excess returns to the standard deviation of excess returns. The tests for normality give the *p*-value of Royston's (1991) test that skewness and kurtosis are normal. The weights for each style are the weights that aggregate the ten styles to the overall Credit Suisse/Tremont index, averaged over the sample period of January 1994 through November 2009. We also report the return to the overall hedge fund index. The market return is the cum dividend value-weighted CRSP return.

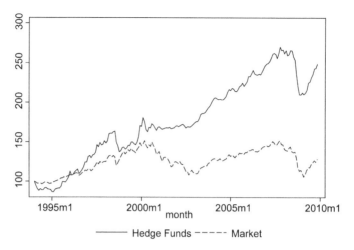

Fig. 4.1   Cumulative returns

Notes: This figure plots cumulative returns for the overall Credit Suisse/Tremont hedge fund index and for the market over the period from January 1994 through November 2009. The market return is the cum dividend value-weighted CRSP return.

4.2.2   Quantile Regressions

In this section, we use bivariate quantile regressions to analyze the tail sensitivities between different hedge fund strategies. Quantile regressions were developed by Koenker and Bassett (1978) and Bassett and Koenker (1978), and a literature review can be found in Koenker (2005).

Consider the q-percent quantile regression of strategy i's returns on strategy j's returns:

$$(1) \qquad R_t^i = \alpha_q^{ij} + \beta_q^{ij} R_t^j + \varepsilon_t^{ij}.$$

To study the tail dependence of strategy i with respect to strategy j, we extract the β_q^{ij} from equation (1).

DEFINITION 1. We denote the q-sensitivity of strategy i with respect to strategy j as the coefficient β_q^{ij} from the q-percent bivariate quantile regression of strategy i's excess returns on strategy j's excess returns.

Our definition of the q-sensitivity captures the degree to which the tail returns of strategy i comoves with the returns of strategy j. By varying the quantile q, we can analyze how the dependencies between hedge fund strategies change between normal times ($q = 50$) and times of crisis (e.g., $q = 5$).

Note that quantile regressions lend themselves to an easy method of calculating the VaR, which we use later in section 4.3.4. In particular, the 5 percent quantile of strategy i's return provides a direct estimate of (the negative of) its VaR. Adrian and Brunnermeier (2009) use this property of quantile regressions to generate a novel measure of systemic risk, CoVaR, which they define as the VaR of the financial sector conditional on a particular institution being in distress.

Table 4.2 reports the 50 percent and 5 percent sensitivities calculated from bivariate quantile regressions among the ten hedge fund strategies. For each strategy i, we calculate its q-sensitivity with respect to each of the nine other strategies, and then average to obtain a single 50 percent and 5 percent sensitivity. For each strategy, we also calculate the percent change in the average 5 percent sensitivity relative to the 50 percent, along with its p-value.

Table 4.2 shows that average hedge fund sensitivities increase in the tails of the return distribution. For all the strategies, except for Dedicated Short Bias, the average 5 percent sensitivity is higher than the 50 percent sensitivity, with the difference statistically significant in five cases. The last row in table 4.2 reports the sensitivities weighted by their average weight in the overall index over this period. By this measure, we find that average sensitivities are nearly 50 percent higher in times of stress compared to normal times, indicating higher dependence between strategies and the potential for simultaneous losses during a crisis. The increase in sensitivities among hedge fund styles in times of stress has previously been noted by Boyson, Stahel, and Stulz (2008).

4.3   Identifying Tail Factors

Having established that sensitivities between hedge fund styles increase during times of stress, in this section we identify factors that explain this tail dependence. We define offloaded returns as the residuals obtained from regressing the raw returns on seven risk factors. We argue that the factor

Table 4.2   **Average q-sensitivities—monthly excess returns**

	50% sensitivity	5% sensitivity	Percent change (%)	p-value
Long/short equity	0.49	0.51	6	0.830
Global macro	0.29	0.44	52	0.275
Event driven	0.29	0.48	68	0.045
Fixed income arbitrage	0.17	0.44	166	0.018
Multistrategy	0.23	0.50	116	0.002
Emerging markets	0.76	0.94	25	0.473
Equity market neutral	0.13	0.20	63	0.799
Managed futures	0.06	0.11	94	0.798
Convertible arbitrage	0.25	0.70	177	0.002
Dedicated short bias	−0.73	−0.09	−87	0.000
Weighted average	**0.33**	**0.48**	**45**	**0.064**

Notes: This table reports the average of the bivariate 50 percent and 5 percent sensitivities for each of the ten Credit Suisse/Tremont hedge fund styles calculated using monthly excess returns. In addition, we calculate the percent change of the 5 percent sensitivity relative to the 50 percent. The p-values test the null hypothesis that the percent change is zero, and are generated via bootstrap with 1,000 draws.

structure explains this tail dependence if the sensitivities of the offloaded returns are much lower than those of the raw returns.

We begin by outlining our seven risk factors, and then create offloaded returns for each of the hedge fund styles and for the financial institution indices. We then generate 50 percent and 5 percent sensitivities using these offloaded returns.

4.3.1   Tail Factors—Description and Data

We select the following seven factors to try to capture the increase in tail dependence among hedge fund strategies. All seven factors have solid theoretical foundations and are included to capture certain aspects of risk. Moreover, they are also all liquid and easily tradable. Our factors are:

1. The CRSP *market return* in excess of the three-month bill rate.

2. The *VIX* (*volatility index*) *straddle excess return* to capture the implied future volatility of the stock market. The VIX is from the Chicago Board Options Exchange (CBOE); we get a tradable excess return series by calculating the hypothetical at-the-money straddle return that is based on the VIX implied volatility and then subtracting the three-month bill rate.

3. The *variance swap return* to capture the associated risk premium for shifts in volatility. The variance swap contract pays the difference between the realized variance over the coming month and its delivery price at the beginning of the month. Since the delivery price is not observable over our whole sample period, we use—as is common practice—the VIX squared, normalized to twenty-one trading days; that is, $((VIX * 21)/360)^2$. The realization of the index variance is computed from daily S&P 500 Index data for each month. Note that, since the initial price of the swap contract is zero, returns are automatically expressed as excess returns.

4. A short-term "*liquidity spread*," defined as the difference between the three-month general collateral repo rate and the three-month bill rate. We use the three-month repo rate available on Bloomberg and obtain the three-month Treasury rate from the Federal Reserve Bank of New York.

5. The *carry-trade excess return* is calculated using the Deutsche Bank carry USD total return index. The index is constructed from a carry strategy on the G10 currencies that is rolled over quarterly. The index is long the three highest-yielding currencies and short the three lowest-yielding currencies.

6. The *slope of the yield curve,* measured by the yield spread between the ten-year Treasury rate and the three-month bill rate from the Federal Reserve Board's H.15 release.

7. The *credit spread* between BAA rated bonds and the ten-year Treasury rate from the Federal Reserve Board's H.15 release.

All data are monthly from January 1994 through November 2009. Summary statistics are presented in table 4.3.

Table 4.3   Summary statistics of risk factors

	Sharpe	Mean	Std dev	Min	Tests for normality		Obs
					Pr(Skew) (%)	Pr(Kurt) (%)	
CRSP market excess return	0.09	0.44	4.65	-18.55	0	0	192
VIX straddle excess return	-1.06	-0.54	0.51	-1.43	0	0	191
Variance swap return	-0.38	-0.30	0.79	-0.84	0	0	191
Repo-Treasury rate	1.00	0.01	0.01	-0.05	12	0	192
Carry-trade excess return	0.18	0.45	2.54	-14.26	0	0	191
10 year, three-month Treasury return	0.11	0.25	2.37	-6.24	27	0	191
Moody's BAA—10 year Treasury return	0.07	0.14	2.05	-14.08	0	0	191

Notes: This table reports summary statistics for excess returns of seven risk factors. The CRSP market excess return is the market return from the Center for Research in Security Prices in excess of the three-month Treasury bill rate. The VIX straddle excess return is computed from the Black-Scholes (1973) formula using the CBOE's VIX implied volatility index, the S&P 500 Index, and the three-month Treasury bill. The variance swap return is the difference between realized S&P 500 variance from closing daily data and the VIX implied variance. The repo-Treasury rate is the difference between the three-month general collateral Treasury repo rate (from ICAP) and the three-month Treasury bill rate. The carry-trade excess return is calculated using the Deutsche Bank carry USD total return index. The ten-year, three-month Treasury return is the return to the ten-year constant maturity Treasury bond in excess of the three-month Treasury bill. Moody's BAA-10 year Treasury return is the return to Moody's BAA bond portfolio in excess of the return to the ten-year constant maturity Treasury.

4.3.2   Offloaded Returns

Having specified our factors, we generate offloaded returns and study their effect on the q-sensitivities. In particular, we look at quantile offloaded returns—that is, the residuals to the 5 percent quantile regression of raw returns on our seven factors. More formally, we define offloaded returns in the following way.

DEFINITION 2. Consider the q percent quantile regression of hedge fund strategy i onto a vector of tail risk factors X_t:

$$R_t^i = \alpha_q^{iX} + \beta_q^{iX} X_t + \varepsilon_t^{iX}.$$

Offloaded returns $\tilde{R}_t^i$ are then defined as

$$\tilde{R}_t^i = R_t^i - \beta_q^{iX} X_t.$$

Monthly raw and offloaded returns for the ten hedge fund strategies, as well as for the overall index, are plotted in figure 4.2. In most cases, offloading the risk associated with our factors reduces the volatility of the monthly returns.

Table 4.4 displays the summary statistics for these offloaded returns.

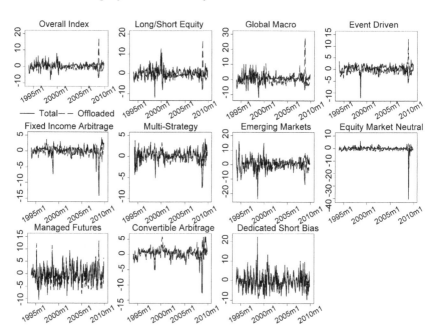

Fig. 4.2   Monthly total and offloaded excess returns

Notes: This figure plots monthly total and 5 percent quantile offloaded returns for the ten Credit Suisse/Tremont hedge fund strategies as well as for the overall index. Offloaded returns are calculated as the residuals from 5 percent quantile regressions of total excess returns on the seven risk factors.

Table 4.4 Summary statistics of monthly offloaded returns

	Sharpe	Mean	Std dev	Skew	Kurt	Min	Tests for normality	
							Pr(Skew) (%)	Pr(Kurt) (%)
Hedge fund strategies								
Long/short equity	-0.14	-0.32	2.37	2.78	19.00	-4.92	0	0
Global macro	0.20	0.83	4.13	2.20	13.43	-6.94	0	0
Event driven	-0.15	-0.25	1.70	3.20	24.87	-3.78	0	0
Fixed income arbitrage	0.04	0.05	1.31	0.13	2.94	-3.59	46	96
Multistrategy	0.13	0.19	1.42	-0.23	3.51	-4.55	20	14
Emerging markets	0.19	0.74	3.92	0.09	3.77	-11.34	59	5
Equity market neutral	-0.16	-0.49	3.08	-9.60	120.40	-38.31	0	0
Managed futures	-0.25	-0.99	3.95	0.66	3.90	-10.48	0	3
Convertible arbitrage	0.40	0.62	1.56	0.34	3.47	-3.12	5	16
Dedicated short bias	0.01	0.02	3.01	0.42	3.06	-6.41	2	67
Weighted average	**0.00**	**0.08**						
Difference relative to total returns	**-0.20****	**-0.43****						

Notes: This table reports summary statistics for monthly 5 percent quantile offloaded returns, calculated as the residuals to the 5 percent quantile regression of raw returns on our seven factors. The weighted average is computed using the weights displayed in the last column of table 4.1. The Sharpe ratio is the ratio of mean excess returns to the standard deviation of excess returns. The tests for normality give the p-value of Royston's (1991) test that skewness/kurtosis are normal.

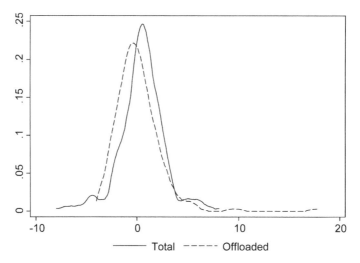

Fig. 4.3   Kernel densities of total and offloaded returns

Notes: This figure plots the kernel densities of the total and 5 percent quantile offloaded returns for the overall Credit Suisse/Tremont hedge fund index.

Table 4.5   CAPM-α of monthly total and offloaded returns

	Total	Offloaded
Long/short equity	0.36**	−0.28
Global macro	0.66***	0.91***
Event driven	0.42***	−0.19
Fixed income arbitrage	0.04	0.02
Multistrategy	0.31***	0.17
Emerging markets	0.20	0.76***
Equity market neutral	0.14	−0.45
Managed futures	0.34	−0.92***
Convertible arbitrage	0.26*	0.65***
Dedicated short bias	−0.01	0.10
Weighted average	**0.40*****	**0.13**

Notes: This table reports the CAPM-α of our monthly total and offloaded returns for each of the ten hedge fund styles. The weighted average is calculated using the weights displayed in the last column of table 4.1, and significance is obtained via bootstrap with 1,000 draws.

Comparing to table 4.1, we see that offloading tail risk markedly reduces the weighted average mean return and Sharpe ratio of the ten hedge fund strategies (and the difference is statistically signficant). Looking at individual styles, some offloaded mean returns and Sharpe ratios even enter negative territory. The kernel densities in figure 4.3 reveal that offloading reduces the fat left tail of the overall index, while having little effect on the right tail.

Table 4.5 compares the CAPM-α's of the total and offloaded returns for

Table 4.6   **Average 5 percent sensitivities for total and offloaded returns**

	Total	Offloaded	Percent change (%)	*p*-value
Long/short equity	0.51	0.05	−90	0.000
Global macro	0.44	0.16	−63	0.015
Event driven	0.48	0.17	−65	0.000
Fixed income arbitrage	0.44	0.04	−91	0.000
Multistrategy	0.50	0.13	−73	0.000
Emerging markets	0.94	0.20	−79	0.000
Equity market neutral	0.20	0.09	−58	0.415
Managed futures	0.11	0.09	−17	0.932
Convertible arbitrage	0.70	0.08	−89	0.000
Dedicated short bias	−0.09%	−0.02%	−79	0.386
Weighted average	**0.48**	**0.11**	**−76**	**0.000**

Notes: This table reports average bivariate 5 percent sensitivities calculated using monthly total and offloaded returns. We also calculate the percent change of the sensitivities using the offloaded returns relative to those using total returns. The *p*-values test the null hypothesis that the percent change is zero, and are generated via bootstrap with 1,000 draws. The weighted average is calculated using the weights displayed in the last column of table 4.1.

the hedge fund strategies. We see that the α's drop notably after offloading the risk associated with our factors; the weighted average α declines from 0.40 to 0.13. Note that we take the simple average of α's rather than the average of the absolute value of the α's since it is not easy to short a hedge fund style.

4.3.3   *q*-Sensitivities of Offloaded Returns

As we did for the raw returns in section 4.2, we replicate the bivariate 5 percent quantile regressions for the offloaded returns. That is, we quantile regress the offloaded returns of style *i* on the offloaded returns of style *j* and calculate the average 5 percent sensitivity for each strategy. Table 4.6 compares the average 5 percent sensitivities calculated using total and offloaded returns, and also displays the percent change of the offloaded sensitivities relative to the total along with their *p*-value.

Table 4.6 shows that, with the exception of only three strategies, using offloaded returns unequivocally decreases the 5 percent sensitivity by a statistically significant margin. In fact, the weighted average shows that offloading the tail risk reduces the 5 percent sensitivity by more than 75 percent. Figure 4.4 confirms these results by plotting the weighted average *q*-sensitivity across the hedge fund styles for all *q* between 5 and 95. We see that the *q*-sensitivity of the offloaded returns are generally well below that of the raw returns.

Beyond looking at sensitivities across states of the world (i.e., for different values of *q*), we can also investigate their evolution over time. To do so, we estimate a multivariate BEKK-ARCH(2) model and extract the evolution of

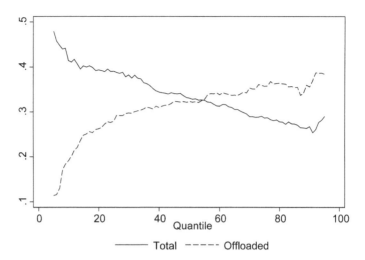

Fig. 4.4   Average *q*-sensitivities by quantile

Notes: This figure plots the weighted average *q*-sensitivity across the ten Credit Suisse/Tremont hedge fund strategies for all *q* between 5 and 95. The solid line plots average sensitivities from total returns, while the dashed line plots sensitivities from the 5 percent quantile offloaded returns. The weighted averages are calculated using the weights displayed in the last column of table 4.1.

covariances across the ten strategies over time. The average of these covariances is shown in figure 4.5.

The average covariance of the offloaded returns is markedly less volatile than that of the total returns. While the average covariance of total returns spiked during the LTCM crisis in the third quarter of 1998, in January 2000, and, most dramatically, following the bankruptcy of Lehman Brothers in September 2008, the average covariance of the offloaded returns increased much less during the same periods.

These results strongly suggest that interdependencies between different hedge fund styles could be significantly reduced were funds to offload the tail risk associated with our seven factors. From a financial stability point of view, this is desirable as it would reduce the potential for simultaneous losses across many strategies during a crisis. However, it is possible that individual fund managers face no such incentive to offload tail risk. We investigate this in the following section.

4.3.4   Incentives to Load on Tail Risk

Because our seven factors were chosen to be tradable and highly liquid, it would be possible for hedge fund managers to offload the risk associated with them without incurring large trading costs. Consequently, offloading is α-neutral within our model. However, as noted previously in our com-

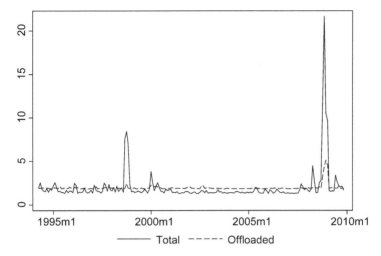

Fig. 4.5   Average ARCH covariances over time

Notes: This figure plots the average covariance across the ten hedge fund strategies, estimated using a multivariate BEKK-ARCH(2) model. The solid line plots the average covariance across total returns, while the dashed line plots the average across the 5 percent quantile offloaded returns.

parison of tables 4.1 and 4.4, offloading this risk significantly reduces the weighted average monthly return of the hedge funds from 0.51 to 0.08. In other words, a large proportion of hedge funds' outperformance relative to the market index appears to be a direct result of their loading on these "tail" factors. Consequently, the question arises whether hedge fund managers have any incentive to offload this risk when doing so would lower their expected return.

Fund managers are typically paid a performance fee of 20 percent of the realized profits plus 2 percent of the value of total assets under management. As such, though offloading tail risk lowers the manager's expected compensation via the performance fee, the expected compensation via the management fee may actually be higher if offloading risk leads to increased inflows into the fund.

To investigate this, we study these flows and compare the effects of average returns and various risk measures on flows across strategies and over time. We use the weights of each strategy within the overall hedge fund index to generate a measure of relative flow—that is, the flow into strategy i is expressed as a proportion of total flow into the hedge fund sector. Recall that w_t^i, the weight of strategy i in the overall index, is determined according to the proportion of total hedge fund assets under management dedicated to funds operating under strategy i. Our flow measure is accordingly defined as

$$(2) \qquad \text{flow}_{t+1}^i = w_{t+1}^i - w_t^i \left(\frac{1 + r_{t+1}^i}{1 + r_{t+1}^{\text{index}}} \right),$$

where r_{t+1}^i and r_{t+1}^{index} are the monthly returns to strategy i and the overall index, respectively. Consequently, our flow variable adjusts changes in the relative weights of each strategy between t and $t + 1$ by the return of each strategy relative to the index return.

Table 4.7 shows that, as expected, flows are very sensitive to past monthly and annual returns. However, we find that taking on more risk, as indicated by higher VaRs, is also associated with larger future flows. This indicates that offloading tail risk not only reduces hedge fund managers' expected compensation via their performance fee (through lower expected returns), but also punishes them with lower management fees by reducing inflows. Consequently, while offloading the risk associated with our factors may be highly desirable from a systemic risk point of view, individual managers have no incentive to do so and, in fact, seem to be rewarded for loading more heavily on these tail risk factors.

4.4 Conclusion

Our chapter documents that sensitivities between hedge fund styles increase in the tails, leading to the potential for simultaneous large losses across different strategies. We identify seven factors that can account for this increase in tail dependence in times of crisis and show that offloading the risk associated with them greatly reduces the sensitivities between hedge fund styles as well as between different financial institutions. However, offloading tail risk might come at the cost of lower compensation for individual hedge fund managers.

References

Ackermann, C., R. McEnally, and D. Ravenscraft. 1999. "The Performance of Hedge Funds: Risk, Return, and Incentives." *Journal of Finance* 54 (3): 833–74.

Adrian, T. 2007. "Measuring Risk in the Hedge Fund Sector." *Current Issues in Economics and Finance by the Federal Reserve Bank of New York* 13 (3): 1–7.

Adrian, T., and M. Brunnermeier. 2009. "CoVaR." Federal Reserve Bank of New York Staff Report no. 348.

Agarwal, V., and N. Y. Naik. 2004a. "Hedge Funds." In *Foundations and Trends in Finance*, vol. 1, edited by L. Jaeger, 130–70. Hanover, MA: Now Publishers.

———. 2004b. "Risks and Portfolio Decisions Involving Hedge Funds." *Review of Financial Studies* 17 (1): 63–98.

Asness, C. S., R. Krail, and J. M. Liew. 2001. "Do Hedge Funds Hedge?" *Journal of Portfolio Management* 28 (1): 6–19.

Table 4.7 Flow-performance regressions

	(1)	(2)	(3)	(4)	(5)	(6)	(7)	(8)	(9)	(10)
Lagged Variables										
Monthly return	0.04***	0.03***	0.04***	0.05***	0.04***	0.03***	0.04***	0.04***	0.04***	0.04***
Annual return	0.01***	0.01***	0.01***			0.01***	0.01***		0.00***	0.01***
α	0.01*							0.01*	0.01*	0.01*
Sharpe ratio	0.01				0.06**	−0.01	0.01			
Standard deviation	0.01	0.01	0.01				0.01			0.01
VaR	0.01***		0.01**	0.01**			0.01**			0.01***
Constant	−3.80***	−0.21	−3.95***	0.68	−2.92***	−3.13***	−3.94***	−2.84***	0.23	−3.80***
Observations	1,680	1,800	1,680	1,680	1,800	1,800	1,680	1,800	1,800	1,680
Adjusted-R^2	10.2%	9.6%	10.1%	9.0%	9.0%	9.6%	10.1%	8.9%	9.7%	10.3%

Notes: This table reports the results of panel regressions run with time and strategy fixed effects. The left-hand side variables are monthly flows into strategies relative to total flows into the hedge fund sector. The right-hand side variables are (1) past monthly returns, (2) past annual returns, (3) the annual rolling α, (4) the annual rolling Sharpe ratio, (5) the annual rolling standard deviation, and (6) the expanding window seven-factor VaR computed as the predicted value from a 5 percent quantile regression on the seven pricing factors with a minimum of twenty-four months of data (i.e., in-sample for the first twenty-four months).

Bali, T. G., S. Gokcan, and B. Liang. 2007. "Value at Risk and the Cross-Section of Hedge Fund Returns." *Journal of Banking and Finance* 31 (4): 1135–66.

Bassett, G. W., and R. Koenker. 1978. "Asymptotic Theory of Least Absolute Error Regression." *Journal of the American Statistical Association* 73 (363): 618–22.

Black, Fischer, and Myron Scholes. 1973. "The Pricing of Options and Corporate Liabilities." *Journal of Political Economy* 81 (3): 637–54.

Boyson, N. M., C. W. Stahel, and R. M. Stulz. 2008. "Is There Hedge Fund Contagion?" *Journal of Finance* 65 (5): 1789–816.

Brown, S. J., W. N. Goetzmann, and R. G. Ibbotson. 1999. "Offshore Hedge Funds: Survival and Performance 1989–1995." *Journal of Business* 72 (1): 91–117.

Brunnermeier, M. K., and S. Nagel. 2004. "Hedge Funds and the Technology Bubble." *Journal of Finance* 59 (5): 2013–40.

Brunnermeier, M. K., and L. H. Pedersen. 2009. "Market Liquidity and Funding Liquidity." *Review of Financial Studies* 22 (6): 2201–38.

Chan, N., M. Getmansky, S. Haas, and A. W. Lo. 2006. "Systemic Risk and Hedge Funds." In *The Risks of Financial Institutions,* edited by M. Carey and R. M. Stulz, 235–339. Chicago: University of Chicago Press.

Dudley, E., and M. Nimalendran. 2011. "Margins and Hedge Fund Contagion." *Journal of Financial and Quantitative Analysis* 45 (5): 1227–57.

Fung, W., and D. A. Hsieh. 2001. "The Risk in Hedge Fund Strategies: Theory and Evidence from Trend Followers." *Review of Financial Studies* 14 (2): 313–41.

———. 2002. "The Risk in Fixed-Income Hedge Fund Styles." *Journal of Fixed Income* 12:6–27.

———. 2003. "The Risk in Hedge Fund Strategies: Alternative Alphas and Alternative Betas." In *Managing Risk in Alternative Investment Strategies,* edited by L. Jaeger, 72–87. Euromoney.

Getmansky, M., A. W. Lo, and I. Makarov. 2004. "An Econometric Model of Serial Correlation and Illiquidity in Hedge Fund Returns." *Journal of Financial Economics* 74 (3): 529–609.

Hasanhodzic, J., and A. W. Lo. 2007. "Can Hedge-Fund Returns Be Replicated? The Linear Case." *Journal of Investment Management* 5 (2): 5–45.

Koenker, R. 2005. *Quantile Regression.* Cambridge: Cambridge University Press.

Koenker, R., and G. W. Bassett. 1978. "Regression Quantiles." *Econometrica* 46 (1): 33–50.

Liang, B. 2000. "Hedge Funds: The Living and the Dead." *Journal of Financial and Quantitative Analysis* 35 (3): 309–26.

Liang, B., and H. Park. 2007. "Risk Measures for Hedge Funds." *European Financial Management* 13 (2): 333–70.

Malkiel, B. G., and A. Saha. 2005. "Hedge Funds: Risk and Return." *Financial Analysts Journal* 61 (6): 80–88.

Patton, A. 2009. "Are 'Market Neutral' Hedge Funds Really Market Neutral?" *Review of Financial Studies* 22 (7): 2495–530.

Royston, P. 1991. "sg3.5: Comment on sg3.4 and an Improved D'Agostino Test." *Stata Technical Bulletin* 3:23–24.

Comment   Ben Craig

This chapter by Adrian, Brunnermeier, and Nguyen has three parts. The first uses quantile regression to show that the correlation between hedge fund strategies increases in times of stress. The second shows that this behavior is mostly due to a common measurable shock. Finally, the chapter tries to assess whether hedge funds that focus on hedging away from common measurable shocks increase their size.

To treat the three contributions in turn, the dependence of hedge funds on other funds is shown to increase during times of stress through the comparison of two sets of quantile regressions, measured at the 50 percent and 5 percent levels. Indeed, this approach turns the previous approach of two of the authors on its head. Whereas before they use quantile regression to assess VaRs to investigate systemic risk, here they focus on the quantile regression itself and leave systemic risk contributions unsaid. The authors find, in table 4.2, that the hedge funds increase their dependence by 45 percent, on average. In the single example where being in a tail event decreased the dependence of a hedge fund on other funds, the dependence became less negative, making it less of a hedge against the direction of the other funds' exposure. So tail events increase the tendency of hedge funds to move together, a finding that is interesting and important for research into contagion. However, the table also indicates considerable heterogeneity in this overall result. What are we to make of this? I would have liked to have known what distinguishes this finding from earlier research by Boyson, Stahel, and Stulz (2006) (which they cite) and others, such as Brown and Spitzer (2006), who have found the same phenomenon. Does the use of quantile methods make this a more reliable finding? What are differences in quantile methods that distinguish these findings from ones given by copula correlations or even simple event studies? Given that so much recent research has focused on the properties of portfolios during tail events, a useful contribution would focus on the features of the quantile approach that make it an advantageous one. (This has been done in the statistical literature by Koenker [2005], which is cited in the chapter. It would be nice to see something said about the properties in this paper.)

The second contribution is to investigate whether this phenomenon is affected when they use residual returns after taking into account seven risk factors, including excess market return, volatility measures, liquidity risk measures, and yield slopes. These are common factors that are all measurable, and they could be used by managers to "offload" their portfolio into investments that are less sensitive to these factors. Once the offloadings are

Ben Craig is a senior economic advisor in the Research Department of the Federal Reserve Bank of Cleveland.

For acknowledgments, sources of research support, and disclosure of the author's material financial relationships, if any, please see http://www.nber.org/chapters/c12058.ack.

removed from the hedge fund returns, the 5 percent quantile regressions are run on the residuals with the result that much of the 5 percent sensitivity is accounted for by these factors. Presumably the factors should also account for the difference between the median sensitivity and the tail sensitivity as well, which it does. I would very much have liked a comparison of these results with similar earlier results such as Boyson, Stahel, and Stulz (2006), along with a discussion of where these results differ and why. Further, it is quite clear from the tables that some funds are much more sensitive to these common factors than others, and are much more sensitive to each other than others. What accounts for this? These hedge funds are actually just aggregates chosen by Credit Suisse to represent differing strategies. To what extent are these strategies consistent with an offloading strategy in a tail event?

The final contribution concerns an observation often made anecdotally about hedge fund managers: these managers have no incentive to offload tail risk. The results from a regression shows that when the tail risk decreases, inflow into that strategy also decreases, suggesting that managerial incentives are not to offload tail risk because this will reduce their management fees. This was a tantalizing result. However, it raised many questions, some of which could have been explored with the data and methods used here. To what extent can a strategy offload risk due to common measurable factors? Do shocks in these dimensions allow such a strategy to work, or do these shocks arise so quickly that managers cannot respond? How do the possible methods of hedging against a common shock relate to the measure defined here, and what does this measure have to do with systemic risk? There was so much I wanted to know about this result, but the brevity of the description prevented me from finding out more.

References

Boyson, N. M., C. W. Stahel, and R. M. Stulz. 2008. "Is There a Hedge Fund Contagion?" *Journal of Finance* 65 (5): 1789–816.
Brown, Stephen, and Jonathan Spitzer. 2006. "Caught by the Tail: Tail Risk Neutrality and Hedge Fund Returns." Unpublished Manuscript. New York Stern School.
Koenker, R. 2005. *Quantile Regression.* Cambridge: Cambridge University Press.

How to Calculate Systemic Risk Surcharges

Viral V. Acharya, Lasse H. Pedersen, Thomas Philippon, and Matthew Richardson

5.1 Introduction

Current and past financial crises show that systemic risk emerges when aggregate capitalization of the financial sector is low. The intuition is straightforward. When a financial firm's capital is low, it is difficult for that firm to perform its intended financial services, and when capital is low in the aggregate, it is not possible for other financial firms to step into the breach. This breakdown in financial intermediation is the reason there are severe consequences for the broader economy in crises. Systemic risk therefore can be broadly thought of as the failure of a significant part of the financial sector leading to a reduction in credit availability that has the potential to adversely affect the real economy.

Existing financial regulation such as the Basel capital requirements seeks to limit each institution's risk. However, unless the external costs of systemic

Viral V. Acharya is the C. V. Starr Professor of Economics at the Leonard N. Stern School of Business, New York University, and a research associate of the National Bureau of Economic Research. Lasse H. Pedersen is the John A. Paulson Professor of Finance and Alternative Investments at the Leonard N. Stern School of Business, New York University, and a research associate at CEPR and the National Bureau of Economic Research. Thomas Philippon is the John L. Vogelstein Faculty Fellow and associate professor of finance at the Leonard N. Stern School of Business, New York University, and a research associate of the National Bureau of Economic Research. Matthew Richardson is the Charles E. Simon Professor of Applied Economics at the Leonard N. Stern School of Business, New York University, and a research associate of the National Bureau of Economic Research.

We are grateful for useful comments from Rob Engle, Jim Poterba, participants at the Research Conference on Quantifying Systemic Risk organized by the NBER and the Federal Reserve Bank of Cleveland, our discussants Mathias Drehmann and Dale Gray, the reviewers, and the organizers Joseph Haubrich and Andrew Lo. For acknowledgments, sources of research support, and disclosure of the authors' material financial relationships, if any, please see http://www.nber.org/chapters/c12063.ack.

risk are internalized by each financial institution, the institution will have the incentive to take risks that are supposedly borne by others in the economy. That is, each individual firm may take actions to prevent its own collapse but not necessarily the collapse of the entire system. It is in this sense that a financial institution's risk can be viewed as a negative externality on the system.[1] An illustration from the current crisis is that financial institutions took bets on securities and portfolios of loans (such as AAA-rated subprime mortgage-backed tranches), which faced almost no idiosyncratic risk, but large amounts of systematic risk.

As a result, a growing part of the literature argues that financial regulation should be focused on limiting systemic risk, that is, the risk of a crisis in the financial sector and its spillover to the economy at large. Indeed, there is a plethora of recent papers that provides measures of systemic risk in this context.[2] Several papers in particular—Acharya, Pedersen, et al. (2010a, 2010b) (hereafter APPR), Korinek (2010), Morris and Shin (2008), and Perotti and Suarez (2011)—provide theoretical arguments and explore the optimality properties of a "Pigovian tax" as a potential regulatory solution to the problem of systemic risk.

In these frameworks, each financial institution must face a "surcharge" that is based on the extent to which it is likely to contribute to systemic risk (defined, for example, by APPR as the realization of states of the world in which the financial sector as a whole becomes undercapitalized). The idea of systemic risk surcharges is that they provide incentives for the financial firm to limit its contributions to systemic risk; that is, to lower its surcharge by reducing size, leverage, risk, and correlation with the rest of the financial sector and the economy.

This chapter analyzes various schemes to estimate such a surcharge: (a) *regulatory stress tests of financial institutions* that measure their capital losses in adverse scenarios; (b) *statistical-based measures of capital losses* of financial firms extrapolated to crisis periods; (c) pricing of *contingent capital insurance for systemic risk,* that is, government-run insurance for each firm against itself becoming undercapitalized when the financial sector as a whole becomes undercapitalized; and (d) *market-based discovery of the price of such risk insurance* that financial institutions must purchase partly from the private sector and mostly from the government or the central bank.

While the chapter provides a discussion of each scheme, we perform a detailed analysis of scheme (c). In particular, we provide an explicit calcu-

---

1. An analogy can be made to an industrial company that produces emissions that lower its own costs but pollute the environment.

2. See, for example, Acharya, Cooley, et al. (2010b); Acharya, Pedersen, et al. (2010a); Adrian and Brunnermeier (2009); Billio et al. (2010); De Jonghe (2009); Gray, Merton, and Bodie (2008); Gray and Jobst (2009); Segoviano and Goodhart (2009); Hartmann, Straetmans, and De Vries (2005); Huang, Zhou, and Zhu (2009); Lehar (2005); Perotti and Suarez (2011); and Tarashev, Borio, and Tsatsaronis (2009), among others.

lation formula for contingent capital insurance and illustrate how the systemic risk surcharge varies with the size of the institution, its leverage, risk (equity volatility), and importantly, its correlation with rest of the economy or with the systemically important part of the financial sector. In applying the method to the period prior to the start of the financial crisis in July 2007, the measure of systemic risk sorts well on the firms that ended up running aground in the crisis (e.g., only eighteen firms show up in the top fifteen systemic firms in all four years from 2004 to 2007). These firms are a who's who of the current crisis, including American International Group (AIG), Bank of America, Bear Stearns, Citigroup, Countrywide, Fannie Mae, Freddie Mac, Goldman Sachs, Hartford Financial, JP Morgan, Lehman Brothers, Lincoln National, Merrill Lynch, Metlife, Morgan Stanley, Prudential Financial, Wachovia, and Washington Mutual. Moreover, the measure is not just size-based. Many of these firms also show up at the top of the list when we reapply the method, while adjusting for their market capitalization.

The chapter is organized as follows. Section 5.2 reviews the recent literature on systemic risk measurement and regulation, focusing in particular on the APPR paper. In the context of the description in section 5.2, section 5.3 describes various approaches to estimating systemic risk surcharges. Section 5.4 presents a detailed analysis of one of the schemes to charge financial firms for their systemic risk contributions, which is based on the price of their contingent capital insurance. We provide an exact formula for the price of each firm's contingent capital insurance and calibrate it using data prior to the start of the financial crisis beginning in the summer of 2007. Section 5.5 concludes.

5.2   Surcharges on Systemic Risk

As described earlier, systemic risk is broadly considered to be the joint failure of financial institutions or markets, which leads to the impairing of the financial intermediation process. In the recent crisis, full-blown systemic risk emerged only when the Government-Sponsored Enterprises (GSEs), Lehman Brothers, AIG, Merrill Lynch, Washington Mutual, Wachovia, and Citigroup, among others, effectively failed in the early fall of 2008. Consider the impact of the financial crisis of 2007 to 2009 on the economy. In the late fall and winter of 2008 and 2009, the worldwide economy and financial markets collapsed. On a dollar-adjusted basis, stock markets fell 42 percent in the United States, dropped 46 percent in the United Kingdom, 49 percent in Europe at large, 35 percent in Japan, and around 50 percent in the larger Latin American countries. Likewise, global GDP fell by 0.8 percent (the first contraction in decades), with a sharp decline in advanced economies of 3.2 percent. Furthermore, international trade fell almost 12 percent. When economists describe the impact of systemic risk, this is generally what they mean.

While the mechanism by which many financial firms fail simultaneously—aggregate shock, a "bank" run, counterparty risk, fire sales—may differ, the end result is invariably a capital shortfall of the aggregate financial sector. Individual firms do not have the incentive to take into account their contribution to this aggregate capital shortfall. By its very nature, therefore, systemic risk is a negative externality imposed by each financial firm on the system. A number of researchers and policymakers have argued that a major failure of the current crisis was that existing financial sector regulation seeks to limit each institution's risk seen in isolation and are not sufficiently focused on systemic risk. As a result, while individual firm's risks are properly dealt with in normal times, the system itself remains, or is in fact encouraged to be, fragile and vulnerable to large macroeconomic shocks.

As mentioned in the introduction, there is a growing literature in economics and finance that analyzes the problem of systemic risk of financial firms. APPR suggest a methodology to get around this market and regulatory failure and induce financial institutions to internalize the negative externality of systemic risk. Firms are often regulated to limit their pollution or charged based on the externality they cause (see, e.g., the classic regulation theory of Stigler [1971] and Peltzman [1976]). Similarly, APPR derive a Pigovian tax on financial firms' contribution to systemic risk.[3]

Specifically, in (a) a model of a banking system in which each bank has limited liability and maximizes shareholder value, (b) the regulator provides some form of a safety net (i.e., guarantees for some creditors such as deposit or too-big-to-fail insurance), and (c) the economy faces systemic risk (i.e., system-wide costs) in a financial crisis when the banking sector's equity capitalization falls below some fraction of its total assets and that these costs are proportional to the magnitude of this shortfall, the welfare costs imposed by each financial firm can be shown to equal the sum of two components:

Costs to society of the financial firm = Expected losses of the firm's

guaranteed debt upon default

+ Expected systemic costs in a crisis per dollar of capital shortfall

× Expected capital shortfall of the firm if there is a crisis.

1. *The expected losses upon default of the liabilities that are guaranteed by the government:* That is, the government guarantees in the system need to be priced, or, in other words, financial firms must pay for the guarantees they receive. Because the price of these guarantees will vary across firms due to the firm's risk characteristics, the firm will choose an optimal level of leverage and risk-taking activities at a more prudent level. Currently, the Federal Deposit Insurance Corporation (FDIC) in the United States chooses the

---

3. See, for example, Baumol (1972) and, in the context of the financial crisis, Korinek (2010) and Perotti and Suarez (2011).

level of FDIC premiums on a risk-adjusted basis. However, in reality, premiums are only charged when the fund is poorly capitalized so the current FDIC scheme will in general not achieve this optimal policy.

2. *The firm's contribution to expected losses in the crisis (i.e., the contribution of each firm to aggregate losses above a certain threshold) multiplied by the expected systemic costs when the financial sector becomes undercapitalized:* The systemic risk also needs to be priced, that is, financial institutions need to internalize the costs of the negative externality imposed on the system. There are two terms to this component of the surcharge. The first term—expected systemic costs—involves estimating the probability of a systemic crisis and the external costs of such a crisis, and represents the level of the surcharge. This can be considered the *time-series* component of the surcharge. There is substantial evidence on what leads to financial crises and the costs to economies of such crises beyond the impact of a normal economic downturn.[4] The second term—the firm's contribution of each institution to the financial sector collapse—measures which institutions pay more surcharge. This can be considered the *cross-sectional* component of the surcharge. The key ingredient is the expected capital shortfall of the firm in a crisis, denoted $E(\text{Capital Shortfall}_{\text{Firm } i} \mid \text{Crisis})$.

The main goal of systemic risk surcharges are to incentivize firms to limit systemic risk taking or to be well capitalized against systemic risk in order to reduce the cost of these surcharges. In the next section, we describe several approaches to calculating systemic risk surcharges.

5.3   Estimating Capital Shortfalls in a Crisis

Within the APPR framework given earlier, calculating the relative contribution of systemic risk surcharges is equivalent to estimating the expected capital shortfall of a financial firm in a financial crisis. The firm's relative contribution is simply its expected shortfall over the expected aggregate shortfall. Interestingly, if a firm had an expected capital surplus in a crisis, then it would actually reduce the systemic costs of the financial sector

---

4. There is a growing evidence of large bailout costs and real economy welfare losses associated with banking crises. For example, Hoggarth, Reis, and Saporta (2002) estimate output losses somewhere between 10 to 15 percent of GDP; Caprio and Klingebiel (1996) argue that the bailout of the thrift industry in the US in the late 1980s cost $180 billion (3.2 percent of GDP). They also document that the estimated cost of episodes of systemic banking crises were 16.8 percent for Spain, 6.4 percent for Sweden, and 8 percent for Finland. Honohan and Klingebiel (2000) find that countries spent 12.8 percent of their GDP to clean up their banking systems. Claessens, Djankov, and Klingebiel (1999), however, set the cost at 15 to 50 percent of GDP. These papers outline the costs of financial crises. Of equal importance is the probability of such crises occurring. In an extensive analysis across many countries and time periods, Reinhart and Rogoff (2008a, 2008b) look at the factors that lead to banking crises, thus providing some hope of probabilistic assessments of such crises. Borio and Drehmann (2009) study leading indicators for banking systems affected by the current crisis.

and should be "subsidized." The intuition is that firms that have plenty of capital, less risky asset holdings, or safe funding can still provide financial intermediation services when the aggregate financial sector is weak. In this section, we describe various ways to estimate and consider related measures of $E(\text{Capital Shortfall}_{\text{Firm } i} \mid \text{Crisis})$.

This measure is closely related to the standard risk measures used inside financial firms, namely value at risk (VaR) and expected shortfall (ES). These seek to measure the potential loss incurred by the firm as a whole in an extreme event. Specifically, VaR is the most that the bank loses with a confidence level of $1 - \alpha$, where α is typically taken to be 1 percent or 5 percent. For instance, with $\alpha = 5\%$, VaR is the most that the bank loses with 95 percent confidence. Hence, $\text{VaR} = -q_\alpha$, where q_α is the α quantile of the bank's return R:

$$q_a = \sup\{z \mid \Pr[R < z] \leq \alpha\}.$$

The ES is the expected loss conditional on something bad happening. That is, the loss conditional on the return being less than the α quantile:

$$ES_\alpha = -E[R \mid R \leq q_\alpha].$$

Said differently, ES is the average returns on days when the portfolio exceeds its VaR limit. The ES is often preferred because VaR can be gamed in the sense that asymmetric, yet very risky, bets may *not* produce a large VaR. For risk management, transfer pricing, and strategic capital allocation, banks need to know how their possible firm-wide losses can be broken down into its components or contributions from individual groups or trading desks. To see how, let us decompose the bank's return R into the sum of each group's return r_i, that is, $R = \Sigma_i y_i r_i$, where y_i is the weight of group i in the total portfolio. From the definition of ES, we see that

$$ES_\alpha = -\sum_i y_i E[r_i \mid R \leq q_\alpha].$$

From this expression we see the sensitivity of overall risk to exposure y_i to each group i:

$$\frac{\partial ES_\alpha}{\partial y_i} = -E[r_i \mid R \leq q_\alpha] \equiv MES_\alpha^i,$$

where MES_α^i is group i's *marginal expected shortfall* (MES). The marginal expected shortfall measures how group i's risk taking adds to the bank's overall risk. In other words, MES can be measured by estimating group i's losses when the firm as a whole is doing poorly.

These standard risk-management practices are then completely analogous to thinking about the overall risk of the financial system. For this, we can consider the expected shortfall of the overall banking *system* by letting R be the return of the aggregate banking sector. Then each bank's contribution to this risk can be measured by its MES. Hence, a financial system is constituted by a number of banks, just like a bank is constituted by a number of groups, and it is helpful to consider each component's risk contribution to the whole. As shown in section 5.3.2, MES is an important component of measuring expected capital shortfall.

5.3.1   Government Stress Tests

One of the advantages of the aforementioned approach is that the regulator has a quantifiable measure of the relative importance of a firm's contribution to overall systemic risk and thus the percentage of total systemic surcharges it must pay. The surcharge component captures in one fell swoop many of the characteristics, that are considered important for systemic risk such as size, leverage, concentration, and interconnectedness, all of which serve to increase the expected capital shortfall in a crisis. But the surcharge measure also provides an important addition, most notably the comovement of the financial firm's assets with the aggregate financial sector in a crisis. The other major advantage of this surcharge component is that it makes it possible to understand systemic risk not just in terms of an individual financial firm but in the broader context of financial subsectors. For example, since expected capital shortfall is additive, it is just one step to compare the systemic risk surcharges of, say, the regional banking sector versus a large complex bank.

Most important, however, is the fact that US regulators can implement the aforementioned approach using current tools at their disposal. In particular, stress tests are a common tool used by regulators and are now mandatory under various sets of regulation including both the Dodd-Frank Act of 2010 and the proposed Basel III accords. Stress tests measure whether financial firms will have enough capital to cover their liabilities under severe economic conditions, in other words, an estimate of $E(\text{Capital Shortfall}_{\text{Firm } i} \mid \text{Crisis})$.

For example, the Supervisory Capital Assessment Program (SCAP) that was initiated in the US in February 2009 and concluded in May 2009 was originated amidst the credit crisis, which had cast into doubt the future solvency of many large and complex financial firms. The idea was to conduct a stress test in order to assess the financial ability of the largest US Bank Holding Companies (BHCs) to withstand losses in an even more adverse economic environment. The SCAP focused on the nineteen largest financial companies, which combined held two-thirds of assets and more than half of loans in the US banking system, and whose failure was deemed to pose a systemic risk. The goal of the SCAP was to measure the ability of these financial firms to absorb losses in the case of a severe macroeconomic shock. In particular, the scenarios were two-years-ahead what-if exercises and considered losses across a range of products and activities (such as loans, investments, mortgages, and credit card balances), as well as potential trading losses and counterparty credit losses. Specifically, the stress test measured the ability of a firm to absorb losses in terms of its Tier 1 capital, with emphasis on Tier 1 Common Capital "reflecting the fact that common equity is the first element of the capital structure to absorb losses." Firms whose capital buffers were estimated small relative to estimated losses under the adverse scenario would be required to increase their capital ratios. The size of the SCAP buffer was determined in accordance with the estimated losses under the worst scenario and the ability of a firm to have a Tier 1 risk-based ratio in excess of 6 percent at year-end 2010 and its ability to have a Tier 1 Common Capital risk-based ratio in excess of 4 percent at year-end 2010.

The idea of conducting joint stress tests across the largest firms was that regulators could cross-check each firm's estimate of its own losses across these products and therefore get a more precise and unbiased estimate of what the losses should be. Table 5.1 summarizes the results for each bank. The main finding was that ten of the nineteen original banks needed to raise

Table 5.1   Banks included in the stress test, descriptive statistics

Bank name	SCAP	Tang. comm.	SCAP/tang. comm. (%)	SCAP/total SCAP (%)	MES (%)	SRISK (%)
GMAC	11.5	11.1	103.60	14.88	n/a	n/a
Bank of America Corp.	33.9	75	45.50	45.44	15.05	22.96
Wells Fargo & Co.	13.7	34	40.41	18.36	10.57	10.50
Regions Financial Corp.	2.5	7.6	32.89	3.35	14.8	1.37
Keycorp	1.8	6	30.00	2.41	15.44	0.96
Citigroup Inc.	5.5	23	24.02	7.37	14.98	18.69
Suntrust Banks Inc.	2.2	9.4	23.40	2.95	12.91	1.66
Fifth Third Bancorp	1.1	4.9	22.45	1.47	14.39	1.18
Morgan Stanley	1.8	18	10.11	2.41	15.17	6.26
PNC Financial Services Grp	0.6	12	5.13	0.08	10.55	2.30
American Express Co.	0	10.1	0.00	0.00	9.75	0.36
BB&T Corp.	0	13.4	0.00	0.00	9.57	0.92
Bank New York	0	15.4	0.00	0.00	11.09	0.63
Capital One Financial	0	16.8	0.00	0.00	10.52	1.47
Goldman Sachs	0	55.9	0.00	0.00	9.97	7.21
JPMorgan Chase & Co.	0	136.2	0.00	0.00	10.45	16.81
MetLife Inc.	0	30.1	0.00	0.00	10.28	4.37
State Street	0	14.1	0.00	0.00	14.79	1.28
US Bancorp	0	24.4	0.00	0.00	8.54	1.07

Notes: This table contains the values of SCAP shortfall (in $ billion), tangible common equity (in $ billion), SCAP shortfall/tangible common equity, SCAP/Total SCAP, MES, and SRISK for the nineteen banks that underwent stress testing. The banks are sorted according to the SCAP/Tangible Common Equity ratio. SCAP shortfall is calculated as max $[0, 0.08\,D - 0.92\,MES\,(1 - 6.13 * MES)]$, where D is the book value of debt and MES is the marginal expected shortfall of a stock given that the market return is below its fifth percentile. SRISK is shortfall divided by the sum of shortfall values for all nineteen firms. MES is measured for each individual company's stock using the period April 2008 till March 2009 and the S&P 500 as the market portfolio.

additional capital in order to comply with the capital requirements set forth in the SCAP. In all ten cases the additional buffer that had to be raised was due to inadequate Tier 1 Common Capital. In total, around $75 billion had to be raised, though there were significant variations across the firms ranging from $0.6 to $33.9 billion. The number is much smaller than the estimated two-year losses, which were at $600 billion or 9.1 percent on total loans. The total amount of reserves already in place was estimated to be able to absorb much of the estimated losses. Only using data up to the end of 2008, the required additional buffer that had to be raised was estimated at $185 billion. However, together with the adjustments after the first quarter of 2009, the amount was reduced to $75 billion.

It should be clear, however, that in the SCAP the regulators in effect were estimating expected capital shortfalls, albeit under a given scenario and over a limited two-year time period. More generally, the methodology would need to be extended to estimate systemic risk, that is, $E(\text{Capital Shortfall}_{\text{Firm}\,i} \mid \text{Crisis})$. Specifically, the first (and most important) step would be to create a range of economic scenarios or an average scenario that *necessarily* leads to an aggregate capital shortfall. This would be a substantial departure from the SCAP and recent stress tests performed in the United States and in Europe. The question here is a different one than asking whether an adverse economic scenario imperils the system, but instead asks, if the system is at risk, which firm contributes to this risk?

In addition, the set of financial firms investigated by these stress tests would have to be greatly expanded beyond the current set of large BHCs. This expansion would in theory include insurance companies, hedge funds, possibly additional asset management companies, and other financial companies. This is not only necessary because some of these companies may be important contributors to the aggregate capital shortfall of the financial sector, but also because their interconnections with other firms may provide valuable information about estimated counterparty losses.[5] Finally, an important element of a financial crisis is illiquidity, that is, the difficulty in

---

5. In order to have any hope of assessing interconnectedness of a financial institution and its pivotal role in a network, detailed exposures to other institutions through derivative contracts and interbank liabilities is a must. This could be achieved with legislation that compels reporting, such that all connections are registered in a repository immediately after they are formed or when they are extinguished, along with information on the extent and form of the collateralization and the risk of collateral calls when credit quality deteriorates. These reports could be aggregated by risk and maturity types to obtain an overall map of network connections. What is important from the standpoint of systemic risk assessment is that such reports, and the underlying data, be rich enough to help estimate *potential exposures* to counterparties under infrequent but socially costly market- or economy-wide stress scenarios. For instance, it seems relevant to know for each systemically important institution (a) what are the most dominant risk factors in terms of losses and liquidity risk (e.g., collateral calls) likely to realize in stress scenarios; and (b) who its most important counterparties are in terms of potential exposures in stress scenarios. A transparency standard that encompasses such requirements would provide ready access to information for purposes of macro-prudential regulation.

converting assets into cash. Basel III has laid out a framework for banks to go through stress test scenarios during a liquidity crisis. It seems natural that liquidity shocks would be part of the "doomsday" scenario of systemic risk. The application of such a scenario would be that firms subject to capital withdrawals, whether through wholesale funding of banks, investors in asset management funds, or even (less sticky) policyholders at insurance companies, would have to take a substantial haircut on the portion of its assets that must be sold and are illiquid in light of these withdrawals. Regulators would need to assess both the level of a financial firm's systemically risky funding and the liquidity of its asset holdings. Cross-checking against likewise institutions would be particularly useful in this regard.

5.3.2   Statistical Models of Expected Capital Shortfall

A major problem with stress tests is that from a practical point of view the analysis is only periodic in nature and is limited by the applicability of the stress scenarios. Financial firms' risks can change very quickly. This problem suggests that the stress tests need to be augmented with more up-to-date information. It is possible to address this question by conducting a completely analogous estimate of systemic risk, that is, $E(\text{Capital Shortfall}_{\text{Firm } i} \mid \text{Crisis})$, using state-of-the-art statistical methodologies based on publicly available data.

Table 5.1 summarizes the stress tests of large BHCs conducted by the US government in May 2009. The table also provides statistical estimates of expected equity return losses in a crisis (denoted as MES) and the percentage capital shortfall in the sector (denoted as SRISK) developed by APPR (2010a), Brownlees and Engle (2010), and the NYU Stern Systemic Risk Rankings described in Acharya, Brownlees et al. (2010).[6] These estimates are based on historical data on equity and leverage, and statistical models of joint tail risk. Table 5.1 implies that these estimates, while not perfectly aligned with the stress tests, load up quite well on the firms that required additional capital. For example, ignoring General Motors Acceptance Corporation (GMAC), for which there is not publicly available stock return data, the eight remaining firms in need of capital based on the SCAP belonged to the top ten MES firms. Moreover, the financial firms that represented the higher percentage of SCAP shortfalls such as Bank of America, Wells Fargo, Citigroup, etc., also had the highest levels of the corresponding statistical measure SRISK. That said, there are Type-I errors with the SRISK measure. Alternatively, one could argue that the stress test was not harsh enough, as it did not generate an aggregate capital shortfall.

In order to better understand the statistical measures, note that a financial

6. For more information on the NYU Stern Systemic Risk rankings, see http://vlab.stern .nyu.edu/welcome/risk.

firm has an expected capital shortfall in a financial crisis if its equity value (denote E_i) is expected to fall below a fraction K_i of its assets (denote A_i); that is, its equity value plus its obligations (denote D_{i0}):

$$E(\text{Capital Shortfall}_{\text{Firm } i} \mid \text{Crisis}) = E[E_i \mid crisis] - K_i E[A_i \mid crisis].$$

Rearranging into return space, we get the following definition:

$$\frac{E(\text{Capital Shortfall}_{\text{Firm } i} \mid \text{Crisis})}{E_{i0}} = (1 - K_i)(1 - MES_i) - K_i L_{i0},$$

where the leverage ratio

$$L_{i0} \equiv \frac{A_{i0}}{E_{i0}} = \frac{D_{i0} + E_{i0}}{E_{i0}}.$$

Estimating the expected capital shortfall in a crisis as a fraction of current equity is paramount to estimation of $MES_{i,t} = E_{t-1}(R_{i,t} \mid crisis)$. Of course, there are a variety of statistical methods at one's disposal for estimating this quantity. For example, APPR (2010a) estimate the crisis as the market's worst 5 percent days and derive a nonparametric measure of MES; Brownlees and Engle (2010) condition on daily market moves less than 2 percent, derive a full-blown statistical model based on asymmetric versions of generalized autoregressive conditional heteroskedasticity (GARCH), dynamic conditional correlation (DCC), and nonparametric tail estimators, and extrapolate this to a crisis (i.e., to MES); and a number of other researchers develop statistical approaches that could easily be adjusted to measure MES, such as De Jonghe (2010), Hartmann, Straetmans, and de Vries (2005), and Huang, Zhou, and Zhu (2009), among others.

Table 5.2 ranks the ten financial firms contributing the greatest fraction to expected aggregate capital shortfall of the 100 largest financial institutions for three dates ranging from July 1, 2007, through March 31, 2009. Estimates of MES are also provided. The methodology used is that of Brownlees and Engle (2010) and the numbers and details are available at www.systemicrisk ranking.stern.nyu.edu. The dates are chosen to coincide with the start of the financial crisis (July 1, 2007), just prior to the collapse of Bear Stearns (March 1, 2008), and the Friday before Lehman Brothers' filing for bankruptcy (September 12, 2008).

The important thing to take from table 5.2 is that the methodology picks out the firms that created most of the systemic risk in the financial system and would be required to pay the greater fraction of systemic risk surcharges. Of the major firms that effectively failed during the crisis, that is, either failed, were forced into a merger, or were massively bailed out—Bear Stearns, Fannie Mae, Freddie Mac, Lehman Brothers, AIG, Merrill Lynch, Wachovia, Bank of America, and Citigroup—all of these firms show up early as having large expected capital shortfalls during the period in ques-

Table 5.2   Systemic risk rankings during the financial crisis of 2007 to 2009

	July 1, 2007 Risk% (Rank)			March 1, 2008 Risk% (Rank)			September 12, 2008 Risk% (Rank)		
	SRISK		MES	SRISK		MES	SRISK		MES
Citigroup	14.3	1	3.27	12.9	1	4.00	11.6	1	6.17
Merrill Lynch	13.5	2	4.28	7.8	3	5.36	5.7	5	6.86
Morgan Stanley	11.8	3	3.25	6.7	6	3.98	5.2	7	4.87
JP Morgan Chase	9.8	4	3.44	8.5	2	4.30	8.6	4	5.2
Goldman Sachs	8.8	5	3.6	5.3	9	3.14	4.2	9	3.58
Freddie Mac	8.6	6	2.35	5.9	7	4.60	—	—	—
Lehman Brothers	7.2	7	3.91	5.0	9	4.88	4.6	8	15.07
Fannie Mae	6.7	8	2.47	7.1	4	5.88	—	—	—
Bear Stearns	5.9	9	4.4	2.9	12	4.16	—	—	—
MetLife	3.6	10	2.57	2.2	15	2.93	1.9	12	3.20
Bank of America	0	44	2.06	6.7	5	3.60	9.6	2	6.33
AIG	0	45	1.51	5.5	8	4.63	9.6	3	10.86
Wells Fargo	0	48	2.38	1.9	16	4.14	3.0	10	5.40
Wachovia	0	51	2.2	4.6	11	4.64	5.7	6	9.61

Source: www.systemicriskranking.stern.nyu.edu.

Notes: This table ranks the ten most systemically risky financial firms among the one hundred largest financial institutions for three dates ranging from July 1, 2007, through September 12, 2008. The marginal expected shortfall (MES) measures how much the stock of a particular financial company will decline in a day, if the whole market declines by at least 2 percent. When equity values fall below prudential levels of 8 percent of assets, the Systemic Risk Contribution, SRISK percent, measures the percentage of all capital shortfall that would be experienced by this firm in the event of a crisis. Note that the SRISK percent calculations here incorporate existing capital shortfalls from failed institutions.

tion. For example, all but Bank of America, AIG, and Wachovia are in the top ten on July 1, 2007. And by March 2008, both Bank of America and AIG have joined the top ten, with Wachovia ranked eleventh.

In addition, most of expected aggregate capital shortfall is captured by just a few firms. For example, in July 2007, just five firms captured 58.2 percent of the systemic risk in the financial sector. By March 1, 2008, however, as the crisis was impacting many more firms, the systemic risk was more evenly spread, with 43 percent covered by five firms. As the crisis was just about to go pandemic with massive failures of a few institutions, the concentration crept back up, reaching 51.1 percent in September 2008 (where we note that the SRISK percent have been scaled up to account for the capital shortfalls of failed institutions). These results suggest, therefore, that had systemic risk surcharges been in place prior to the crisis, a relatively small fraction of firms would have been responsible for those surcharges. As the theory goes, these surcharges would have then discouraged behavior of these firms that led to systemic risk.

To the extent systemic risk remains, these levies would have then gone toward a general "systemic crisis fund" to be used to help pay for the remaining systemic costs, either injecting capital into solvent financial institutions affected by the failed firms or even supporting parts of the real economy hurt by the lack of adequate financial intermediation. Going back to section 5.2, only those losses due to the default of the liabilities that are guaranteed by the government would be covered by a separate FDIC-like fund. The purpose of the systemic crisis fund is not to bail out failed institutions but to provide support to financial institutions, markets, and the real economy that are collateral damage caused by the failed institution.

5.3.3 Contingent Claim Pricing Models of Expected Capital Shortfall

An alternative methodology to estimating expected capital shortfalls would be to set an economic price for such shortfalls, that is, *contingent capital insurance*.[7] These insurance charges would allow the regulator to determine the proportionate share of expected losses contributed by each firm in a crisis (i.e., the relative systemic risk of each firm in the sector). This would be used to determine who pays their share of the overall systemic surcharge. The regulator would then take this proportionate share of each firm and multiply it by the expected systemic costs of a crisis to determine the level of the surcharge.

Putting aside for the moment who receives the insurance payments, suppose we require (relying on results and insights from APPR) that each financial firm take out government insurance against itself becoming undercapitalized when the financial sector as a whole becomes undercapitalized. This would be similar in spirit to how deposit insurance schemes are run. The pricing of such an insurance contract fits into the literature on pricing multivariate contingent claims (see, e.g., Margrabe 1978, Stulz 1982, Stapleton and Subrahmanyam 1984, Kishimoto 1989, Rosenberg 2000, and Camara 2005). This literature develops contingent-claim valuation methodologies for cases in which the valuation of claims depends on payoffs that are based on the realizations of multiple stochastic variables. Here, the insurance contract only pays off if the financial institutions' results are extremely poor when the aggregate sector is in distress.[8]

To make the argument more formal, let X_{it} and M_t be the value of the financial institution i's and the aggregate market's (e.g., financial sector or

---

7. A related method would be to require financial institutions to hold in their capital structure a new kind of "hybrid" claim that has a *forced* debt-for-equity conversion whenever a prespecified threshold of distress (individual and systemic) is met. These hybrid securities have been called contingent capital bonds. Examples in the literature of such approaches are: Wall (1989) propose subordinated debentures with an embedded put option; Doherty and Harrington (1997) and Flannery (2005) propose reverse convertible debentures; and Kashyap, Rajan, and Stein (2008) propose an automatic recapitalization when the overall banking sector is in bad shape, *regardless of the health of a given bank at that point.*

8. For related contingent claim analyses that focus on the balance sheets of financial institutions, see also Lehar (2005), Gray and Jobst (2009), and Gray, Merton, and Bodie (2008).

public equity market) particular measure of performance (e.g., equity value, equity value/debt value, writedowns, etc.), respectively. It is well-known that the value of any contingent claim that depends on X_{iT} and M_T can be written as

(1) $$V_t = E_t[F(X_{iT}, M_T)SD_T]$$

where $F(\cdot)$ is the payoff function depending on realizations of X_{iT} and M_T at maturity of the claim, and SD_T is the stochastic discount factor or the pricing kernel.

Beyond assumptions about the stochastic process followed by the variables, the problem with equation (1) is that it requires estimates of preference parameters, such as the level of risk-aversion and the rate of time discount. Alternatively, assuming continuous trading, one can try and set up a self-financing strategy that is instantaneously riskless. Then, as in Black and Scholes (1973), one can solve the resulting partial differential equation with the preference parameters being embedded in the current value of the assets. Valuation techniques such as Cox and Ross (1976) can then be applied.

Appealing to Brennan (1979) and Rubinstein (1976), Stapleton and Subrahmanyam (1984) show that risk-neutral valuation can be applied in a multivariate setting even when the payoffs are functions of cash flows and not traded assets, as may be the case for our setting. In particular, under the assumption that aggregate wealth and the stochastic processes are multivariate lognormal and the representative agent has constant relative risk aversion preferences, one can apply risk neutral valuation methods to the pricing of equation (1).[9]

As described earlier, assume that the financial institution is required to take out insurance on systemic losses tied to the market value of equity of the firm and the overall sector. Formally, a systemic loss is defined by:

1. The market value of the equity of the aggregate financial sector, S_{MT}, falling below K_{S_M}.
2. The required payment at maturity of the claim is the difference between some prespecified market value of the equity of the financial institution, K_{S_i}, and its actual market value, S_{iT}.

The payoff at maturity T can be represented mathematically as

(2) $$F(S_{MT}, S_{iT}) = \frac{\max(K_{S_M} - S_{MT}, 0)}{K_{S_M} - S_{MT}} \times \max(K_{S_i} - S_{iT}, 0).$$

---

9. Obviously, in practice, one of the advantages of this methodology is that it allows for more complex joint distributions that are not multivariate normal such as ones that involve either time varying distributions (e.g., Bollerslev and Engle 1986, 1988, Engle 2002) or tails of return distributions described by extreme value theory (e.g., Barro 2006, Gabaix 2009, and Kelly 2009). The pricing framework would need to be extended for such applications (e.g., Engle and Rosenberg 2002).

Applying the results in Stapleton and Subrahmanyam (1984), equation (1) can be rewritten as

$$(3) \qquad V_t = \frac{1}{r^{T-t}} \int_0^\infty \int_0^\infty \frac{\max(K_{S_M} - S_{MT}, 0)}{K_{S_M} - S_{MT}}$$

$$\times \max(K_{S_i} - S_{iT}, 0) \phi'(S_{MT}, S_{iT}) dS_{MT} dS_{iT}$$

$$= \frac{1}{r^{T-t}} \int_0^{K_{S_M}} \int_0^{K_{S_i}} (K_{S_i} - S_{iT}) \phi'(S_{MT}, S_{iT}) dS_{MT} dS_{iT},$$

$$\phi'(S_{MT}, S_{iT}) = \frac{1}{2\pi(T-t)\sigma_{S_M}\sigma_{S_i}(1 - \rho_{Mi})S_{MT}S_{iT}} e^{-1/[2(1-\rho_{Mi}^2)]\varpi_T}$$

$$\varpi_T = \left[\frac{\{\ln S_{MT} - (T-t)\ln r - \ln S_{Mt} + [(T-t)\sigma_{S_M}^2/2]\}}{\sigma_{S_M}\sqrt{T-t}} \right]^2$$

$$+ \left[\frac{\{\ln S_{iT} - (T-t)\ln r - \ln S_{it} + [(T-t)\sigma_{S_i}^2/2]\}}{\sigma_{S_i}\sqrt{T-t}} \right]^2$$

where

$$- 2\rho_{Mi} \left[\frac{\{\ln S_{MT} - (T-t)\ln r - \ln S_{Mt} + [(T-t)\sigma_{S_M}^2/2]\}}{\sigma_{S_M}\sqrt{T-t}} \right]$$

$$\times \left[\frac{\{\ln S_{iT} - (T-t)\ln r - \ln S_{it} + [(T-t)\sigma_{S_i}^2/2]\}}{\sigma_{S_i}\sqrt{T-t}} \right],$$

and σ_{S_M}, σ_{S_i}, and ρ_{S_M} are the volatility of the financial sector return, the volatility of the return of the financial institution i, and the correlation between them, respectively. And r is the risk-free rate.

Equation (3) provides one way regulators could set the price for contingent capital insurance. As an illustration, section 5.4 presents a detailed analysis of equation (3) in the context of the financial crisis of 2007 to 2009. As described in section 5.3.2, the insurance charges would be placed in a general systemic crisis fund to be used to help cover systemic costs and not to bail out the failed institution per se. In other words, there is no question of moral hazard here.

5.3.4   Market-Based Estimates of Expected Capital Shortfall

One of the issues with estimating expected capital shortfalls in a crisis is that the statistical approach of section 5.3.2 and the contingent claim methodology of 5.3.3 rely on projecting out tail estimates of capital shortfall of a firm to an even more extreme event; that is, when the aggregate sector suffers a shortfall. The assumption is that the cross-sectional pattern amongst financial firms is maintained as events get further in the tail of the distribution. This is not necessarily the case. For example, interconnectedness might rear its problems only under the most extreme circumstances. If some firms are more interconnected than others, then the estimation and pricing methodology will not capture this feature.

Moreover, measurement errors are likely, especially if some financial firms have fatter tail distributions, or face different individual term structure volatilities than other firms. A natural way to rectify this problem would be to allow market participants to estimate and trade on these insurance costs. In a competitive market, it is likely that the measurement errors would be reduced.

A market-based approach that uses market prices, assuming market efficiency will reflect all available information, may be able to uncover the tail distributions and give a more robust estimate of the cross-sectional contribution of each firm to aggregate expected capital shortfall. The core idea of a market-based plan to charge for systemic risk is that each financial firm would be required to buy private insurance against its own losses in a systemic risk scenario in which the whole financial sector is doing poorly. In the event of a payoff on the insurance, the payment would not go to the firm itself, but to the regulator in charge of managing systemic risk and stabilizing the financial sector. This contingent capital insurance cost, however, is not necessarily equal to the systemic risk surcharge. It would be used to determine the proportionate share of each financial firm's contribution to the total systemic risk surcharge. The level of the systemic risk surcharge would be determined by the expected systemic costs of a financial crisis times the proportionate share of each firm.[10] The important point is that each firm's share would be determined by the private market for insurance.

This scheme would in theory not only provide incentives for the firm to limit its contributions to systemic risk, but also provide a market-based estimate of the risk (the cost of insurance), and avoid moral hazard (because the firm does not get the insurance payoff). The problem with private insurance markets, however, is that they are not set up to insure against systemic risks. By their very nature, systemic risks cannot be diversified away. The underlying capital required to cover these losses, therefore, is quite large even though the possibility of such an event is very small. Examples of this problem can be found in the recent financial crisis with the major monoline insurers, such as Ambac Financial Group and Municipal Bond Insurance Association (MBIA), and, of course, the division of AIG named AIG Financial Products. These monolines guarantee repayment when an issuer

---

10. The expected systemic costs may be higher or lower than the contingent capital insurance costs. The insurance costs assume a dollar systemic cost for every dollar of loss of the firm in a systemic risk scenario.

defaults. Going into the crisis, their businesses focused more and more on structured products, such as asset-backed securities, collateralized debt obligations, and collateralized loan obligations, which already represent well-diversified portfolios. Moreover, the majority of insurance was placed on the so-called AAA super senior portions. Almost by construction, the AAA tranches' only risk is systemic in nature.[11] Undercapitalized relative to the systemic event, almost all the monolines and AIG Financial Products were effectively insolvent.

Since the role of the private sector in providing such insurance is primarily for price discovery and the amount of private capital available to provide such systemic insurance is likely to be limited, it seems natural that most of the insurance would be purchased from the government. APPR (2009, 2010b) describe how private-public contingent capital insurance might work in practice. Each regulated firm would be required to buy insurance against future losses, but only losses during a future general crisis. For example, each financial institution would have a "target capital" of, say, 8 percent of current assets in the event of a crisis.[12] For every dollar that the institution's capital falls below the target capital in the crisis, the insurance company would have to pay N cents to the regulator (e.g., a systemic risk fund).[13] This way, the insurance provider would have every incentive to correctly estimate the systemic risk of a firm in a competitive market and charge the firm accordingly. The financial firms would need to keep acquiring insurance, and thus pay surcharges, on a continual basis to ensure continual monitoring and price discovery, and to prevent sudden high insurance premiums from causing funding problems because the purchases of premiums are spread out. For example, each month, each firm would need to buy a fractional amount of insurance to cover the next five years. Hence, the coverage of the next month would be provided by the insurance purchased over the last five years.

Note that the surcharge proceeds are *not* meant to bail out failed institutions, but to support the affected real sector and solvent institutions. In other words, to the extent systemic risk still remains once the surcharge has been imposed, the proceeds of the surcharge are to cover systemic risk costs. Future expected bailouts (i.e., government guarantees) need to be priced

11. Coval, Jurek, and Stafford (2009) call these securities economic catastrophe bonds and show that the securities' underlying economics is akin to out-of-the-money put options on the aggregate market.

12. A crisis would be ex ante defined by the regulator as a time when the aggregate losses in the financial industry (or the economy at large) exceed a specified amount.

13. N cents represent the proportional share of the private market's participation in the insurance component of the public-private plan. If the proposal were simply contingent capital insurance in which the firm got recapitalized if the firm were doing poorly in a crisis, then the government's share of the payout to the firm would be $100 - N$ cents on the dollar, and the government would receive $(100 - N/100)$ percent of the insurance premiums. To avoid double taxation, the fees paid to the insurance company would be subtracted from the firm's total systemic surcharge bill paid to the regulator.

separately. As described in section 5.2, this portion equals the expected loss on its guaranteed liabilities, akin to the FDIC premium, but they need to be charged irrespective of the size of the resolution fund.

As described before, the major disadvantage of private insurance is that, even for extremely well-capitalized institutions, the insurance sector has struggled for a number of years to provide open-ended (albeit diversifiable) catastrophe insurance. An extensive literature has studied this topic. While the models differ, the primary reason boils down to the inability of insurers to be capitalized well enough to cover large losses. See, for example, the evidence and discussion in Jaffee and Russell (1997), Froot (2001, 2007), and Ibragimov, Jaffee, and Walden (2008). The solution in the catastrophe insurance markets has generally been greater and greater backing by the Federal and state governments (e.g., Federal primary coverage against floods in 1968, insurance against hurricanes after 1992 by Florida, and earthquake coverage by California after 1994). The idea behind these approaches is that private insurers help price the insurance while the government provides significant capital underlying the insurance.

The question arises whether such public-private insurance markets can exist for systemic risk. While some reinsurance schemes have been looked at by the FDIC, most recently in 1993, with the conclusion that the market is not viable, there do exists such markets today. Financial markets in general have become much more sophisticated in how they develop niche markets. A case in point is that coinsurance programs are not without precedent; indeed, motivated by the events of September 11, 2001, the Terrorism Risk Insurance Act (TRIA) was first passed in November 2002, and offers federal reinsurance for qualifying losses from a terrorist attack. It remains an open question whether this can be extended to financial crises.

5.4   Contingent Capital Insurance and the Financial Crisis of 2007 to 2009

Section 5.3.3 described a methodology for uncovering the price of expected capital shortfalls of financial firms in a crisis. In this section, we explore this idea in greater detail. First, for a given set of parameter values describing the multivariate process for the financial firm's stock price and the final sector's stock price, we can estimate the value of the insurance contract using Monte Carlo simulation. We provide some examples and comparative statics to describe some of the underlying economic intuition for the price of this insurance contract. Second, we apply this analysis to the financial crisis of 2007 to 2009.

5.4.1   Comparative Statics

Figure 5.1 graphs the insurance costs as a percentage of the equity of the financial firm as a function of the correlation between the firm's equity return and the market return, and as a function of the strike rate of the insur-

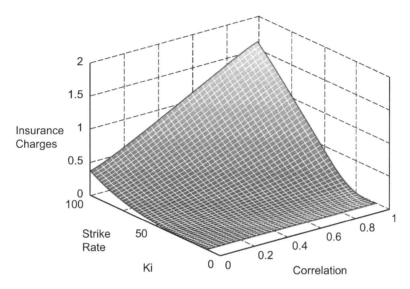

Fig. 5.1   **The graph depicts simulated insurance charges as a percent of equity as a function of the correlation between the firm's equity return and the market return, and as a function of the strike rate of the insurance contract**

Notes: Specifically, the payoff is triggered when the market drops 40 percent and the firm's ratio of market value of equity to (total liabilities + market equity value) falls below the strike rate, ranging from 1 percent to 10 percent (i.e., $K_i = 10$ to 100). We assume the following parameters based on recent history: market volatility of 16 percent, firm equity volatility of 27 percent, risk-free rate of 4 percent, and a current firm's ratio of market value of equity to (total liabilities + market equity value) equal to 10 percent. The contract has a four-year maturity.

ance contract. Specifically, the payoff is triggered when the market drops 40 percent and the firm's ratio of market value of equity to (total liabilities + market equity value) falls below some strike rate, ranging from 1 to 10 percent. For example, 1 percent would be a very weak capital requirement while 10 percent would be strict. We assume the following parameters based on recent history: market volatility of 16 percent, firm equity volatility of 27 percent, risk-free rate of 4 percent, and a current firm's ratio of market value of equity to (total liabilities + market equity value) equal to 10 percent. The contract has a four-year maturity.

Figure 5.1 shows that the insurance costs are nonlinearly increasing the stronger the capital requirement and the higher the correlation between the firm's equity return and the market's return. Most important, these factors interact nonlinearly, so the greatest impact by far is when the trigger takes place closer to 10 percent *and* the correlation is very high. To better understand the magnitude of the insurance cost, consider a firm with $100 billion market value of equity, $1 trillion of assets, highly correlated with the market, and facing a trigger close to 10 percent. Even for these extreme

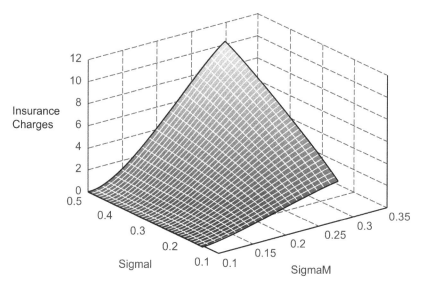

Fig. 5.2   The graph depicts simulated insurance charges as a percent of equity as a function of the volatility of the firm's equity return and the volatility of the market return for a given strike rate of the insurance contract

Notes: Specifically, the payoff is triggered when the market drops 40 percent and the firm's ratio of market value of equity to (total liabilities + market equity value) falls below the strike rate of 10 percent. We assume the following parameters based on recent history: correlation between the firm equity return and the market return of 55 percent, risk-free rate of 4 percent, and a current firm's ratio of market value of equity to (total liabilities + market equity value) equal to 10 percent. The contract has a four-year maturity.

values, the four-year cost is only around $1 billion, which illustrates the fact that the likelihood of both the firm and the market collapsing is a rare event.

While clearly the insurance trigger and the correlation are key factors, what else drives the magnitude of the insurance cost? Figure 5.2 depicts insurance charges as a percent of equity value as a function of the volatility of the firm's equity return and the volatility of the market return for three given strike rates of the insurance contract, namely 10 percent, 7.5 percent, and 5 percent. As before, the payoff is triggered when the market drops 40 percent and the firm's ratio of market value of equity to (total liabilities + market equity value) falls below the strike rate of 10 percent. We also assume the following parameters based on recent history: correlation between the firm equity return and the market return of 55 percent, risk-free rate of 4 percent, and a current firm's ratio of market value of equity to (total liabilities + market equity value) equal to 10 percent. The contract again has a four-year maturity.

Figure 5.2 shows the importance of the interaction between firm volatility, market volatility, and the triggers. A few observations are in order. First, across the different strike rates, the three-dimensional shape is quite

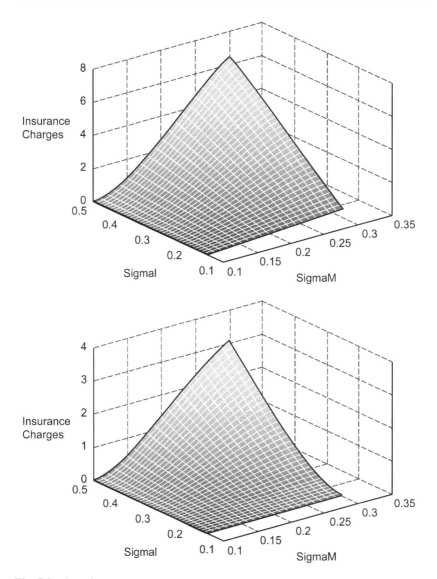

Fig. 5.2 **(cont.)**

similar. The pattern shows a highly nonlinear relationship that requires both the firm and market volatilities to be high. This should not be surprising given that the payoff occurs only in states where both the firm and market are undercapitalized. Second, in comparison to figure 5.1, the key factor in determining the insurance cost is the level of volatility. For example, for firm and market volatilities of 50 percent and 25 percent, respectively, the insurance costs run as high as 6 percent, 4 percent, and 2 percent of equity value for the strike rates of 10 percent, 7.5 percent, and 5 percent. This is important for understanding the properties of contingent capital insurance. Since volatility tends to be procyclical (high in bad times and low in booms), the cost of contingent capital insurance in general will be procyclical as well. Therefore, to reduce procyclicality of insurance charges, the regulator would have to make the strike rates countercyclical (higher strikes in good times), setting the overall insurance cost such as to avoid an overleveraged financial sector and an overheated economy. This design issue is similar to the trade-off the Federal Open Market Committee (FOMC) must evaluate when setting interest rates.

In the next subsection, we apply the insurance model of section 5.3.3 to available data preceding the financial crisis of 2007 to 2009. In particular, we comment on both the insurance charges and systemic risk contributions that would have emerged if the plan had been put in place during the 2004 to 2007 period.

5.4.2 The Financial Crisis of 2007 to 2009

This section empirically analyzes systemic risk surcharges based on contingent capital insurance for US financial institutions around the recent financial crisis. Here, the institutions have been selected according to (a) their role in the US financial sector, and (b) their market cap as of end of June 2007 being in excess of $5 billion. The companies can be categorized into the following four groups: *Depository Institutions* (e.g., JPMorgan, Citigroup, Washington Mutual, etc.); *Security and Commodity Brokers* (e.g., Goldman Sachs, Morgan Stanley, etc.); *Insurance Carriers* (e.g., AIG, Berkshire Hathaway, etc.) and *Insurance Agents, Brokers and Service* (e.g., Metlife, Hartford Financial, etc.); and a group called *Others* consists of nondepository institutions, real estate firms, and so forth. The total number of firms that meet all these criteria is 102.

Table 5.3 contains descriptive year-by-year statistics of the implied insurance charge for these 102 firms across the four groups—that is, Depository Institutions, Security and Commodity Brokers, Insurance, and Others—over the period 2004 to 2007. As with the simulations provided in section 5.4.1, the insurance payoff is triggered when the aggregate stock market falls 40 percent, and the payoff is based on the fall in the firm's equity value when the ratio of equity value over total assets drops below 10 percent. The amounts are in millions and represent the cost over a four-year period. The main parameter inputs—volatilities and correlations—are estimated over the prior year, and the current ratio of equity value over total assets is computed accordingly from the Center for Research in Security Prices (CRSP) and COMPUSTAT.

Several observations are in order. First, there is a clear ordering of the insurance cost across the type of institution. In particular, brokers/dealers face the highest costs every year; insurance companies face the lowest. Sec-

Table 5.3   Descriptive statistics of the dollar insurance charge across groups

	2004	2005	2006	2007
All				
Mean	42.80	8.22	3.41	3.22
Median	1.77	0.33	0.07	0.02
Std. dev.	102.00	19.20	9.11	8.35
Max	540.00	90.30	48.90	39.10
Min	0.00	0.00	0.00	0.00
Depository				
Mean	36.06	6.00	2.53	3.19
Median	4.99	0.86	0.43	0.34
Std. dev.	88.20	13.80	6.32	8.57
Max	425.78	65.70	32.34	38.06
Min	0.06	0.00	0.00	0.00
Nondepository				
Mean	29.68	8.56	1.76	2.06
Median	0.00	0.00	0.00	0.00
Std. dev.	124.00	25.70	8.02	6.65
Max	540.00	90.30	41.00	25.50
Min	0.00	0.00	0.00	0.00
Insurance				
Mean	24.51	4.20	1.71	1.13
Median	0.77	0.05	0.02	0.00
Std. dev.	51.40	8.90	4.14	2.69
Max	226.24	33.32	17.39	11.43
Min	0.00	0.00	0.00	0.00
Broker-Dealer				
Mean	162.00	30.00	17.70	14.00
Median	184.00	30.50	16.30	8.81
Std. dev.	165.77	32.11	18.74	15.76
Max	461.00	87.80	48.90	39.10
Min	0.00	0.00	0.00	0.00

Notes: This table contains descriptive statistics of the dollar insurance charge across the groups by year: Depository Institutions, Security and Commodity Brokers, Insurance, and Others. The insurance payoff is triggered when the aggregate stock market falls 40 percent with the payoff based on the fall in the firm's equity value below a 10 percent equity value over total assets. The amounts are in millions and represent the cost over a four-year period.

ond, for most years, and most of the institution types, there is significant skewness in the cross-section of insurance charges, that is, the mean is multiple times the median. While this finding is mostly due to skewness in the distribution of asset size across firms, the results of section 5.4.1 showed that high costs are due to simultaneous extreme parameters and the moneyness of the option, properties likely to affect just a few firms. Third, there is considerable variation through time in the insurance fees, with a general decline in the level of these fees from 2004 to 2007. The reason for this variation is the general decline of volatilities over this same period.

The latter finding points to the need to state a few caveats. Table 5.3 provides results on insurance fees based on short-term volatility estimates of the financial firms and the market. Acharya, Cooley et al. (2010a) present evidence showing that during the latter years of the relevant period the term structure of volatility was sharply upward sloping. While higher expected volatility in the future may not affect the cross-sectional rankings or proportional share estimates of who pays the systemic risk surcharge, it clearly impacts the contingent capital insurance costs. The latter year calculations provided in table 5.3 therefore are underestimated. Similarly, the contingent capital insurance pricing model of section 5.3.3 makes a number of assumptions about equity return distributions, most notably multivariate normality. To the extent conditional normality produces unconditional fat tails, this assumption may not be as unpalatable as it first seems. Nevertheless, there is evidence that return distributions have some conditional fat tailness, which would also increase the level of the insurance fees.

To better understand what determines the fees during this period, table 5.4 provides results of cross-sectional regressions of the insurance charges for each firm, both in dollar amounts (panel A) and as a percentage of equity value (panel B) against parameters of interest, including leverage (i.e., the moneyness of the trigger), correlation with the market, the firm's volatility, and the institutional form. Generally, across each year, the adjusted R-squared's roughly double from the mid-twenties to around 50 percent when the institutional form is included in the regression. The broker/dealer dummy is especially significant. This is interesting to the extent that much of the systemic risk emerging in the crisis derived from this sector. Table 5.4 shows that, as early as 2004, the contingent capital insurance costs of the broker/dealer sector would have been a red flag.

Table 5.4 brings several other interesting empirical facts to light. First, in every year, leverage is a key factor explaining the insurance costs across firms. This result should not be surprising given that the contingent capital trigger is based on leverage. But if one believes the trigger *does* capture systemic risk, it suggests that higher capital requirements will have a first-order effect in containing systemic risk. Second, the correlation between the firm's return and the market return is a key variable, possibly more important than the firm's volatility itself. The reason is that without sufficient correlation the probability that both the firm and market will run aground is remote, pushing down the cost of insurance. Finally, table 5.3 showed that there was significant variation in the mean insurance costs from 2004 to 2007. Table 5.4 runs a cross-sectional stacked regression over the 2004 to 2007 period but also includes market volatility as an additional factor. While the adjusted R-squared does drop from the mid-twenties in the year-by-year regressions to 16 percent (in panel A) and to 19 percent (in panel B) for the stacked regressions, the drop is fairly small. This is because the market volatility factor explains almost all the time-series variation.

This result highlights an important point about contingent capital insur-

Table 5.4   Cross-sectional regression analysis of insurance charges on firm characteristics

A. Dependent variable is $ insurance charge of each firm

	2004		2005		2006		2007		2004–2007	
Intercept	−31.5		−11.4		−8.1		−12.4		−259.2	
	(−0.60)		(−1.08)		(−1.85)		(−2.86)		(−3.64)	
Equity/assets	−148.4	−178.9	−33.5	−40.3	−14.0	−15.8	−10.1	−11.9	−46.2	−54.3
	(−3.92)	(−2.98)	(−3.92)	(−3.61)	(−3.75)	(−3.02)	(−4.65)	(−1.55)	(−5.06)	(−3.80)
Correlation w/ mkt.	169.6	87.1	32.2	19.3	22.3	9.9	25.2	13.9	68.4	35.6
	(2.39)	(1.11)	(2.21)	(1.88)	(2.74)	(1.73)	(3.59)	(2.03)	(2.95)	(1.37)
Firm equity vol.	120.3	−88.2	60.7	14.0	22.0	9.0	28.8	6.1	80.7	16.1
	(0.98)	(−0.71)	(1.90)	(0.56)	(2.45)	(1.41)	(3.10)	(0.64)	(3.08)	(0.55)
Dummy: Broker/dealer		169.7		24.6		13.0		7.3		−201.6
		(1.85)		(2.26)		(1.84)		(0.93)		(−3.18)
Dummy: Depository		33.0		−1.0		−1.9		−3.6		−246.1
		(0.53)		(−0.14)		(−0.56)		(−0.82)		(−3.71)
Dummy: Nondepository		91.3		15.5		3.3		0.1		−226.7
		(0.92)		(1.25)		(0.55)		(0.01)		(−3.55)
Dummy: Insurance		56.6		4.9		0.6		−2.4		−238.4
		(0.88)		(0.63)		(0.16)		(−0.49)		(−3.61)
Market volatility									2147.4	2228.6
									(3.52)	(3.64)
Adj. R^2	19.0%	41.5%	19.9%	45.0%	25.1%	47.9%	29.6%	46.4%	16.2%	25.7%

(*continued*)

Table 5.4 (continued)

B. *Dependent variable is insurance charge of each firm as a % of market value of equity*

	2004		2005		2006		2007		2004–2007	
Intercept	0.00023		-0.00081		-0.00014		-0.00021		-0.01038	
	(0.09)		(-0.33)		(-1.62)		(-2.45)		(-4.49)	
Equity/assets	-0.00684	-0.00783	-00118	-0.00102	-0.00039	-0.00044	-0.00026	-0.00031	-0.00197	-0.00220
	(-4.26)	(-4.54)	(-5.16)	(-4.87)	(-4.86)	(-4.34)	(-5.00)	(-4.43)	(-5.20)	(-5.08)
Correlation w/ mkt.	0.00301	0.00138	0.00051	0.00018	0.00042	0.00019	0.00039	0.00017	0.00121	0.00498
	(1.00)	(0.50)	(1.66)	(0.46)	(2.76)	(1.67)	(3.44)	(1.83)	(1.28)	(0.53)
Firm equity vol.	0.00860	0.00108	0.00175	0.00066	0.00067	0.00013	0.00078	0.00027	0.00363	0.00156
	(2.05)	(0.27)	(2.59)	(0.37)	(3.31)	(2.90)	(3.29)	(1.42)	(3.99)	(1.83)
Dummy: Broker/dealer		0.00700		0.00048		0.00030		0.00021		-0.00855
		(1.90)		(2.16)		(2.24)		(1.63)		(-4.74)
Dummy: Depository		0.00117		0.00031		-0.00005		-0.00004		-0.01029
		(0.49)		(0.56)		(-0.60)		(-0.54)		(-4.85)
Dummy: Nondepository		0.00337		0.00036		0.00010		0.00007		-0.00961
		(1.20)		(1.73)		(0.87)		(0.60)		(-4.83)
Dummy: Insurance		0.00337		0.00044		0.00005		0.00002		-0.0961
		(1.30)		(1.53)		(0.68)		(0.24)		(-4.82)
Market volatility									0.09261	0.09480
									(4.32)	(4.47)
Adj. R^2	22.1%	52.1%	25.7%	59.6%	33.3%	61.5%	36.4%	59.7%	19.3%	30%

Notes: This table provides results of cross-sectional regressions of the insurance charges for each firm, both in dollar amounts (panel A) and in a percentage of equity value (Panel B), against parameters of interest, including leverage (i.e, the moneyness of the trigger), correlation with the market, the firm's volatility, and the institutional form; *t*-statistics in parentheses.

ance. Just prior to the crisis starting in June 2007, market volatility was close to an all-time low. Putting aside the previously mentioned issues of short- versus long-term volatility and conditional fat tails, this low volatility necessarily implies low insurance charges. Consistent with table 5.3's summary, table 5.5 presents the dollar and percent insurance charges firm by

Table 5.5   **US financial firms' ranking by insurance charges**

Ranking (based on %)	Company	Percent of equity	$ charge	Ranking (based on $)	Contribution to costs (%)
1	Bear Stearns Companies Inc.	0.000978	16.292	9	4.96
2	Federal Home Loan Mortgage Corp.	0.000636	25.521	6	7.77
3	Lehman Brothers Holdings Inc.	0.000524	20.719	8	6.31
4	Merrill Lynch & Co. Inc.	0.000478	34.649	3	10.55
5	Morgan Stanley Dean Witter & Co.	0.000443	39.129	1	11.92
6	Federal National Mortgage Assn.	0.000387	24.616	7	7.50
7	Goldman Sachs Group Inc.	0.000311	27.558	5	8.39
8	Countrywide Financial Corp.	0.000263	5.6808	14	1.73
9	MetLife Inc.	0.000239	11.426	10	3.48
10	Hartford Financial Svcs Group I	0.000235	7.3309	13	2.23
11	Principal Financial Group Inc.	0.000182	2.8404	18	0.87
12	Lincoln National Corp. IN	0.000178	3.421	17	1.04
13	Prudential Financial Inc.	0.000175	7.8739	12	2.40
14	JPMorgan Chase & Co.	0.000167	27.645	4	8.42
15	Citigroup Inc.	0.00015	38.058	2	11.59
16	Ameriprise Financial Inc.	0.000147	2.1912	19	0.67
17	E Trade Financial Corp.	0.000141	1.326	21	0.40
18	CIT Group Inc. New	0.000137	1.4368	20	0.44
19	Washington Mutual Inc.	0.000116	4.351	16	1.33
20	Commerce Bancorp Inc. NJ	8.7E-05	0.61563	28	0.19
21	Sovereign Bancorp Inc.	8.34E-05	0.84257	26	0.26
22	Genworth Financial Inc.	6.59E-05	0.98527	24	0.30
23	National City Corp.	6.07E-05	1.1636	22	0.35
24	Wachovia Corp. 2nd New	5.66E-05	5.549	15	1.69
25	Keycorp New	5.22E-05	0.70366	27	0.21
26	SLM Corp.	4.83E-05	1.1444	23	0.35
27	Unum Group	4.58E-05	0.41017	32	0.12
28	UnionBanCal Corp.	4.45E-05	0.36689	34	0.11
29	State Street Corp.	4.28E-05	0.98425	25	0.30
30	Bank of America Corp.	4.21E-05	9.1278	11	2.78
31	Huntington Bancshares Inc.	3.82E-05	0.20437	39	0.06
32	Comerica Inc.	3.63E-05	0.33666	35	0.10
33	MBIA Inc.	2.42E-05	0.19672	40	0.06
34	Regions Financial Corp. New	1.81E-05	0.42231	31	0.13
35	Capital One Financial Corp.	1.8E-05	0.58626	29	0.18

(continued)

Table 5.5   (continued)

Ranking (based on %)	Company	Percent of equity	$ charge	Ranking (based on $)	Contribution to costs (%)
36	Bank New York Inc.	1.64E-05	0.5158	30	0.16
37	Zions Bancorp	1.52E-05	0.12619	43	0.04
38	Suntrust Banks Inc.	1.28E-05	0.39277	33	0.12
39	BB&T Corp.	1.15E-05	0.25406	38	0.08
40	Northern Trust Corp.	9.69E-06	0.13695	42	0.04
41	M&T Bank Corp.	9.16E-06	0.10596	44	0.03
42	Hudson City Bancorp Inc.	6.82E-06	0.044336	48	0.01
43	Fifth Third Bancorp	6.43E-06	0.13698	41	0.04
44	Marshall & Ilsley Corp.	4.12E-06	0.050894	46	0.02
45	New York Community Bancorp Inc.	4.07E-06	0.021705	50	0.01
46	PNC Financial Services Grp IN	3.79E-06	0.093488	45	0.03
47	TD Ameritrade Holding Corp.	2.46E-06	0.029364	49	0.01
48	Wells Fargo & Co. New	2.42E-06	0.28287	36	0.09
49	Schwab Charles Corp. New	1.83E-06	0.047105	47	0.01
50	American International Group IN	1.55E-06	0.28175	37	0.09
51	CNA Financial Corp.	1.36E-06	0.017655	51	0.01
52	CIGNA Corp.	9.95E-07	0.014958	53	0.00
53	Aetna Inc. New	6.95E-07	0.017586	52	0.01
54	Compass Bancshares Inc.	6.12E-07	0.005615	54	0.00
55	CB Richard Ellis Group Inc.	3.09E-07	0.002583	56	0.00
56	Berkley WR Corp.	2.55E-07	0.001611	57	0.00
57	Assurant Inc.	1.92E-07	0.001372	58	0.00
58	Allstate Corp.	1.22E-07	0.004564	55	0.00
59	Synovus Financial Corp.	3.74E-08	0.000375	61	0.00
60	NYSE Euronext	3.14E-08	0.00061	60	0.00
61	Travelers Companies Inc.	2.56E-08	0.000909	59	0.00
62	Humana Inc.	2.09E-08	0.000214	62	0.00
63	IntercontinentalExchange Inc.	1.30E-09	1.35E-05	68	0.00
64	Loews Corp.	1.25E-09	3.41E-05	63	0.00
65	Aon Corp.	7.56E-10	9.46E-06	69	0.00
66	AFLAC Inc.	5.89E-10	1.48E-05	67	0.00
67	Peoples United Financial Inc.	4.93E-10	2.63E-06	71	0.00
68	Berkshire Hathaway Inc. Del	4.83E-10	2.38E-05	66	0.00
69	US Bancorp Del	4.28E-10	2.45E-05	64	0.00
70	American Express Co.	3.32E-10	2.41E-05	65	0.00
71	MasterCard Inc.	2.67E-10	3.53E-06	70	0.00
72	Union Pacific Corp.	4.90E-11	1.52E-06	72	0.00
73	NYMEX Holdings Inc.	2.69E-11	3.11E-07	73	0.00
74	Chubb Corp.	1.27E-11	2.77E-07	74	0.00
75	AMBAC Financial Group Inc.	5.94E-12	5.28E-08	75	0.00
76	Western Union Co.	2.57E-12	4.14E-08	76	0.00
77	Fidelity National Finl Inc. New	1.94E-12	1.02E-08	78	0.00
78	Legg Mason Inc.	1.92E-12	2.49E-08	77	0.00
79	Janus Cap Group Inc.	1.72E-12	8.88E-09	79	0.00
80	Edwards AG Inc.	1.26E-12	8.07E-09	80	0.00

Table 5.5   (continued)

Ranking (based on %)	Company	Percent of equity	$ charge	Ranking (based on $)	Contribution to costs (%)
81	Safeco Corp.	6.11E-13	4.04E-09	82	0.00
82	Health Net Inc.	3.85E-13	2.28E-09	84	0.00
83	Blackrock Inc.	3.42E-13	6.21E-09	81	0.00
84	American Capital Strategies Ltd.	1.46E-13	1.13E-09	86	0.00
85	Progressive Corp. OH	1.25E-13	2.18E-09	85	0.00
86	UnitedHealth Group Inc.	3.71E-14	2.54E-09	83	0.00
87	Cincinnati Financial Corp.	2.28E-14	1.70E-10	87	0.00
88	Marsh & McLennan Cos. Inc.	7.75E-15	1.33E-10	88	0.00
89	Torchmark Corp.	7.25E-16	4.64E-12	89	0.00
90	Chicago Mercantile Exch. Hldg. IN	5.69E-17	1.06E-12	90	0.00
91	Fidelity National Info. Svcs. Inc.	1.12E-17	1.17E-13	91	0.00
92	Coventry Health Care Inc.	2.57E-20	2.32E-16	93	0.00
93	Wellpoint Inc.	1.42E-20	6.96E-16	92	0.00
94	Berkshire Hathaway Inc. Del	2.79E-22	3.32E-17	94	0.00
95	Loews Corp.	4.34E-23	3.64E-19	95	0.00
96	Leucadia National Corp.	1.18E-23	9.04E-20	96	0.00
97	CBOT Holdings Inc.	1.78E-25	1.94E-21	98	0.00
98	Alltel Corp.	1.36E-25	3.15E-21	97	0.00
99	Franklin Resources Inc.	1.83E-34	6.05E-30	99	0.00
100	T Rowe Price Group Inc.	2.36E-41	3.25E-37	100	0.00
101	SEI Investments Company	3.69E-51	2.10E-47	101	0.00
102	Eaton Vance Corp.	5.56E-59	3.08E-55	102	0.00

Notes: This table contains the list of US financial firms with a market cap in excess of $5 billion as of June 2007. The firms are listed in descending order according to their insurance costs. The insurance payoff is triggered when the market drops 40 percent and the firm's ratio of market value of equity to (total liabilities + market equity value) falls below 10 percent at the end of a four-year period. The payoff equals the difference between the equity value implied by the 10 percent ratio and the final equity value. The volatility of the firm's equity, the volatility of the market, and the correlation between the two, are estimated using daily data over the prior year. The insurance costs calculation assumes a multivariate normal distribution of equity returns. The first three columns represent, respectively, the insurance charge as a percent of equity, the total dollar insurance charge in millions, and the ranking based on the total dollar amount.

firm. For almost all the financial firms, the capital contingent insurance costs seem quite low, especially in light of what happened just a few months later.

Interestingly, table 5.5 shows an important difference between contingent capital insurance and the systemic risk surcharge. Recall that the systemic risk surcharge separates into the product of two components—the expected systemic costs and the proportional share of systemic risk. Table 5.5 provides an estimate of this share across the 102 firms, and therefore is a measure of the latter component of the systemic risk surcharge. Using the capital insurance charge as its basis, just five firms provide over 50 percent of all the risk, and fifteen firms 92 percent of the risk. This is a key finding and perhaps not surprising given the outcome of the crisis that followed, namely that most of the systemic risk is concentrated in just a few places. Note that in order of importance, table 5.5 lists Morgan Stanley, Citigroup, Merrill Lynch, JP Morgan, Goldman Sachs, Freddie Mac, Fannie Mae, Lehman Brothers, Bear Stearns, Metlife, Bank of America, Prudential Financial, Hartford Financial, Countrywide, and Wachovia as the leading systemic firms. At least nine of these firms either failed or required extraordinary capital infusions or guarantees. In fact, probably only JP Morgan (and to a lesser extent, Goldman Sachs) was considered somewhat safe at the height of the crisis in the late fall of 2008 and the winter of 2009.

Table 5.6 shows that this finding is not a fluke by also reporting the rankings of the insurance costs in the earlier periods of 2004, 2005, and 2006. For example, panel B reports the dollar charges in all four periods and shows that the exact same firms (albeit in different order) show up consistently in the top fifteen. In fact, the only additions to the list are Washington Mutual, AIG, and Lincoln National, two of which failed in the crisis. On a preliminary basis, these results suggest that a measure like the one calculated here (i.e., the cost of contingent capital insurance), does a good job of deciphering which firms are systemic and should pay the share of the surcharge. Of some importance, panel A shows that these rankings are not solely size-based as most of these firms also show up on a percentage of equity basis as well, and APPR provide more extensive evidence of this type for predicting the realized performance of financial firms during the stress test (SCAP) exercise, the crisis period of 2007 to 2009, and other crises of the past.

The APPR approach to measuring systemic risk has its limitations. The basic assumption in that paper is that the negative externality gets triggered in a proportional amount to each dollar of aggregate capital that falls below the aggregate capital threshold level. Therefore, irrespective of the type of financial institution or how that institution is funded, its capital loss contribution is treated the same below the threshold. To take just one example, in table 5.5, large insurance companies like Metlife, Prudential Financial, and Hartford Financial show up as systemically quite risky. Their presence is due to their large offerings of guaranteed investment products that exposed them to aggregate risk and a large MES. Is this a fair outcome? While their funding via insurance premiums is stickier than a large bank, which relies on wholesale funding, it is not obvious that these firms do not pose systemic risk. For example, insurance premiums represent almost 10 percent of GDP, insurance policies are subject to limited runs and, most important, as the largest buyer of corporate debt, insurance companies provide an important financial intermediation service. Disruptions in any of these activities would have important consequences. A final comment on the APPR concept of systemic risk is that the basic intuition is all financial firms are part of the entire system in that well-capitalized financial institutions could take over

Table 5.6 Ranking by insurance charge

A. Ranking by percent of market value of equity

July 2003–June 2004	July 2004–June 2005	July 2005–June 2006	June 2006–June 2007
1. Bear Stearns Companies Inc.	Bear Stearns Companies Inc.	Bear Stearns Companies Inc.	Bear Stearns Companies Inc.
2. Genworth Financial Inc.	Federal Home Loan Mortgage Corp.	Federal National Mortgage Assn.	Federal Home Loan Mortgage Corp.
3. Lehman Brothers Holdings Inc.	Federal National Mortgage Assn.	Morgan Stanley Dean Witter & Co.	Lehman Brothers Holdings Inc.
4. Prudential Financial Inc.	Morgan Stanley Dean Witter & Co.	Lehman Brothers Holdings Inc.	Merrill Lynch & Co. Inc.
5. Morgan Stanley Dean Witter & Co.	Lincoln National Corp. IN	Goldman Sachs Group Inc.	Morgan Stanley Dean Witter & Co.
6. Lincoln National Corp. IN	Lehman Brothers Holdings Inc.	Merrill Lynch & Co. Inc.	Federal National Mortgage Assn.
7. Federal National Mortgage Assn.	Goldman Sachs Group Inc.	MetLife Inc.	Goldman Sachs Group Inc.
8. Hartford Financial Svcs Group I	Merrill Lynch & Co. Inc.	Hartford Financial Svcs Group I	Countrywide Financial Corp.
9. MetLife Inc.	Hartford Financial Svcs Group I	Prudential Financial Inc.	MetLife Inc.
10. Merrill Lynch & Co. Inc.	Prudential Financial Inc.	Lincoln National Corp. IN	Hartford Financial Svcs Group I
11. Goldman Sachs Group Inc.	Genworth Financial Inc.	Ameriprise Financial Inc.	Principal Financial Group Inc.
12. JPMorgan Chase & Co.	MetLife Inc.	Countrywide Financial Corp.	Lincoln National Corp. IN
13. Principal Financial Group Inc.	Principal Financial Group Inc.	JPMorgan Chase & Co.	Prudential Financial Inc.
14. E Trade Financial Corp.	JPMorgan Chase & Co.	Unum Group	JPMorgan Chase & Co.
15. Unum Group	E Trade Financial Corp.	Sovereign Bancorp Inc.	Citigroup Inc.
16. Travelers Companies Inc.	Unum Group	Principal Financial Group Inc.	Ameriprise Financial Inc.
17. CIGNA Corp.	Washington Mutual Inc.	E Trade Financial Corp.	E Trade Financial Corp.
18. Sovereign Bancorp Inc.	CNA Financial Corp.	Washington Mutual Inc.	CIT Group Inc. New
19. Washington Mutual Inc.	Countrywide Financial Corp.	Commerce Bancorp Inc. NJ	Washington Mutual Inc.
20. Commerce Bancorp Inc. NJ	Commerce Bancorp Inc. NJ	Huntington Bancshares Inc.	Commerce Bancorp Inc. NJ

(*continued*)

Table 5.6 (continued)

B. Ranking by total dollar amount

July 2003–June 2004	July 2004–June 2005	July 2005–June 2006	June 2006–June 2007
1. Federal National Mortgage Assn.	Federal National Mortgage Assn.	Morgan Stanley Dean Witter & Co.	Morgan Stanley Dean Witter & Co.
2. Morgan Stanley Dean Witter & Co.	Morgan Stanley Dean Witter & Co.	Federal National Mortgage Assn.	Citigroup Inc.
3. JPMorgan Chase & Co.	Federal Home Loan Mortgage Corp.	Goldman Sachs Group Inc.	Merrill Lynch & Co. Inc.
4. Merrill Lynch & Co. Inc.	JPMorgan Chase & Co.	Merrill Lynch & Co. Inc.	JPMorgan Chase & Co.
5. Goldman Sachs Group Inc.	Merrill Lynch & Co. Inc.	JPMorgan Chase & Co.	Goldman Sachs Group Inc.
6. Lehman Brothers Holdings Inc.	Goldman Sachs Group Inc.	Lehman Brothers Holdings Inc.	Federal Home Loan Mortgage Corp.
7. Prudential Financial Inc.	Lehman Brothers Holdings Inc.	MetLife Inc.	Federal National Mortgage Assn.
8. Citigroup Inc.	Prudential Financial Inc.	Bear Stearns Companies Inc.	Lehman Brothers Holdings Inc.
9. Bear Stearns Companies Inc.	MetLife Inc.	Prudential Financial Inc.	Bear Stearns Companies Inc.
10. MetLife Inc.	Citigroup Inc.	Hartford Financial Svcs Group I	MetLife Inc.
11. Hartford Financial Svcs Group I	Bear Stearns Companies Inc.	Citigroup Inc.	Bank of America Corp.
12. Bank of America Corp.	Bank of America Corp.	Bank of America Corp.	Prudential Financial Inc.
13. Wachovia Corp. 2nd New	American International Group IN	Washington Mutual Inc.	Hartford Financial Svcs Group I
14. Washington Mutual Inc.	Hartford Financial Svcs Group I	Countrywide Financial Corp.	Countrywide Financial Corp.
15. Lincoln National Corp. IN	Wachovia Corp. 2nd New	Wachovia Corp. 2nd New	Wachovia Corp. 2nd New
16. Genworth Financial Inc.	Washington Mutual Inc.	Lincoln National Corp. IN	Washington Mutual Inc.
17. Principal Financial Group Inc.	Lincoln National Corp. IN	Ameriprise Financial Inc.	Lincoln National Corp. IN
18. Travelers Companies Inc.	Principal Financial Group Inc.	American International Group IN	Principal Financial Group Inc.
19. CIGNA Corp.	Genworth Financial Inc.	Principal Financial Group Inc.	Ameriprise Financial Inc.
20. Suntrust Banks Inc.	Countrywide Financial Corp.	Sovereign Bancorp Inc.	CIT Group Inc. New

Notes: This table contains the names of the top twenty companies ranked in descending order according to their insurance charge for the specified periods as a percent of their market value of equity. The insurance payoff is triggered when the market drops 40 percent and the firm's ratio of market value of equity to (total liabilities + market equity value) falls below 10 percent at the end of a four-year period.

poorly capitalized institutions. This is, of course, not possible when aggregate capital losses exceed a large enough threshold.

5.5   Concluding Remarks

Based on a recent literature that focuses on systemic risk surcharges, the centerpiece underlying these surcharges is the measurement of a firm's share of expected losses conditional on the occurrence of a systemic crisis. In this chapter, we describe and analyze various ways to estimate these expected capital shortfalls. As an example of one particular way to measure the firm's share of systemic risk, we analyze the pricing of contingent capital insurance from both a theoretical and empirical point of view. Using the current crisis as an illustration, the measure appears to successfully choose the systemic firms, consistent with recent statistical-based measures of systemic risk (e.g., APPR 2010a and Brownlees and Engle 2010, among others).

Appendix

This appendix contains the names of the US financial institutions used in the analysis of the recent crisis. The institutions have been selected according to their inclusion in the US financial sector and their market cap as of end of June 2007, where all firms had a market cap in excess of $5 billion.

The companies can be categorized into the following four groups: *Depository Institutions* (JPMorgan, Citigroup, WAMU, etc.); *Security and Commodity Brokers* (Goldman Sachs, Morgan Stanley, etc.); *Insurance Carriers* (AIG, Berkshire Hathaway, Countrywide, etc.); *Insurance Agents, Brokers, Service* (Metlife, Hartford Financial, etc.); and a group called *Others* consisting of nondepository institutions, real estate, and so forth.

Table 5A1

Depository institutions: 29 companies, 2-digit SIC code = 60	Other: Nondepository institutions, etc.: 27 companies, 2-digit SIC code = 61, 62(except 6211), 65, 67	Insurance: 36 companies, 2-digit SIC code = 63 and 64	Security and commodity brokers: 10 companies, 4-digit SIC code = 6211
1. BB&T Corp.	1. Alltel Corp.	1. AFLAC Inc.	1. Bear Stearns Companies Inc.
2. Bank New York Inc.	2. American Capital Strategies Ltd.	2. Aetna Inc. New	2. E Trade Financial Corp.
3. Bank of America Corp.	3. American Express Co.	3. Allstate Corp.	3. Edwards AG Inc.
4. Citigroup Inc.	4. Ameriprise Financial Inc.	4. AMBAC Financial Group Inc. American	4. Goldman Sachs Group Inc.
5. Comerica Inc.	5. Blackrock Inc.	5. International Group Inc.	5. Lehman Brothers Holdings Inc.
6. Commerce Bancorp Inc. NJ	6. CBOT Holdings Inc.	6. Aon Corp. Assurant Inc.	6. Merrill Lynch & Co. Inc.
7. Hudson City Bancorp Inc.	7. CB Richard Ellis Group Inc.	7. Berkley WR Corp.	7. Morgan Stanley Dean Witter & Co.
8. Huntington Bancshares Inc.	8. CIT Group Inc. New	8. Berkshire Hathaway Inc. Del	8. NYMEX Holdings Inc.
9. JPMorgan Chase & Co.	9. Capital One Financial Corp.	9. Berkshire Hathaway Inc. Del	9. Schwab Charles Corp. New
10. Keycorp New	10. Chicago Mercantile Exch Hldg Inc.	10. CIGNA Corp.	10. T Rowe Price Group Inc.
11. M&T Bank Corp.	11. Compass Bancshares Inc.	11. CNA Financial Corp.	
12. Marshall & Ilsley Corp.	12. Eaton Vance Corp.	12. Chubb Corp.	
13. National City Corp.	13. Federal Home Loan Mortgage Corp.	13. Cincinnati Financial Corp.	
14. New York Community Bancorp Inc.	14. Federal National Mortgage Assn.	14. Countrywide Financial Corp.	

15. Northern Trust Corp.
16. PNC Financial Services Grp Inc.
17. Peoples United Financial Inc.
18. Regions Financial Corp. New
19. Sovereign Bancorp Inc.
20. State Street Corp.
21. Suntrust Banks Inc.
22. Synovus Financial Corp.
23. US Bancorp Del
24. UnionBanCal Corp.
25. Wachovia Corp. 2nd New
26. Washington Mutual Inc.
27. Wells Fargo & Co. New
28. Western Union Co.
29. Zions Bancorp

15. Fidelity National Info. Svcs Inc.
16. Fifth Third Bancorp
17. Franklin Resources Inc.
18. IntercontinentalExchange Inc.
19. Janus Cap Group Inc.
20. Legg Mason Inc.
21. Leucadia National Corp.
22. MasterCard Inc.
23. NYSE Euronext
24. SEI Investments Company
25. SLM Corp.
26. TD Ameritrade Holding Corp.
27. Union Pacific Corp.

15. Coventry Health Care Inc.
16. Fidelity National Finl Inc. New
17. Genworth Financial Inc.
18. Hartford Financial
19. SVCS Group IN
20. Health Net Inc.
21. Humana Inc.
22. Lincoln National Corp. IN
23. Loews Corp.
24. Loews Corp.
25. MBIA Inc.
26. Marsh & McLennan Cos. Inc.
27. MetLife Inc.
28. Principal Financial Group Inc.
29. Progressive Corp.
30. Prudential Financial Inc.
31. Safeco Corp.
32. Torchmark Corp.
33. Travelers Companies Inc.
34. UnitedHealth Group Inc.
35. Unum Group
36. Wellpoint Inc.

Notes: The total number of firms in the sample is 102. Note that although Goldman Sachs has a SIC (standard industrial classification) code of 6282, thus initially making it part of the group called *Others*, we have nonetheless chosen to put in the group of *Security and Commodity Brokers*.

References

Acharya, Viral V., Christian Brownless, Farhang Farazmand, Robert Engle, and Matthew Richardson. 2010. "Measuring Systemic Risk." In *Regulating Wall Street: The Dodd-Frank Act and the New Architecture of Global Finance,* edited by Viral V. Acharya, Thomas Cooley, Matthew Richardson, and Ingo Walter, 87–120. Princeton, NJ: Princeton University Press.

Acharya, Viral V., Thomas Cooley, Matthew Richardson, and Ingo Walter. 2010a. "Manufacturing Tail Risk: A Perspective on the Financial Crisis of 2007–2009." *Foundations and Trends in Finance* 4 (2009): 247–325.

———. 2010b. *Regulating Wall Street: The Dodd-Frank Act and the New Architecture of Global Finance.* Princeton, NJ: Princeton University Press.

Acharya, Viral V., Lasse H. Pedersen, Thomas Philippon, and Matthew Richardson. 2009. "Regulating Systemic Risk." In *Restoring Financial Stability: How to Repair a Failed System,* edited by Viral V. Acharya and Matthew Richardson, 283–304. New York: New York University Stern School of Business, John Wiley and Sons.

———. 2010a. "Measuring Systemic Risk." Working Paper. New York University Stern School of Business.

———. 2010b. "Taxing Systemic Risk." In *Regulating Wall Street: The Dodd-Frank Act and the New Architecture of Global Finance,* edited by Viral V. Acharya, Thomas Cooley, Matthew Richardson, and Ingo Walter, 121–42. Princeton, NJ: Princeton University Press.

Adrian, Tobias, and Markus Brunnermeier. 2009. "CoVaR." Working Paper. Federal Reserve Bank of New York.

Barro, R. 2006. "Rare Disasters and Asset Markets in the Twentieth Century." *The Quarterly Journal of Economics* 121:823–66.

Baumol, W. J. 1972. "On Taxation and the Control of Externalities." *American Economic Review* 62 (3): 307–22.

Billio, Monica, Mila Getmansky, Andrew W. Lo, and Loriana Pelizzon. 2010. "Econometric Measures of Systemic Risk in the Finance and Insurance Sectors." NBER Working Paper no. 16223. Cambridge, MA: National Bureau of Economic Research, July.

Black, Fischer, and Myron Scholes. 1973. "The Pricing of Options and Corporate Liabilities." *The Journal of Political Economy* 81 (3): 637–54.

Bollerslev, Tim, and Robert F. Engle. 1986. "Modelling the Persistence of Conditional Variances." *Econometric Reviews* 5 (1): 1–50.

———. 1988. "A Capital Asset Pricing Model with Time-Varying Covariances." *The Journal of Political Economy* 96 (1): 116–31.

Borio, Claudio, and Mathias Drehmann. 2009. "Assessing the Risk of Banking Crises—Revisited." *BIS Quarterly Review* March:29–46.

Brennan, Michael J. 1979. "The Pricing of Contingent Claims in Discrete Time Models." *Journal of Finance* 34:53–68.

Brownlees, Christian, and Robert F. Engle. 2010. "Volatility, Correlation and Tails for Systemic Risk Measurement." Working Paper. NYU Stern School of Business.

Camara, A. 2005. "Option Prices Sustained by Risk-Preferences." *Journal of Business* 78:1683–708.

Caprio, Gerard, and Daniela Klingebiel. 1996. "Bank Insolvencies: Cross Country Experience." World Bank, Policy Research Working Paper no. 1620. Washington, DC: World Bank.

Claessens, Stijn, Simeon Djankov, and Daniela Klingebiel. 1999. "Financial Restructuring in East Asia: Halfway There?" World Bank, Financial Sector Discussion Paper no. 3. Washington, DC: World Bank.

Cox, J., and S. A. Ross. 1976. "The Valuation of Options for Alternative Stochastic Processes." *Journal of Financial Economics* 3:145–66.

Coval, J., J. Jurek, and E. Stafford. 2009. "Economic Catastrophe Bonds." *American Economic Review* 99 (3): 628–66.

De Jonghe, Olivier. 2010. "Back to the Basics in Banking? A Micro-Analysis of Banking System Stability." *Journal of Financial Intermediation* 19 (3): 387–417.

Doherty, Neil A., and Scott Harrington. 1997. "Managing Corporate Risk with Reverse Convertible Debt." Working Paper. The Wharton School.

Engle, Robert F. 2002. "Dynamic Conditional Correlation." *Journal of Business and Economic Statistics* 20 (3): 339–50.

Engle, Robert F., and Joshua Rosenberg. 2002. "Empirical Pricing Kernels." *Journal of Financial Economics* 64 (3): 341–72.

Flannery, Mark J. 2005. "No Pain, No Gain? Effecting Market Discipline via 'Reverse Convertible Debentures.'" In *Capital Adequacy beyond Basel: Banking, Securities, and Insurance,* edited by Hal S. Scott, 171–96. New York: Oxford University Press.

Froot, Kenneth. 2001. "The Market for Catastrophe Risk: A Clinical Examination." *Journal of Financial Economics* 60 (2): 529–71.

———. 2007. "Risk Management, Capital Budgeting, and Capital Structure Policy for Insurers and Reinsurers." *The Journal of Risk and Insurance* 74 (2): 273–99.

Gabaix, Xavier. 2009. "Power Laws in Economics and Finance." *Annual Review of Economics* 1 (1): 255–94.

Gray, Dale F., and Andreas A. Jobst. 2009. "Higher Moments and Multivariate Dependence of Implied Volatilities from Equity Options as Measures of Systemic Risk." In *Global Financial Stability Report,* 128–31. Washington, DC: International Monetary Fund.

Gray, Dale F., Robert C. Merton, and Zvi Bodie. 2008. "New Framework for Measuring and Managing Macrofinancial Risk and Financial Stability." Working Paper no. 09-015. Boston: Harvard Business School, August.

Hartmann, P., S. Straetmans, and C. de Vries. 2005. "Banking System Stability: A Cross-Atlantic Perspective." NBER Working Paper no. 11698. Cambridge, MA: National Bureau of Economic Research, October.

Hoggarth, Glenn, Ricardo Reis, and Victoria Saporta. 2002. "Costs of Banking System Instability: Some Empirical Evidence." *Journal of Banking and Finance* 26 (5): 825–55.

Honohan, Patrick, and Daniela Klingebiel. 2000. "Controlling Fiscal Costs of Bank Crises." World Bank, Working Paper no. 2441. Washington, DC: World Bank.

Huang, Xin, Hao Zhou, and Haibin Zhu. 2009. "A Framework for Assessing the Systemic Risk of Major Financial Institutions." *Journal of Banking & Finance* 33 (11): 2036–49.

Ibragimov, Rustam, Dwight Jaffee, and Johan Walden. 2009. "Nondiversification Traps in Catastrophe Insurance Markets." *Review of Financial Studies* 22 (3): 959–93.

Jaffee, Dwight, and Thomas Russell. 1997. "Catastrophe Insurance, Capital Markets, and Uninsurable Risks." *Journal of Risk and Insurance* 64 (2): 205–30.

Kashyap, Anil, Raghuram Rajan, and Jeremy Stein. 2008. "Rethinking Capital Regulation." Paper presented at the Kansas City Symposium, "Maintaining Stability in a Changing Financial System." Jackson Hole, WY. August 21–23.

Kelly, Bryan. 2009. "Risk Premia and the Conditional Tails of Stock Returns." Working Paper. NYU Stern School of Business.

Kishimoto, N. 1989. "Pricing Contingent Claims under Interest Rate and Asset Price Risk." *Journal of Finance* 45 (3): 571–89.

Korinek, Anton. 2010. "Systemic Risk-Taking: Amplification Effects, Externalities, and Regulatory Responses." Working Paper. University of Maryland.

Lehar, A. 2005. "Measuring Systemic Risk: A Risk Management Approach." *Journal of Banking and Finance* 29:2577–603.

Margrabe, William. 1978. "The Value of an Option to Exchange One Asset for Another." *Journal of Finance* 33:177–86.

Morris, Stephen, and Hyun Song Shin. 2008. "Financial Regulation in a System Context." *Brookings Papers on Economic Activity* Fall:229–74.

Peltzman, Sam. 1976. "Toward a More General Theory of Regulation." *Journal of Law and Economics* 19:211–40.

Perotti, Enrico, and Javier Suarez. 2011. "A Pigovian Approach to Liquidity Regulation." CEPR Discussion Paper no. DP8271. Washington, DC: Center for Economic and Policy Research.

Reinhart, Carmen M., and Kenneth S. Rogoff. 2008a. "Is the 2007 US Sub-Prime Financial Crisis So Different? An International Historical Comparison." *American Economic Review: Papers & Proceedings* 98 (2): 339–44.

———. 2008b. "This Time Is Different: A Panoramic View of Eight Centuries of Financial Crises." NBER Working Paper no. 13882. Cambridge, MA: National Bureau of Economic Research, March.

Rosenberg, Joshua. 2000. "Asset Pricing Puzzles: Evidence from Options Markets." Leonard N. Stern School Finance Department Working Paper Series 99-025. New York University.

Rubinstein, Mark. 1976. "The Valuation of Uncertain Income Streams and the Pricing of Options." *Bell Journal of Economics and Management Science* 7:407–25.

Segoviano, Miguel, and Charles Goodhart. 2009. "Banking Stability Measures." IMF Working Paper 09/04. Washington, DC: International Monetary Fund.

Stapleton, R. C., and M. G. Subrahmanyam. 1984. "The Valuation of Multivariate Contingent Claims in Discrete Time Models." *Journal of Finance* 39:207–28.

Stigler, George. 1971. "The Theory of Economic Regulation." *Bell Journal of Economics and Management Science* 2:3–21.

Stulz, Rene M. 1982. "Options on the Minimum or the Maximum of Two Risky Assets: Analysis and Applications." *Journal of Financial Economics* 10 (2): 161–85.

Tarashev, Nikola, Claudio Borio, and Kostas Tsatsaronis. 2009. "Allocating Systemic Risk to Individual Institutions: Methodology and Policy Applications." Working Paper. Bank for International Settlements. Basel: BIS.

Wall, Larry. 1989. "A Puttable Subordinated Debt Plan for Reducing Future Deposit Insurance Losses." *Federal Reserve Bank of Atlanta Economic Review* 74 (4): 2–17.

Comment   Mathias Drehmann

In response to the global financial crisis, many policymakers have called for supplementing microprudential regulation focusing on institution-specific

Mathias Drehmann is a senior economist in the Monetary and Economic Department of the Bank for International Settlements.

The views expressed in this comment are those of the author and do not necessarily reflect those of the BIS. I would like to thank Nikola Tarashev for helpful comments. For acknowledgments, sources of research support, and disclosure of the author's material financial relationships, if any, please see http://www.nber.org/chapters/c12064.ack.

risks with a macroprudential approach, taking account of system-wide interactions and externalities (e.g., G20 2009; FSF 2009). Broadly speaking, the macroprudential approach can be separated along two dimensions (see BIS 2009). First, there is a time dimension related to the procyclical nature of the financial system. Second, there is the cross-sectional dimension, as the failure of one institution may have severe ramifications for other participants in the system. Recent reforms by the Basel Committee (2010, 2011) address both dimensions by proposing countercyclical capital buffers and surcharges for globally systemically important banks. Yet many questions remain open.

The chapter by Acharya, Pedersen, Philippon and Richardson (henceforth APPR) provides a valuable contribution in this area, as it discusses several methods to determine potential regulatory surcharges to force banks to internalize the externalities of financial crises: regulatory stress tests, statistical-based measures of capital losses, pricing of contingent capital insurance, and market-based prices of insuring this risk. I will abstain from discussing each method separately.[1] Instead, I want to highlight that the authors take one particular perspective on what constitutes systemic risk and the systemic importance of individual banks. And as I will show, different perspectives can lead to materially different conclusions.

The Nature of Systemic Risk

The chapter begins by defining "that systemic risk emerges when the aggregate capitalization of the financial sector is low." Also, that the breakdown of intermediation in such a situation would lead to severe consequences to the real economy. While there is no universally agreed-upon definition of systemic risk, this definition shares important elements with most other definitions (Borio and Drehmann 2009). First, it focuses on the financial system as a whole, as opposed to individual institutions. Second, it does not consider the financial system in isolation, but thinks about welfare in terms of the real economy.

Ideally, systemic risk measurement would not only assess the aggregate capitalization of the financial sector, but it would also capture other important facets of systemic risk such as liquidity. In addition, the measurement approach would be broad enough to take into account other determinants such as substitutability or complexity, which have been identified to influence the systemic importance of banks (BCBS 2011). Operationally, though, such a broad scope is impossible to implement, unless simple indicators are used. However, an indicator approach clearly has its own drawbacks. The

---

1. Given current technologies it is highly unlikely that stress tests can be effectively used as a tool to measure a bank's systemic importance ahead of crisis (see Borio, Drehmann, and Tsatsaronis 2011).

focus on capital is therefore a useful first step, which I will also adopt for the remainder of my discussion.

Different Perspectives on Measuring the Systemic Importance of Banks

At the heart of the chapter is the idea that the regulatory system has to be changed to set incentives for financial firms to limit their contributions to systemic risk, or alternatively, to reduce their systemic importance. I fully support this, and the question—which is also the main question of the chapter—is how. But before engaging in this discussion, let me distinguish what I mean by systemic risk and systemic importance. Within the context of APPR, I would prefer to define the expected system-wide capital shortfall (conditional on crises) as a measure of system-wide risk, and each bank's expected capital shortfall (conditional on crises) as a bank-specific measure of systemic importance. This would also underline a nice feature of their approach, as their framework of the sum of bank-specific measures of systemic importance adds up to the level of overall system-wide risk.

APPR suggest a range of methods to calibrate capital surcharges. Nonetheless, the authors take one specific perspective of what constitutes systemic importance. Other perspectives are possible. For example, the Basel Committee (2011) associates a banks' systemic importance by its impact on the rest of the system, should it default. This system-wide "LGD" is then proxied by indicators. CoVar, as suggested by Adrian and Brunnermeier (2009), is another alternative.

As APPR, Drehmann and Tarashev (2011a) (henceforth DT 2011a) measure a bank's systemic importance as its share in the overall level of system-wide risk. They differ from APPR along two dimensions.

First, DT (2011a) measure system-wide risk differently. Drehmann and Tarashev (2011a) adopt the perspective of a macroprudential regulator, which measures system-wide risk by the expected credit losses that the banking system as a whole may impose on nonbanks in systemic events. These events, in turn, are characterized by aggregate losses exceeding a critical level; that is, financial crises in the language of APPR.

Second and more important, DT (2011a) explore two approaches, which decompose the same quantum of system-wide risk, but allocate it differently across individual institutions. This is illustrated in figures 5C.1 and 5C.2, taken from Drehmann and Tarashev (2011b).

The first approach is equivalent to the perspective taken by APPR, which starts by focusing on systemic events or, in the language of APPR, financial crises (shaded area in the left-hand panel of figure 5C.1). It then measures the systemic importance of a bank, say bank i, as the expected losses incurred by its nonbank creditors in these events. This approach equates systemic importance with the expected participation of individual banks in systemic events. Thus, DT (2011a) label it the participation approach

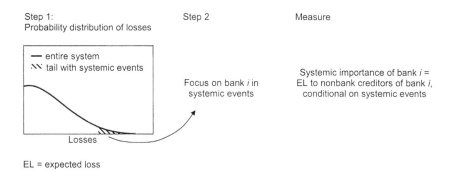

Step 2

Measure

Focus on bank *i* in
systemic events

Systemic importance of bank *i* =
EL to nonbank creditors of bank *i*,
conditional on systemic events

EL = expected loss

Fig. 5C.1   Participation approach (PA)

(PA). Economically, PA equals the actuarially fair premium that the bank would have to pay to a provider of insurance against losses it may incur in a systemic event.

Importantly, a bank's participation in systemic events is conceptually different from its contribution to system-wide risk. Consider, for example, a bank that is small in the sense that it can impose only small losses on its nonbank creditors. As this bank can participate little in systemic events, PA assigns only limited systemic importance to it. The same bank, however, might be highly interconnected in the interbank market and contribute materially to system-wide risk by transmitting distress from one bank to another. As PA is not designed to capture such transmission mechanisms, DT (2011a) propose an alternative: the contribution approach (CA). The

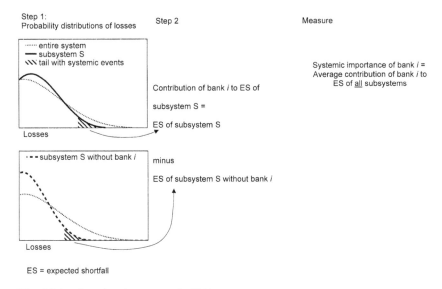

Step 1:
Probability distributions of losses

Step 2

Measure

Contribution of bank *i* to ES of

subsystem S =

ES of subsystem S

minus

ES of subsystem S without bank *i*

Systemic importance of bank *i* =
Average contribution of bank *i* to
ES of all subsystems

ES = expected shortfall

Fig. 5C.2   Contribution approach (CA)

CA accounts explicitly for the fact that a bank contributes to systemic risk through its exposure to exogenous shocks, by propagating shocks through the system, and by being itself vulnerable to propagated shocks.

Contribution approach is rooted in a methodology first proposed by Shapley (1953) for the allocation across individual players of the value created in a cooperative game. As a measure for systemic importance it was first suggested by Tarashev, Borio, and Tsatsaronis (2010) and extended by DT (2011a) to allow for interbank markets.[2] Details are discussed in these papers but the intuition behind this methodology is quite simple. One could use the level of risk an individual bank generates in isolation as a measure of systemic importance. But such an approach would miss the contribution of each bank to the risk of others. Similarly, it is not enough to consider only the marginal-risk contribution of a single bank, calculated as the difference between the system-wide risk with and without the bank. The reason is that this calculation ignores the complexity of bilateral relationships, which is especially pronounced when interbank exposures can propagate shocks within the system through a potentially long chain of market participants. The Shapley methodology accounts fully for such interactions by ascribing to individual institutions a weighted average of the marginal contributions each makes to the risk in each possible subsystem. The derivation of such a marginal contribution for a given subsystem S is illustrated in figure 5C.2.

Analyzing a system of twenty large globally active banks, DT (2011a) show that the participation and contribution approach can disagree substantially about the systemic importance of a particular bank. This can affect not only the level but also the rank-ordering of the systemic importance of banks in a system.

The differences between PA and CA can be most easily explained with a stylized system of five banks, shown in figure 5C.3. Four banks are typical in that they borrow to and lend from nonbanks. DT (2011a) label them periphery banks (PB) as they only engage in one-sided interbank transaction: two of these banks are interbank lenders and the other two are interbank borrowers. The fifth bank is a central counterparty, which only intermediates between these four banks and does not engage with nonbank customers. The balance sheets and the measures of systemic importance under PA and CA are shown in table 5C.1.[3]

Intuitively, the central counterparty should be systemically important as contagion can only spread via this bank. However, the perspective taken by

2. The contribution approach in a setting with interbank markets has also been studied by Gauthier, Lehar, and Souissi (2010) and Liu and Staum (2010).

3. The technical derivation of the measures is discussed in detail by DT (2011a). It is based on a simulation procedure that starts by drawing a set of correlated exogenous shocks, which determines which banks experience fundamental defaults. If there is a fundamental default, the ensuing contagion defaults are derived via the "clearing algorithm" of Eisenberg and Noe (2001). To construct a probability distribution of these losses, one million sets of exogenous shocks are drawn.

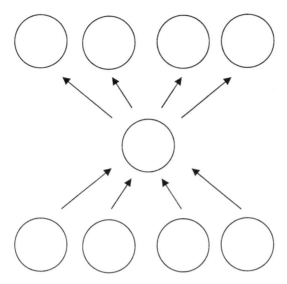

Fig. 5C.3   The hypothetical interbank system

APPR—the participation approach PA—assigns it *zero* systemic importance (last column of table 5C.1). The reason for this is twofold. First, the
central counterparty does not lend to nonbanks, therefore it can only default
because of counterparty credit risk in the interbank market. Second, since
it does not borrow from nonbanks, the expected loss of nonbank creditors
conditional on a crisis is zero. Thus, by design it can *never participate* in
systemic events. That said, this bank creates indirect links between lending
and borrowing periphery banks, thereby *contributing* to system-wide risk,
which the contribution approach CA captures correctly.

The difference in the measured systemic importance of the peripheral
interbank lenders and borrowers (last two rows in table 5C.1) between the
two approaches also reflects fundamental factors. To understand why, consider an interbank transaction without a central counterparty, which the
interbank lender funds by nonbank deposits and the interbank borrower
uses to buy assets. Assume also that this interbank link leads to contagion
from the borrower to the lender in some systemic events. Thus, the link raises
the expected participation of the lending bank in systemic events but leaves
the participation of the borrowing bank unchanged. And since participation
in systemic events is all that matters to PA, this approach attributes the entire
risk associated with this interbank link to the interbank lender. By contrast,
a key property of the Shapley value is that risk is split equally between the
two counterparties. In this way, CA captures the idea that an interconnected
bank can contribute to system-wide risk through two channels: by directly
imposing losses on its own nonbank creditors, and by indirectly imposing
losses on the nonbank creditors of banks from which it has borrowed.

Table 5C.1   Differences in measure of systemic importance

	Balance sheets[a]				Measures of systemic importance[b]	
	EQ	NBL	IBL	IBA	CA	PA
Central counterparty	3	0	32	32	**0.22**	**0**
PB lender	5	87	0	8	**0.58**	**0.70**
PB borrower	5	87	8	0	**0.58**	**0.52**

[a]PB: periphery bank; EQ: equity; NBL: nonbank liabilities (= size); IBL: interbank liabilities; IBA: interbank assets. There are two PB lenders and two PB borrowers in the system. To satisfy the balance sheet identity, we assume that the central counterparty invests three units in a risk-free asset.
[b]All values are in percent. The PA and CA values are expressed per unit of system size. All other values pertain to a bank in the particular group. The f.PD and c.PD are fundamental and contagion PDs, respectively. For further details see Drehmann and Tarashev (2011a).

Since PA and CA are valid alternative measures of systemic importance but provide materially different results, it is essential that users have a clear understanding of which measure is designed to address which question. If the goal is to design a scheme for insuring against losses in systemic events, then the participation approach provides the natural measure. And this is what APPR propose to do, most clearly with their third and fourth measure. Yet, the authors argue repeatedly that "the idea of systemic risk surcharges is that they provide incentives for the financial firm to limit its *contributions* to systemic risk" (my emphasis). If this is the case, however, the contribution approach should be used.

Measuring Systemic Risk with Market Prices

With the exception of stress tests, the authors rely on markets either directly, to price systemic risk, or indirectly, as market data are used to derive the measures. For listed banks, data availability is therefore not an issue. Computationally, the calculations are also relatively straightforward. Together, this makes the implementation very simple.[4] Yet, it puts the onus on markets to price systemic risk correctly.

It is more than doubtful that markets can be effective in pricing systemic risk because of what we call the "paradox of financial instability" (Borio and Drehmann 2009): the system looks strongest precisely when it is most vulnerable. Credit growth and asset prices are unusually strong, leverage mea-

4. The approach by Tarashev, Borio, and Tsatsaronis (2010) or DT (2011a) is computationally more cumbersome as it involves the derivation of expected shortfall of all 2^N subgroups in a system of N banks.

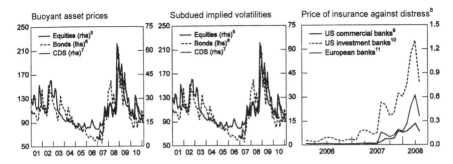

Fig. 5C.4   Footprints of the paradox of financial instability, the US example

Source: Drehmann, Borio, and Tsatsaronis (2011).

Notes:

[1]End 2001 = 100.

[2]S&P 500.

[3]S&P Case Shiller index, twenty cities.

[4]Five-year on-the-run CDX.NA.HY 100 spread, in basis points.

[5]VIX index (implied volatility on S&P 500).

[6]MOVE index (implied volatility on treasury options).

[7]Implied volatility on the five-year-on-the-run CDX.NA.HY 100 spread.

[8]In percent, based on CDS spreads. Risk neutral expectation of credit losses that equal or exceed 15 percent of the corresponding segments' combined liabilities in 2006 (per unit of exposure to these liabilities); risk neutral expectations comprise expectations of actual losses and attitudes toward risk. Taken from Tarashev and Zhu (2008).

[9]Ten banks headquartered in the United States.

[10]Eight banks headquartered in the United States.

[11]Sixteen universal banks headquartered in Europe.

sured at market prices is artificially low, profits and asset quality are especially healthy, and risk premia and volatilities are unusually low precisely when risk is highest. What looks like low risk is, in fact, a sign of aggressive risk taking. Figure 5C.4 illustrates this point based on the behavior of market prices during the run-up to the crisis in the United States (left-hand and center panels). This perverse behavior infects more formal measures of systemic risks that use market prices, including correlations. This is also the case for implied price of insurance against systemic event (right-hand side panel), which is a measure of system-wide risk very much along the lines of APPR (see Tarashev and Zhu 2008). Clearly, these measures were unusually subdued ahead of the crisis and showed signs of trouble only once overt financial market stress emerged in mid-2007.

The authors are aware of this problem. Their measures, for example, decline in the run-up to the crisis (e.g., table 5.3 in APPR). They argue that more sophisticated methods using long-run volatilities can partly address this issue. Given the behavior of credit default swap (CDS) spreads (left-hand panel, figure 5C.4), which should focus on downside risks in the future, I am skeptical that this will truly help.

Nonetheless, there is value in these measures as they seem to be successful in identifying systemically important firms, as judged, for example, by out-of-sample tests for the recent crisis. This is clearly useful information for policymakers and practitioners. Given the state of the literature, more generally, it seems most prudent anyhow to analyze a diverse range of tools to measure systemic risk and systemic importance such as simulation models, network approaches, general equilibrium models, simple indicators, and the like.[5] The method proposed in this chapter could be one of these tools and the conference as a whole could be a good starting point to explore potential avenues.

References

Adrian, T., and M. Brunnermeier. 2009. "CoVarR." Working Paper. Federal Reserve Bank of New York.
Bank for International Settlements (BIS). 2009. *Annual Report.* Basel: BIS.
Basel Committee on Banking Supervision (BCBS). 2010. *Basel III: A Global Regulatory Framework for More Resilient Banks and Banking Systems.* Basel: BIS.
———. 2011. *Global Systemically Important Banks: Assessment Methodology and the Additional Loss Absorbency Requirement.* Basel: BIS.
Borio, C., and M. Drehmann. 2009. "Towards an Operational Framework for Financial Stability: 'Fuzzy' Measurement and Its Consequences." BIS Working Paper 284. Basel: BIS.
Borio, C., M. Drehmann, and K. Tsatsaronis. 2011. "Stress-Testing Macro Stress Testing: Does It Live Up to Expectations?" Paper presented at the Office of Financial Research/Financial Stability Oversight Council (OFR/FSOC) conference on Macroprudential Tools.
Drehmann, M., C. Borio, and K. Tsatsaronis. 2011. "Characterizing the Financial Cycle: Don't Lose Sight of the Medium Term!" Paper presented at the Reserve Bank of Chicago-ECB 14th Annual International Banking Conference, "The Role of Central Banks in Financial Stability: How Has It Changed?" Chicago, Illinois. November 10–11.
Drehmann, M., and N. Tarashev. 2011a. "Measuring the Systemic Importance of Interconnected Banks." BIS Working Paper 342. Basel: BIS.
———. 2011b. "Systemic Importance: Some Simple Indicators." BIS Quarterly Review, March. Basel: BIS.
Eisenberg, L., and T. H. Noe. 2001. "Systemic Risk in Financial Systems." *Management Science* 47:236–49.
Financial Stability Forum (FSF). 2009. *Report of the Financial Stability Forum on Addressing Procyclicality in the Financial System.*
G20. 2009. "Declaration on Strengthening the Financial System." London. April 2.
Gauthier, C., A. Lehar, and M. Souissi. 2010. "Macroprudential Regulation and Systemic Capital Requirements." Bank of Canada Working Paper 2010-4.

---

5. Besides the chapters in this conference volume, Borio and Drehmann (2009) provide a recent survey about different approaches to measure financial instability.

Liu, M., and J. Staum. 2010. "Systemic Risk Components in a Network Model of Contagion." Working Paper. Northwestern University.

Shapley, L. 1953. "A Value for n-Person Games." In *Annals of Mathematical Studies,* vol. 28, edited by H. Kuhn and A. Tucker, 307–17. Princeton, NJ: Princeton University Press.

Tarashev, N., C. Borio, and K. Tsatsaronis. 2010. "Allocating Systemic Risk to Individual Institutions: Methodology and Policy Applications." Unpublished Manuscript. Olin Business School at Washington University in St. Louis.

Tarashev, N., and H. Zhu. 2008. "Market Perceptions of Systemic Risk in the Banking Industry." *BIS Quarterly Review* March:6–8. Basel: BIS.

The Quantification of Systemic Risk and Stability
New Methods and Measures

Romney B. Duffey

6.1 The Risk Measures and Assumptions

Financial markets do not just involve money and statistics; just like all other modern systems, they include people. Therefore, to understand and predict markets it is essential to understand people, predicting their actions, mistakes, skills, decisions, responses, learning, and motivation. To understand people we must explicitly include their learned and unlearned behaviors with experience and risk exposure. This is what we attempt here, based on what has been learnt from other systems data. We treat all outcomes—such as failures, crises, busts, and collapses—as occurring with some probability, and that these adverse or unwelcome events reflect the inherent stability characteristics of financial markets. As noted by a well-known investor (Soros 2009): "Since markets are unstable, there are systemic risks in addition to risks affecting individual market participants. . . . Participants may ignore these systemic risks . . . but regulators cannot."

We wish to make a failure *prediction,* using objective measures for risk and risk exposure, since all homo-technological systems have failures and we learn from them.[1] The past outcomes for all homo-technological *sys-*

Romney B. Duffey was the Principal Scientist at Atomic Energy of Canada Limited and is presently the principal and founder of DSM Associates Inc.

The author thanks the discussers and reviewers from the economic and financial community for their insightful reactions, encouragement, criticism, comments, and suggestions on the chapter; the NBER for providing both the opportunity and the forum to present this work; Joseph Haubrich for proposing and pursuing the entire publication process; and AECL for supporting this research. For acknowledgments, sources of research support, and disclosure of the author's material financial relationships, if any, please see http://www.nber.org/chapters/c12060.ack.

1. We define a homo-technological system as the complex and inseparable involvement of humans in any and all aspects of design, construction, operation, management, maintenance, regulation, production, control, conduct, and decisions.

tems (industrial, transportation, production facilities) show clear evidence of trends, and the failures, busts, and crises are due to both known and unknown causes and may be "rare" or "unlikely."

Inability to predict failures is due to the improper and incomplete treatment of human error, learning, and risk taking as part of the overall system. Traditional risk analysis and prediction techniques do not explicitly include the dynamic variability due to the inherent human characteristics embedded in and inseparable from the system. All major events and disasters, especially financial ones, include the dominant contribution not only from individual mistakes, but also management failures and corporate-wide and regulatory errors and blunders. *Risk is a measure of our uncertainty, and that uncertainty is determined by the probability of error.* We must also estimate and predict risk that also includes the unknown or rare event.

We try to find a dynamic objective measure that would actually anticipate instability, thus allowing predicting the onset of failure or large excursions (i.e., hence managing that risk and its consequences—equivalent to "emergency preparedness"). In the popular finance articles, the risk mitigation process seems to be referred to as "pricking bubbles," and traditionally involves some kind of ad-hoc debt, credit and trading limitations, and/or restraints. These types of regulation or reactions are very much a posteriori and case-by-case, but are neither predictive nor general. As noted for risk in *Nature Nanotechnology:* "the real issue is how to regulate in the face of uncertainty" (Brown 2009, 209). Our work suggests that learning is effective as a risk management and predictive tool, but only if we have adopted the "correct" risk exposure and uncertainty measures that we now attempt to determine.

Obviously, as humans we learn from experience, both good and bad. We also take risks and must make mistakes in order to improve. A universal curve is derived for both collective and individual learning trends, naturally including the inevitability of outcomes and risk. Based on our work studying and analyzing over 200 years of real data on and for risk in technological, medical, industrial, and financial systems, five measures are presented and discussed for the objective measure of risk, failure probability, and risk exposure. Correct measure(s) for experience enable the prediction and uncertainty estimation for the entire range of rare, repeat, and unknown outcomes (e.g., major industrial disasters, facility accidents and explosions, everyday auto accidents, aircraft crashes, financial busts, and market collapses).

We also introduce and present the unifying concept of risk and uncertainty derived from the information entropy as a quantitative measure of randomness and disorder. We show how this allows comparative risk estimation and the discerning of insufficient learning. Since these risk measures and learning trends have been largely derived from data including the financial arena, we show how to generalize these to include the presence of market pressures, financial issues, and risk measures. We define and present the bases, analyses, and results for new risk measures for the quantitative *predictions* of risk exposure, failure, and collapse using relevant experience including:

1. Universal Learning (ULC), similar to the Black-Scholes concept
2. Risk Ratios (RR) and exposure, as derived from empirical hazard curves
3. Repeat Event Predictions (REP) or never happening again, equivalent to birthday matching and reoccurring echoes
4. Rare and Unknown Outcome occurrences (UU), as in the black swan concept
5. System and Organizational Stability (SOS) or resilience criteria, using the information entropy concept

We provide quantified examples for production processes, transportation losses, major hazards, and financial exposure. These new concepts also provide the probability of success, the emergence of order, and the understanding and quantification of risk perception. Note that these measures replace and do not include in any way the standard financial techniques utilizing net value, value at risk, or variations about or from the mean.

In our analysis we assume financial markets are just another homo-technological system and the past failure rates inform the future, and that the inherent apparent randomness and chaos conveys and contains information. We avoid using traditional statistical approaches where past failure frequencies define invariant future failure probability distributions. We also explicitly avoid the impossible modeling of all the internal details of assets and trading, and avoid any filtering of data; we consider only emergent trends at system level based on what we know. We treat risk as determined by experience or risk exposure, thus avoiding using comfortable calendar time intervals (i.e., as in daily, hourly, monthly, quarterly, or annual reporting) as markets operate according to their experience. As in medical and other systems, this risk measure is often determined by the dynamic accumulated "volume," which also provides the learning opportunity. Our research approach is predicated on extrapolating known and unknown past failure rates based on *experience* and future dynamic risk exposure, and is tested against data, so the concept and measures of risk and stability are truly falsifiable.

6.2   Risk: How We Learn from Experience and What We Know about Risk Prediction

Risk is measured by our *uncertainty,* and the measure of uncertainty is probability.

The definition, use, and concepts of risk adopted in this chapter utilizes measures for risk exposure and for uncertainty that encompass and are consistent with that proposed before in the financial literature (Holton 2004, 19):

Risk entails two essential components:

- Exposure, and
- Uncertainty

Risk, then, is exposure to a proposition of which one is uncertain.

What is the risk of system failure? What is the measure for exposure? What is the measure of uncertainty? To answer those questions we must understand how and why systems fail, and show how to make a prediction, noting that while financial systems constitute a distinct discipline with its own terminology, they actually must behave just like all others that are prone to the all too common vagaries, actions, and motivations of humans. We use probability and information entropy to quantify uncertainty, and past and future experience to quantify exposure.

We first review what is known and not known about predicting and managing risk in industrial, energy, transportation, nuclear, medical, and manufacturing systems, and the associated risk exposure measures. We address the question of the predictability of a large systems failure, or collapse, and the necessary concepts related to risk quantification and system stability that are emerging from the physical sciences, cognitive psychology, information theory, and multiple industrial arenas that are relevant to current financial and economic market and stability concerns. We have defined the risk of any outcome (being a proposition of which one is uncertain) as caused by uncertainty, and that the measure of the uncertainty is probability, p. We attempt to use some of these risk concepts, learning, and applications from mainly operational systems to inform risk prediction for financial systems.

Risks are due to the probability/possibility of an adverse event, outcome, or accident. Simply put, we learn from our mistakes, correcting our errors along the way. We all know that we have had a serious failure of the financial and investments markets due to excessive risk exposure and losses. The key observation is that markets are random, which is confirmed by sampling distributions, but we also know that conventional statistics of normal distributions (such as used in VaR and CoVaR techniques) do not work when applied to predicting dynamically changing accident, event, and outcome trends (Taleb 2007; Duffey and Saull 2008). So while the instantaneous behavior appears to be random and hence unpredictable, *the failure to predict is due to the failure to properly include the systematic influence of human element, which is nonlinear, dynamic, and varies with experience and risk exposure.*

In industrial operations, the cardinal rule of operation applicable to *any* system is due to Howlett (2001), which is:

> Humans must remain in control of their machinery at all times. Any time the machine operates without the knowledge, understanding and assent of its human controllers, the machine is out of control. (5)

Furthermore, the limits to operation are defined by a Safe Operating Envelope, with limits that include margins and uncertainty that define "guarantees" for the avoidance of failure. Risk management is then employed to protect or *mitigate* the consequences of failures that might occur anyway (Howlett 2001). These well-tried concepts are all translatable to and usable in financial systems, just as they are for industrial systems, since *all systems include human involvement and hence involve the uncertainty due to risk taking and learning.*

We have previously shown that the *dominant* contribution to *all* management and system failures, outcomes, and accidents is from that same inextricable and inseparable human involvement. Be they airplane, auto, train, or stock market crashes, the same learning principles also apply. We have shown that to quantify risk we must include the learning behavior, quantifying outcomes rates, and probabilities due to our experience from human decision making and involvement with modern technological and social systems, including industrial, transportation, chemical, financial, and manufacturing technologies (Duffey and Saull 2002, 2008). These ideas and concepts include naturally not only the collective system (e.g., a bank, railway, power plant, or airline) but also the individual human reliability (e.g., an investor, driver, manager, or pilot).

What we know is that provided we have prior (outcome or failure) data we can now predict accurately the future outcome rates, and define the risk exposure based on the past known and the future expected experience. That we can learn from experience is what all the data show, and that experience is the past risk exposure we have all so painfully acquired as a human society. The experience measure is a surrogate for our very human risk exposure, of how long, how many, and how much we have been exposed to the chance of an outcome, or to the risk of an error.

The prediction of the future rate of failures or outcomes is given from the Learning Hypothesis, being simply the principle that humans naturally learn from their mistakes, by correcting and unlearning during and from the accumulated experience, both good and bad. The experience—however it is defined or measured—represents also not only the learning opportunity, but a measure of the risk exposure. The probability of error, accident, catastrophe, or mistake (p) is determined by the failure rate, which derives from the number of either a successful or a failed (unsuccessful) outcome. The rate of outcomes decreases exponentially with experience, in the form of a Universal Learning Curve (ULC). Over 200 years of experience and millions of prior, past, or historic data allow the ULC to be defined. The validation derives from massive data sets of both frequent and rare events (Duffey and Saull 2002, 2008), which now includes multiple sources and outcomes, with the historical time spans covering the past 200 years, and major data available from the last 50 or more years.

We analyzed auto passenger deaths, railway injuries, coal mining deaths, oil spills at sea, commercial airline near-misses, and recreational boating deaths. Globally, the learning data set we have amassed now contains multiple technologies worldwide: coal and gold mining, 20 million pulmonary disease deaths, cataract operations, infant heart surgeries, the international total of rocket launches, pilot deaths in Australia, train derailments and danger signals passed on railways, and notably, the anti-missile interception and destruction effectiveness over England of German VI bombs in World War II. Economic data on specific unit price variations with increasing output or commercial sales demonstrating the learning trends and so-called "progress curves" for manufacturing are observed for millions of units produced in factories and production lines.

The millions of outcome data analyzed are well represented by the Learning Hypothesis (Duffey and Saull 2002, 2008), which states that the rate of decrease of the outcome or failure rate, λ, with experience units, τ, is proportional to that same rate. Thus, very simply, the differential equation is the proportionality:

$$\left(\frac{d\lambda}{d\tau} \right) \propto - \lambda.$$

The previous cases and data sets show variations in the learning constant: when learning trends are present an average learning rate "constant" of proportionality value of $k \sim 3$ is reasonable (see also figure 6.1).

Systems exist that do not show significant learning, as measured by decrease or declining loss and error trends, are those where the continuing influence and reliance on the human element and historic practices overrides massive changes in technology and the robustness of system design.

6.3   Individual Actions: Predictable and Unpredictable

It is reasonable to ask how the behavior of entire systems reflect the individual interactions within them, and vice versa, including the myriads of managers, accountants, traders, investors, speculators, lawyers, and regulators that make up a financial market or system. This link is between the unobserved multitudinous and microscopic interactions and the observed macroscopic and emergent system trends, distributions, responses, and outcomes. For just individual actions (as opposed to system outcomes), data are available in the psychological literature from many thousands of individual human subject task and learning trials. These trials have established the rate of skill acquisition as described by the so-called Laws of Practice. We have shown (Duffey and Saull 2008) that these laws are entirely consistent with the ULC for entire systems and have the same learning constant (or K value) with repeated trials. Thus, the data show that external system-learning behavior mirrors the internal learning trends of the individuals within. The

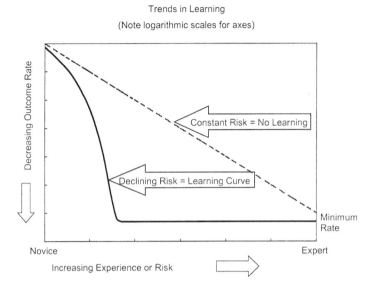

Fig. 6.1   **The ULC and Constant Risk Lines: Failure rates with increasing experience and/or risk exposure**

predicted probability of error also agrees with published nuclear plants events, simulator tests, and system recovery action times. Probabilities for power restoration for power losses at over 100 US nuclear power plants are also in agreement, as is the power blackout repair probability for customers over a period of several days.

In all these data, we have n outcomes occurring in some experience, τ. The resulting form of the learning curve is shown in figure 6.1, which is a log-log plot with arbitrary units on each axis of the rate of the undesirable errors and outcomes, $dn/d\tau$, versus the accumulated experience, which is a surrogate for the risk exposure during actual system operation. This *risk exposure* or *experience measure, τ,* is unique for each and every system: for aircraft it is the number of flights flown, for railways the train-miles traveled, for ships the shipping-years afloat, for manufacturing the number of units produced, for human errors in decision making, skill acquisition, and response time it is the number of repetitive trials.

As we increase our experience and risk exposure as both individuals and systems, the event or outcome rate depends on whether, either collectively and/or individually, we follow a learning curve of decreasing risk or not, or if we are somewhere in between. In figure 6.1, the line labeled "learning curve" (from the Minimum Error Rate Equation, or MERE) is the desirable ULC, where learning occurs to rapidly reduce the rate. This is the most likely path, and is also that of the *least* risk as we progress from being a "novice" with little experience to becoming an "expert with progressively more exposure and experience." There are no "zero defects"; there is always a finite, nonzero residual rate of error, λ_m, so say all of the world's data. The equation that describes the learning curve is an exponential with experience:[2]

Failure rate, $\lambda(\tau)$ = Minimum rate, λ_m

+ (Initial rate, λ_0 − Minimum rate, λ_m) × exp−$(k\tau)$.

If we simply replace the rate, λ, by the value or specific cost, C, and change the sign, the MERE turns out to be identical in form to that of the trending part of the Black-Scholes equation for portfolio cost and value. For manufacturing or production there is a "tail" of nonzero value that corresponds to the minimum possibly achievable, C_m, in any competitive market system. Reducing cost with increasing volume, or units produced, thus also holds for manufacturing and production cost decreases, just as patient volume does for improving individual surgical skill, thus reducing inadvertent deaths with increasing patient count (practice or trials). The difference is that in these cases the experience parameter, τ, is conventionally taken as either time (for stock or equity values variation) or accumulated units manufactured (for production prices changes), and a key question is what measure to adopt in financial systems for the relevant experience and risk exposure.

Since figure 6.1 is a log-log plot (scale units are factors of ten on each axis), any line of *constant risk* is then a straight line of slope minus one, where the event rate, λ, times experience, τ, is the constant number of events, n. Hence, $\lambda = n/\tau$, and for the first or rare event, $n = 1$, which is the dashed "constant risk" line for any first or rare event shown in figure 6.1. The rate decreases inversely with the risk exposure or experience, so importantly, at little or no experience or little learning, *the initial rate is given by* $\lambda_0 = 1/\tau$, which is exactly the form of the rare events as derived from commercial aircraft crashes. As we shall see, this risk path is the initial rate and also emphasizes the "fat tail" that worries and confounds conventional risk and value analysts. We call this prediction a White Elephant when it underestimates the risk, since it has no value as a prediction.

In terms of probabilities as a measure of risk, instead of rates, the previous equation can be integrated to yield an expression that in words implies:

Risk exposure probability is due to the minimum risk *plus* the initial risk exposure *less* the reduction in risk due to learning.

For any real, not hypothetical system the minimum achievable failure rate does not appear to change and has not changed for over 200 years, depending solely on our experience and risk exposure measure for a given system. So conversely, the *systemic risk (the probability of failure or a bust) is dependent on the risk exposure measure.*

---

2. See the definitions and derivations in the appendix.

6.4   The Seven Commonalities of Rare and Terrible Events: Risk Ratios and Predictions

What do large disasters, crises, busts, and collapses in financial systems like the Great Crash of 2008 (IMF 2009b) have in common with the other major events? These have happened in multiple technologies and industries, such as in industries as diverse as aerospace (Columbia and Challenger Shuttle losses) (CAIB 2003), nuclear (Davis-Besse plant vessel corrosion) (NRC 2008), oil (Deepwater Horizon explosion and leak) (US National Commission 2011), chemical (Toulouse ammonia plant explosion) (Barthelemy 2001), transportation (the Quebec overpass collapse) (Commission of Inquiry 2007a, 2007b), and the recent devastating nuclear reactor meltdowns at the Fukushima plants in Japan. The common features, or, as we may call them, the Seven Themes, cover the aspects of causation, rationalization, retribution, and prevention, ad nauseam.

First, these major losses, failures, and outcomes all share the same very same and very human Four Phases or warning signs: the unfolding of the precursors and initiating circumstances, the confluence of events and circumstances in unexpected ways, the escalation where the unrecognized unknowingly happens, and afterward, denial and blame shift before final acceptance.

Second, as always, these incidents all involved humans, were not expected but clearly understandable as due to management emphasis on production and profit rather than safety and risk, were from gaps in the operating and management requirements, and from lax inspection and inadequate regulations.

Third, these events have all caused a spate of media coverage, retroactive soul-searching, "culture" studies and surveys, regulation review, revisions to laws, guidelines, and procedures, new limits, and reporting legislation, which all echo perfectly the present emphasis on limits to the bonus culture and risk taking that are or were endemic in certain financial circles.

Fourth, the failures were so-called "rare events" and involved obvious dynamic human lapses and errors, and as such do not follow the usual statistical rules and laws that govern large quasi-static samples, or the multitudinous outcome distributions (like normal, lognormal, and Weibull) that dominate conventional statistical thinking, but clearly require analysis and understanding of the role of human learning, experience, and skill in making mistakes and taking decisions.

Fifth, these events all involve humans operating inside and/or with a system, and contain real information about what we know about what we do not know—being the unexpected, the unknown, the rare and low occurrence rate events—with large consequences and highlighting our own inadequate predictive capability, so that to predict we must use Bayesian-type likelihood estimation.

Sixth, there is the learning paradox that if we do not learn we have more risk, but to learn perversely we must have the very events we seek to avoid, which also have a large and finite risk of reoccurrence. Ultimately, we have more risk from events we have not had the chance to learn about, being the unknown, rare, or unexpected.

Seventh, these events were all preventable but only afterward. Hindsight, soul-searching, and sometimes massive inquiries reveal what was so obvious time after time—the same human fallibilities, performance lapses, supervisory and inspections gaps, bad habits, inadequate rules and legislation, management failures, and risk-taking behaviors that all should have been and were self-evident, and were uncorrected.

We claim to learn from these each time, perhaps introducing corrective actions, revised rules, and lessons learned (Ohlsson 1996), thus hopefully reducing the outcome rate or the chance of reoccurrence. All of these aspects were also evident in the financial failure of 2008, in the collapse of major financial institutions and banks. These rare events are worth examining further as to their repeat frequency and market failure probability: recessions have happened before but 2008 was supposedly somewhat different, as it was reportedly due to unbridled systemic risk, and uncontrolled systemic failure in credit and real estate sectors. This failure of risk management in financial markets led to the analysis that follows, extending the observations, new thinking, and methods developed for understanding other technological systems to the prediction and management of so-called "systemic risk" in financial markets and transactions. We treat and analyze these financial entities as systems that function and behave by learning from experience just like any other system, where we observe the external outcomes and failures due to the unobserved internal activities, management decisions, errors, and risks taken.

The past outcome data provide the past failure rate. To determine the future risk, we must distinguish between the past (statistically, the known prior) and the future (statistically, the unknown posterior). So what does the past tell us about the future? To predict an outcome, any event, we must go beyond what we know, that is, the prior knowledge. Somehow, we have to project ourselves into an unknown future, with some measure of confidence and uncertainty, based on both our rational thoughts and our irrational fears, using what we know about what we do not know. This leads us into the somewhat controversial arena of prediction using statistical reasoning, a subject addressed in great detail elsewhere (Jaynes 2003).

The *conditional* future is dependent, albeit with uncertainty, on the past, as per Bayes reasoning (Jaynes 2003; Bayes 1763, 376). The probability or chance of an unknown event is dependent on something called the *likelihood,* which itself is uncertain but provides a rational framework for projection. The likelihood itself is inversely dependent on the prior number of outcomes, and if there are none so far, we just have the Bayesian failure rate of the past based on our (known) experience to date.

The Likelihood formally adjusts the past, prior, or known probability and produces the future or posterior probability. So conditionally dependent on what we already know we know has already happened in the past, according to the thinking of the Reverend Thomas Bayes (1763) and of Edwin Jaynes' (2003) rigorous analysis:

Future chance (posterior probability, $p(P)$)

= Past or prior probability, p, times Likelihood.

The Likelihood multiplier, $p(L)$, whatever it is and however derived (by physical argument, guess, judgment, evidence, probabilistic reasoning, mathematical rigor, or data analysis) is the conditioning factor that always alters the past whatever and however it is estimated. Even if the past was indeed "normal," the likelihood can even change the future to include rare events and unknown unknowns.

The risk ratio (RR) can then be defined as ratio of the future posterior probability, $p(P)$, of an adverse event (accident, outcome, error, or failure in the future) to some known past or present failure probability, $p(\tau)$, based on the prior accumulated experience, as a function of the future risk exposure or experience, or

$$RR = \frac{p(P)}{p(\tau)}.$$

From the above Bayesian equation this risk ratio is equivalent to defining the Likelihood, $p(L)$, where for low probabilities or rare events the posterior, $p(P)$, itself is numerically very nearly equal to the rate of events, or the failure rate, $p(P) \sim f(\tau) \sim \lambda$. This result follows directly from the so-called "generalized Bayes formula" (Sveshnikov 1968 49, 80; Duffey and Saull 2008) that defines the Likelihood as the ratio of the probability of outcomes occurring in the next experience interval to the probability that outcomes have already occurred during the past experience.

So for low probability events, outcomes, or disasters ($p(\tau) \ll 1$), the risk ratio becomes simply the future predicted by the past since:

$$RR = \frac{p(P)(1 - p(\tau))}{p(\tau)} \sim \frac{p(P)}{p(\tau)} \sim \frac{\lambda(\tau)}{p(\tau)},$$

which is the ratio of the known past rate and prior probability.

We show the risk ratio prediction for rare events with little learning ($k \sim 0.0001$) in figure 6.2 versus a series of curves (k from $0.1 - 0.001$) representing slow to negligible learning, where the risk ratio clearly has a slope varying as, $1/\tau$. The key observation is that the future risk predicted by the risk ratio, RR, still does not fall much below $\sim 10^{-5}$ at large risk exposure, which corresponds to the plateau, or "fat tail," caused by the lowest attainable but finite and nonzero failure rate that is observed for any system anywhere and everywhere in the world.

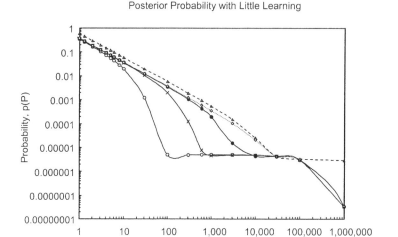

Fig. 6.2   Comparisons of the Risk Ratio Predictions

So what, then, is the resulting Posterior probability, $p(P)$ in the future? It is shown in figure 6.2 for a series of cases with varying learning or knowledge acquisition from increasing risk exposure or accumulated experience. These cases are represented by the range of values shown for the learning "constant," k, where progressively lower values mean less and less learning. As can be seen, if learning is negligible so that k is very small (say, 0.0001) then the event probability decreases almost as a straight line of constant risk, $1/\tau$, as it should; for larger k values a distinct kink or plateau occurs due to the presence of the always finite, nonzero failure rate due to the human involvement.

6.5   Predicting Rare Events: Fat Tails, Black Swans, and White Elephants

Colloquially, a Black Swan is an unexpected and/or rare event, one that dramatically changes prior thinking and expectations.

Because rare events do not happen often, they are also widely misunderstood. Perhaps even previously unobserved, they are called "unknown unknowns" (Rumsfeld 2002), or "Black Swans" (Taleb 2007) precisely because they do not follow the same rules when already having many or frequent events. Think of the space shuttle crashes, the global collapse of financial companies, or an aircraft apparently falling from the sky as it did recently over the Atlantic. These are the things we may or may not have seen before, but certainly did not expect to happen. So when they do happen, perhaps even when being thought not possible, they do not apparently follow the trends, expectations, rules, or knowledge we have built up for more frequent happenings.

There is no assured, easy, or obvious "alarm," indicator, or built-in warning signal, derivable by adjusting filters or data smoothing techniques. As noted in World Bank (2009),

> Whether these alarms are deemed informative depends on their association with subsequent busts. The choice of a threshold above which an alarm is raised presents an important trade-off between the desire for some warning of an impending bust and the costs associated with a false alarm. Nonetheless, even the best indicator failed to raise an alarm one to three years ahead of roughly one-half of all busts since 1985. Thus, asset price busts are difficult to predict.

This is a 50 percent or even chance, which are no better odds than just tossing a coin.

In statistical language and usage, the rare events do not follow or fit in with the usual distributions of previous or expected occurrences. The frequency and/or probability of occurrence lies somewhere outside the usual many expected multiples of the standard deviation for any sample distribution. We may not even have a distribution of prior data anyway. In fact, Taleb (2007) spends a considerable part of his popular book *The Black Swan* discussing, discounting, and dismissing the use of so-called normal distributions such as the Gaussian or bell-shaped curves simply because they do not and cannot account for rare events even though many humans may think that they do. Also rare events, like all events, as we have said, are always due to some apparently unforeseen combination of circumstance, conditions, and combination of things that we did not foresee, and all include the errors in our human made and managed systems (the Seven Themes).

By citing many empirical cases, Taleb (2007) also further argues forcibly that this scale variation destroys any and all credibility of using any Gaussian or normal distribution for *prediction.* In that limited sense, he is right, as conventional sampling statistics based on fitting to some normal distributions using many observations is totally inapplicable for low probability, one-of-a-kind rare, so-far-unobserved or unknown events. To make a true prediction we must still use what we know about what we do not know, and we now know that the *relevant "scale" is in fact our experience or risk exposure,* which is what we have anyway, and is the basis for what we know or do not know about everything.

In figure 6.3, we show the one-on-one head-to-head comparison of a normal (Gaussian) bell-shaped distribution,[3] compared to the reality of

---

3. The example Gaussian (or normal) distribution shown in figure 6.3 is $p(P) = 23 \exp(-0.5 (\tau + 290)/109)^2$, and was fitted to the MERE learning curve using the commercial statistical software routine TableCurve 2D.

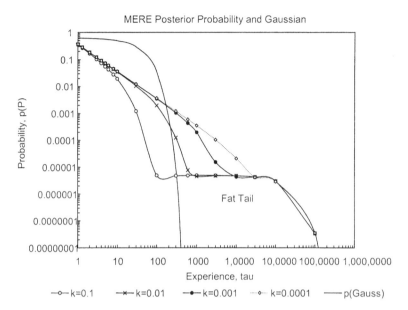

Fig. 6.3   **Predictions: Illustrating the Gaussian distribution failure to include the "fat tail" due to the influence of the human element**

learning variations as they affect probability: it is clear that the Gaussian or normal distribution seriously underestimates risk, in this case the probability of an outcome, for large experience. This inability of standard methods to predict the extremes of the distributions in itself is well-known, but less well-known is that the probability increase or plateau is due to the human element.

So the future chance, or posterior, of any event, even of an unknown unknown, *is* in fact given by estimating the Likelihood, $p(L)$, something Taleb does not discuss at all. Instead, the concept of scalability was invoked, which we have now shown and will demonstrate is actually the same thing as a conditional probability of whether it will occur, but disguised as another White Elephant.

The impact of rare events can vary, particularly because they were somehow disruptive, unexpected, or not predicted. So impacts can be large, as for a financial crisis that affects everyone's credit or bank account (Taleb 2007), or they can be negligible because they do not affect the overall industry but only the participants, as for a commercial airplane crash. But both do not happen very often. Because events occur randomly, we find it difficult to predict when and where they will happen, and can do so only with uncertainty. So with rare events we are more uncertain, as we have had limited learning opportunity and we fear the unknown. The risk we determine or sense can be defined as the uncertainty in the chance of such an event happening. It is perceived by us, individually and collectively, as being a high risk or not based on how we feel about it, and have been taught, trained, experienced, learned, or indoctrinated. The randomness is then inherent in the learning processes, in the myriad of learned and unlearned patterns, neural firings, legal rules, acquired skills, written procedures, unconscious decisions, and conscious interactions that any and all humans have in any and all systems. Perversely, only by having such randomness, learning, skill, trial, and error can order and learning patterns emerge. We create order from disorder, learning as we go from experience and risk exposure, discerning the right and unlearning the wrong behaviors and skills. So a rare Black Swan, even if of major impact, is indeed a White Elephant of no intrinsic value unless and only if we are learning.

We need to know what we do not know. We cannot know what happens inside our brains and see the how the trillions of neural patterns, pathways, and possibilities are wired, learned, interconnected, rationalized, and unlearned. We cannot know the millions of things that any group of people will talk about, learn, exchange, review, revise, argue, debate, reject, use and abuse, each and every day. We cannot know all about how a machine or system will behave when subjected to the whims of inadequate design, poor maintenance, extreme failure modes, external damage, and poor or unsafe operation. What we do know is that, because *we are human,* we do learn from our mistakes: this is the Learning Hypothesis (Petroski 1985; Ohlsson 1996; Duffey and Saull 2002). The rate at which we make errors, produce outcomes, and cause events reduces both as we gain experience and if and as we learn. We make mistakes because we are human: the fat tail, the rare event, occurs because we are human. If and as we gain experience, this is equivalent to increasing our risk exposure too. The risk increases whether by driving on the road, by trading stocks and investments, or by building and operating a technological system like a ship, train, rocket, or aircraft.

Consistent with the principles of natural selection, those who do not learn, those who do not adapt and survive, are the failures and extinctions of history, overtaken by the unexpected and mistakes, the errors and the Black Swans *of the past.*

6.6   Failure to Predict Failure: Scaling Laws and the Risk Plateau

What do we know about what we do not know? We know that the four categories of knowns and unknowns are the Rumsfeld quartet:

Known knowns: What is expected and already observed (in the past)
Known unknowns: Unexpected but observed outcomes (past outcomes)
Unknown knowns: Expected and not yet observed (in the future)
Unknown unknowns: Unexpected and not yet observed (future outcomes or rare events)

This is analogous to drawing both outcomes and nonoutcomes from Bernoulli's urn (Duffey and Saull 2008), and the probability of a rare (unknown) event is determined if all we do is assume that it exists. Thus, we have turned a Black Swan into a White Elephant—the fact that we have not observed it, do not know if it exists, but can rationally discuss it allows the fear, dread, and risk perception to be quantified. This is precisely what Taleb recommends—taking precautions against what it is we do not know about what we do now know.

We have defined a risk ratio that depends on the prior failure rate. But for a rare or unknown event the posterior probability of an unknown unknown, $p(U, U)$ that has not happened yet is finite and is given by analogy to the "case of zero failures" in purely statistical analysis (Coolen 2006, 105). We can then obtain the mathematical estimate for knowing the posterior (future) probability of the unknowable as Duffey and Saull (2008):

$$P(U, U) \sim \left(\frac{1}{U\tau^2}\right) \exp\text{-}U,$$

where U is some constant of proportionality. This order of magnitude estimate shows a clear trend of the probability decreasing with increasing experience as an inverse square power law, τ^2. For every factor of ten increase in experience measured in some tau units, τ, the posterior probability falls by one hundred times. It does not matter if we do not know the exact numbers: the trend is the key for decision making and risk taking. *The rational choice and implication is to trust experience and not to be afraid of the perceived Unknown.*

But although useful for comparative trending purposes, such a purely statistical analysis *excludes* the key human involvement and uncertainty contribution. Hence the risk of an unknown unknown decreases inexorably with our increasing experience, or risk exposure, only until a risk plateau is reached and no further decrease in probability is possible. Therefore, continuing to extrapolate using such scaling power laws will always ultimately underestimate risk. So the White Elephant is precisely the case of little or no learning corresponding exactly to a scaled probability inverse law, that is, $p(P) = n/\tau$, where the number of events, n, is one ($n = 1$), simply because it is that first and rare event that was never previously observed or known. So the probability, p, of any single rare event is always, $1/\tau$, the inverse of (one divided by) the exposure or experience measure, or scale. As shown before in figure 6.2, this is also a measure of the risk ratio and is equivalent numerically to the failure rate, λ. So also shown in figure 6.4 are the so-called "scalable" or pure "power" laws discussed by Taleb (2007), where the probability is assumed to fall as the more general inverse power law, $p(P) = 1/\tau^\alpha$.

Corresponding to the prior and the posterior variations without significant learning, for illustration, the "slope" parameter, α, is often taken as lying in the range between 1 and 2, which assumed values nicely cover the

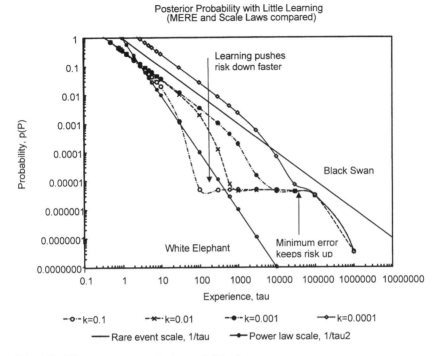

Fig. 6.4   **The rare event prediction and risk plateau**

"true" curves for novice or zero experience, varying as $1/\tau$, and for unknown unknowns varying as, $1/\tau^2$. But these are constant risk lines that do not give the detailed shape or slope variations since they do *not* reflect the learning opportunity and the ultimate irreducible, finite, residual, and nonzero risk rate. Basically the *incorrect* inexorable decrease in risk predicted by a scale law is offset by the inevitability of risk due to the human element, causing the fat tail or plateau in the probability graph. At a future (posterior) probability of order $p < 10^{-5}$ the line intersects the learning curves, and the rare event or Black Swan truly becomes a White Elephant, being of less value or lower risk than the actual and hence of no *predictive* value.

Popular because of its simplicity, the inapplicable power law form is widely used in the field of economics (known as an "elasticity") when fitting the exponent to price or response time reduction (Duffey 2004); in cognitive psychology (known as a "law of practice") when applied to trials that constitute repetitive learning (Stevens and Savin 1962); and in damage estimation for industrial failures and collapses (Hanayasu and Sekine 2004). This general power law form also fits social trends, such as word usage, books sold, website hits, telephone calls, and city populations, leading Taleb (2007) to further argue that this form represents true scalability that we can now recognize as the *fundamental* connection to learning and risk exposure. Arbitrary adjustment of the exponent, α, in economics, social science, and cognitive psychology is an attempt to actually account for and fit what we observe, but without trying to understand why the exponent is not unity nor placing limits on the extrapolations made beyond the known data used for the original fits.

The exponent is roughly constant only over limited ranges of data, otherwise it fails in extrapolating magnitude or trend (Duffey and Saull 2008). In fact in statistics, this form of inverse power law type of relation is often known as a Pareto distribution[4] and Woo (1999, 224) explicitly further cautions that "parameterizing a natural hazard loss curve cannot be reliably reduced to a statistical analysis of loss data, e.g., fitting a Pareto curve: damaging events are too infrequent for this to be sound."

In fact, this failure to predict may even explain the proven poor capability of many economic models, which by using a constant elasticity between price and demand and extrapolating we now know from data do not predict well! We now know and can see from figure 6.4 that the exponent is not constant and the variation *in reality* is due to the presence and effects of learning, with the larger exponent values and steeper slope encompassing the variation between the learning curves (figure 6.3). This variation represents uncertainty and constitutes the measure of risk if taken as a technique for making investment decisions.

Figures 6.3 and 6.4 contain much useful information. Not only are the trends with learning clear, there is the tendency for risk to be smaller initially with more learning; and greater at larger experience due to the forming of a plateau of nearly constant risk (a fat tail, or potential Black Swan). If we neglect this large human contribution and effect at large risk exposure then Pareto lines, power laws, normal and log-normal distributions become White Elephants of little value, as being extrapolated they underestimate the risk. A similar argument can be made for not using results from static or equilibrium VaR and CoVaR techniques (see Taleb [2007], the papers presented at the NBER systemic risk conference, and the chapters in this book). These techniques fit standard statistical distributions to financial asset data and then seek significance in the differences and trends out at the 1 to 2 percent tail, while ignoring again the dynamic human contribution and hence unaware of and not accounting for the systematic existence of the systemic risk plateau.

This presence of learning effects nicely explains the actual range of empirical values for the exponent, α, quoted by Taleb and others of between 1 and 2—*some systems evidently exhibit more or less initial learning than others,* as is shown in figure 6.4. Including the statistical limit of unknown unknowns, the inverse power law simplification shows by definition that if

---

4. Also termed the hyperbolic or power law distribution, the form given by Woo for natural catastrophes is $p(\tau) = ba^b/\tau^{b+1}$, where a and b are constants, the so-called "location" and "shape" parameters.

there are no events there is and can be no learning. Strictly, we know this is not true, as we also learn something from the many and often irritating nonevents, minor losses, and near misses. This so-called incidental learning leads to the other extreme case of "perfect learning" (Duffey and Saull 2008), where the event outcome probability still follows a learning curve until we have just one event, and then subsequently plummets to zero.

We stress here that the power law form is a natural, simplified limiting variant of the more general "learning curve," which naturally then also encompasses the occurrence of rare events.

The analysis of risk ratios due to the financial cost of individual events assumes that big losses or damage occur less often (i.e., are rare or lower in frequency). For example, Hanayasu and Sekine (2004) argue that the rate of financial damage of events in industry decreases with the inverse of the damage or loss. So generally the frequency of an event decreases with increasing cost as the probability density,

$$\frac{dp}{d\tau} \approx \frac{\text{constant}}{h^{q+1}}.$$

Here, q is yet another power law exponent chosen to fit some damage data, and is always such that $q > 1$, so Hanayasu and Sekine assume that it lies in the range $2 < q < 3$. When the slope is an inverse cube such that $\alpha \sim 3$, there is a very rapid decline. We analyzed this approach (Holton 2004, 19) and found the risk ratio or damage ratio referenced to some initial known value, h_0, and probability, p_0, is then given by:

$$RR = \left(\frac{h}{h_0}\right) = \left(\frac{p}{p_0}\right)^{1/q}.$$

Extrapolation of the fitted line beyond the data range given shows a much faster decrease in risk ratio than usually observed or expected from a learning curve with a finite minimum that flattens out. So the basic problem is that extrapolation of the size of the loss according to this power law (although it is not really a law at all) produces inaccuracy outside the known data range, does not account for learning, and also does not allow for the finite nonzero contribution of the human element (the extra fat tail shown in figure 6.2). We have fitted a MERE curve also to these damage data, and as a result the forward risk exposure, financial loss, or uncertainty is grossly *underestimated* because of omitting the human learning element. This is really uncertainty: we are predicting the variation in how big the losses will be for unknown events, based on what we know.

The chance of an unknown unknown or rare event also depends on whether or not you learn! Conversely, rare events and Black Swans are also simply events for which we have little or no learning. The argument is then wrong that this type of inverse power variation represents true randomness, where there is no pattern other than that which is scale invariant (like fractals). In fact, the variation in probability or risk in reality is all due to whether we have been learning or not, at what rate we make or have made mistakes both in the past and in the future. The true natural scale for all human-based systemic risk we have shown repeatedly is our experience, however that is defined and accumulated, as learning is not invariant with risk exposure. What we know about the unknown is that we are human and remain so, learning as we go.

For the future unknown experience, the average future failure rate, $\langle \lambda \rangle$, we will observe over any future risk exposure or operating interval, $\tau - \tau_0$, that is obtained by averaging the varying failure rate over that same observation or risk exposure interval, so:

$$\langle \lambda \rangle = \frac{1}{(\tau - \tau_0)} \int_\tau^{\tau_0} \lambda(\tau) d\tau.$$

Clearly, the apparent average rate also depends on the risk exposure interval, $\tau - \tau_0$, over which we start and finish observing, or choose to record outcomes, or happen to be present, or are risk exposed.

We can show how these ideas work in practice by comparing to actual data for rare events, although this is strictly an oxymoron, as if the outcomes occur they are no longer rare or become known unknowns. The data available is the case we have analyzed in detail before (Duffey and Saull 2002, 2008), for fatal commercial airline crashes between 1970 and 2000. The case is relevant as the airline industry is regarded as relatively safe, and having perhaps attained the lowest possible event rate. Over this thirty-year period using modern jets, some 114 commercial passenger airlines accumulated about 220 million flights, and there were about 270 fatal crashes, excluding hull losses (plane write-offs), with no deaths. The data show a lack of further learning trends, as airline crashes attain the lowest rate currently known or achievable of about one per 200,000 flying experiences or risk exposure hours. What has actually happened is that because they have become rare events there is an almost constant risk, as shown in figure 6.5, where the fatal crash rate indeed varies inversely as, $\lambda \sim 1/\tau$, the number of accumulated flights being the measure of both the learning experience and risk exposure.[5]

The analysis shows that the airlines having the least experience have the highest rate per flight, the airlines overall having descended the learning curve and achieved their lowest possible rare crash rate. So for this case, flights accumulated represent a convenient measure of the risk exposure and learning scale. The only larger interval found is for systems like dams, where humans are passive and not actively and/or continuously involved in the day-to-day system performance and operation.

But the relative future risk of a mature technology, as measured by the

---

5. The seeming paradox with using event rate as a measure of risk for rare events is that the rate and number seemingly fall with increasing experience (not just time), giving an apparent decrease, when in fact the risk of a random outcome is effectively still constant.

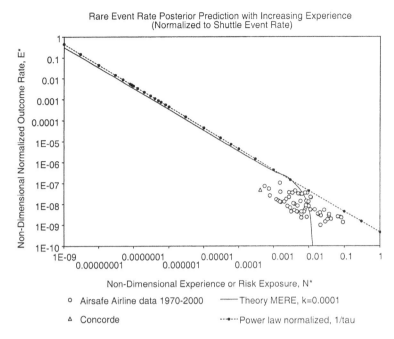

Fig. 6.5   The prediction for rare aircraft crashes

nondimensional posterior outcome rate, is negligible compared to that for new technology. The plunge in the future prediction, $p(P)$, of the risk at large experience, or the thin tail appearing in the end of the fat tail, is due to the prior probability becoming nearer and nearer to certainty ($p \to 1$) at large enough experience or risk exposure since the failure rate (according to all the world's known outcome data) is never, ever zero. Thus, we have found a basis on which to make predictions of all such rare unknown unknowns, based on the (equally) rare prior outcomes from many disparate sources.

We have already recently used the methods and ideas discussed here and in our book (Duffey and Saull 2008) to risk, failure rate, and reliability prediction for many important cases. These include human errors and recovery actions in nuclear power plants (Duffey and Ha 2010); predicting rocket launch failures and space crew safety for new systems (Fragola 2009, 657); the time it takes for restoration of power following grid failure (or "blackout") (Duffey and Ha 2009); predicting the rate of failure of heat exchanger tubing in new designs (Duffey and Tapping 2009); and the quantitative tracking of learning trends ("safety culture") in management and operation of large offshore oil and gas facilities (Duffey and Skjerve 2008); and about thirty other key examples. While each case has its own fascinating and unique experience and data, all examples and cases can be reduced to the common learning basis, and all follow the universal laws and rules for the outcomes due to us, as humans, functioning in modern society and technological systems, whether we know it or not.

6.7   The Financial Risk: Trends in Economic Growth Rates, Failure, and Stability

The fundamental question is, what are the relevant prior data, predictive failure rate, and risk exposure measures in financial and economic systems when including the essential influence of the human involvement?

Like other systems with failures and outcomes, there are a lot of financial system data out there, both nationally and globally, and these data are key to our understanding and analysis. What are the right measures for failure (errors) and experience in financial systems? Can the market collapse be predicted using these measures? As an exercise in examining these questions, we explored the publicly available global financial data from the World Bank and the IMF, covering the years up to the great crash or "bust" of 2008. This was widely attributed to the failure of the credit markets, due to the collateralizing of risky (real estate) debt assets as leveraged securities in the developed economies and financial markets. The present analysis is to determine the presence or not of precursors, the evidence or not of learning trends, and prediction of the probability of failure using the prior data.

Let us make a financial market system prediction based solely on what we know about other system failures. According to the data (and as shown in figures 6.2, 6.3, and 6.4), we have learned that there is an apparent fundamental and inherent inability, due to the inseparable involvement of humans in and with the technological systems, for the posterior (future) probability of an outcome to occur with a probability of less than $p(P) < 10^{-5}$. This corresponds to the lowest observed rate of one outcome or failure in about 100,000 to 200,000 experience or risk exposure units (Duffey and Saull 2002, 2008). If the global financial market, including real estate equities and stocks, is now defined as the relevant *system with human involvement,* and a trading or business experience of 24/7/365 taken as the appropriate risk exposure or experience measure, this implies we may *expect and predict an average "market failure" rate* ranging from not less than about once every ten years and not more than every twenty years. If lack of economic (GWP and/or GDP)[6] growth, with financial credit and market collapse is taken as a surrogate measure of an outcome or failure,[7] there has been apparently four relatively recent "crises" in the world (in about 1981–1982, 1992–1993, 1997–1998, and 2008–2009), and five "recessions" in the United States (circa 1972, 1980, 1982, 1990, and 2008) in the forty-year interval of 1970 to 2010 (IMF 2009a), being an *average* risk interval of between eight (nationally) to ten (globally) years. In fact, in the full interval of 1870 to 2008, the IMF listed eight globally significant financial crises in those 138 years (the above four listed plus

---

6. GWP and GDP are conventional acronyms for Gross World Product and Gross Domestic Product.

7. The recent IMF World Economic Outlook 2009 in fact shows for the 2008 crisis there is a relation between household liabilities and credit growth in relation to GDP growth (18, figure 3.10).

1873, 1891–1892, 1907–1908, 1929–1931), or ten when including the two world wars (IMF 2009b). All these various crises give an *average* interval of about one failure somewhere between every eight to seventeen years, an agreement surprisingly close to and certainly within our present predictive uncertainty range of one about every ten to twenty years of risk exposure.

This present purely rare event prediction is a result that was not anticipated beforehand, and is based on failure data from other global and national nonfinancial systems, implying that the very same and very human forces are at work in financial systems due to human fallibility and mistakes. The present rate-of-failure approach contrasts squarely with many other unsuccessful predictive measures (IMF 2009), and short- and long-term bond rate spreads using probit probability curves tuned to the market statistical variations (Estrella and Mishkin 1996, 1). So although we cannot yet predict exactly when, we can now say that the economic market place (EMP) is behaving and failing on average in the same manner and rates as all other known homo-technological systems. We presume for the moment that this is not just a coincidence, and that the prior historical data are indeed telling us something about the commonality and causes of random and rare fiscal failures, and our ability or inability to predict systemic risk. So we can now seek new measures for predictors or precursors of market failure and stability based on what we know.

We already know that the chance of such a major event "ever happening again" is given by the matching probability using conventional statistics, and this has the value of ~0.63, or about an equal chance of happening or not (Duffey and Saull 2008). This is a repeat event prediction (REP) of a nearly equal chance. So for managing risk, we should expect another collapse based solely on this analysis, and probably with about the same average ten to twenty-year interval unless some change is made that impacts the human contribution. The inevitably of failure is rather disheartening, and although uncomfortable seems to be the reality, so we should all at least proactively plan for it and hence be able to manage and survive the outcome, which is risk mitigation.

Having established the possible relevance of GWP and GDP, as an initial step the measure of the outcome rate is taken to be the percent growth in GWP and GDP (positive growth being success, negative growth being failure), and the relevant measure for experience and risk exposure for the global financial system as the gross world product, GWP (T\$), not in the usual calendar years as the interval over which the data are usually presented.[8]

The result of the ULC analysis is shown in figure 6.6 for the interval 1980 to 2003 (World Bank 2009), where the GDP growth rate, R, is the MERE learning curve form:

8. A reviewer noted that for systemic risk it is reasonable and not unexpected that GWP is an alternative measure to calendar year, and that experience may also be reflected in and by trading volumes. Indeed, for establishing learning trends we need available and open measures that are relevant to experience and risk exposure, and encourage the study and search for relevant measure.

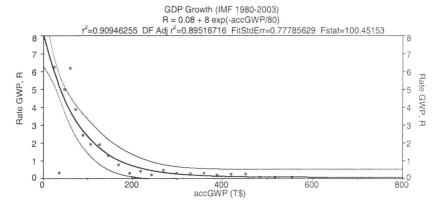

Fig. 6.6   The GWP growth rate curve

$$R, \%\text{GWP} = R_m + (R_0 - R_m) \exp - k(acc\text{GWP}),$$

where numerically, from the data comparison in figure 6.6,

$$R = 0.08 + 8 \exp - \left(\frac{acc\text{GWP}}{80} \right).$$

The growth rate, R, is decreasing exponentially, and this expression is correlated with the data to an $r^2 = 0.9$, and importantly shows that by a GWP of order \$600T the overall global growth rate is trending toward being negligible ($<0.1\%$).

In nondimensional form, relative to some initial growth rate, R_0, this equation can be written as:

$$R^* = \frac{R}{R_0} = \left(\frac{1}{R_0} \right) \left\{ 0.08 + 8 \exp - \left(\frac{acc\text{GWP}}{80} \right) \right\}.$$

It is worth noting that, as might be expected in global trading, the magnitude and growth of many economies are apparently highly correlated with the accumulated GWP, so will follow similar trends, as we see later. For example, the straight line that gives the relation between the US GDP and the GWP for the interval 1981 to 2004 is:

$$\text{GDP(USA, \$}B) = 15\{acc\text{GWP(\$}T)\} + 3{,}210,$$

with a correlation coefficient of $r^2 = 0.99$. The magnitudes are hence very tightly coupled; but here we do not have to decide which is cause and which is effect (i.e., is the change in one due to the other, or vice versa?).[9]

To be clear, we really wish to determine a global financial failure rate and

9. As pointed out by one of the discussers of this chapter, the "tight coupling" condition is one of those qualities proposed for the occurrence of so-called "normal accidents" (Perrow 1984).

the rate we are learning. So what is the relevant measure of the failure rate? Now, global governments and economies usually aim for increasing, or more slowly declining and hopefully nonnegative, growth. We postulate that either of the following extremes can be taken as an equivalent and immediately useful measure of economic failure, both varying with increasing accumulated GWP as a measure of total risk exposure: (a) the rate of decline in GWP growth rate; or (b) the rate of GWP growth rate itself.

By straightforward differentiation of the growth rate, R, we have the global failure or decline rate, λ_f, given by:

$$\lambda_f \equiv -\frac{dR}{dGWP} = k(R_0 - R_m)\exp - k(accGWP).$$

Thus, numerically, we may expect the rate of decline of growth (the global financial failure rate) to decrease with increasing risk exposure and experience and be given very nearly by, in units of percent/GWP:

$$\lambda_f = 0.1 \exp - \left(\frac{accGWP}{80}\right),$$

with the natural limit, $\lambda_0 = 0.1$, so the relevant nondimensional equation is,

$$E^* = \frac{\lambda_f}{\lambda_0} = \exp - \left(\frac{accGWP}{80}\right).$$

The equations for R^* and E^* now allow a direct comparison to the systemic learning trends given by the ULC form, $E^* = \exp - 3N^*$, so we also plotted these two growth decline predictions (shown as the large crosses and circles)[10] in nondimensional form against all other world outcome data with the result shown in figure 6.7. The data are bracketed by the two extreme assumptions, basically: (a) the rate of decline of growth rate, λ_f, when equivalent to financial failure, is tracking somewhat below other adverse outcome data; while (b) the simple decline in growth rate R is somewhat above other adverse data. We can indeed establish and cover the range with these two failure measures, generally within the data scatter.

To our knowledge this is the first time that financial and economic systems have been compared to other modern systems. We take the extraordinary fact that we can bring all these apparently disparate data together using the learning theory as evidence that the human involvement is dominant, not just in accidents and surgeries but also in economics, through the common basis of the fundamental decision and learning processes. Globally, therefore, we can state that we have indeed learned to reduce and manage the rate of overall economic decline, just as we have learned to correct errors and failures in other systems.

10. This graph and comparison now responds to a point arising in the discussion at the first draft presentation of this chapter as to the relevant measure for failure in global systems that exhibit varying growth rates.

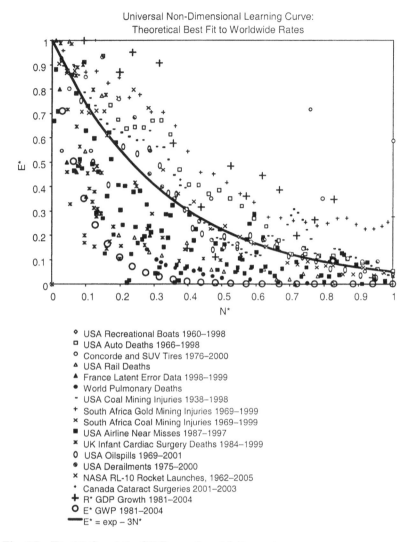

Fig. 6.7   The ULC and the GWP growth and failure rates

The implication is intriguing: if a declining rate of economic growth decline is indeed equivalent to an error, then the economies suffering declines in growth had even learned to further reduce their rate of decline in growth. They have learned or managed how not to grow, eventually reaching an almost infinitesimal asymptotic rate of decline. Further, this result suggests that GWP is a useful measure for estimating risk exposure and the learning opportunity.

6.8   Developing and Developed Economies: The Learning Link

It has been suggested that this decline in growth rate represents saturation of the developed economies, and that major growth then only occurs in the developing economies. To compare growth rates, the IMF and World Bank have also separated out the percentage GDP growth rates for "emerging" or developing countries/economies from "developed" or "advanced" countries/economies (World Bank 2009).

Now the percentage growths are based on very different totals, so just for a comparison exercise, the percent growth rate, πGR, in each grouping was defined relative to the absolute growth in the world, or GWP, as:

$$\pi GR\left(\frac{\%}{\$T}\right) = \frac{\% \text{ GDP Growth}}{(\text{GWP } \$T \times \text{World } \% \text{ Growth})}.$$

In effect, this is a measure of the rate of economic growth rate relative to the total available economic growth pie. The relative growth rate data calculated in this manner for the two groupings are shown in figure 6.8 as a function still of the accumulated GWP, as well as the delta (or difference) in relative growth rate, $\{\pi GR \text{ (developed)} - \pi GR \text{ (emerging)}\}$, between the two types of economies. The reason for taking the *accumulated* GWP as the experience measure is this is presumable some measure of available learning

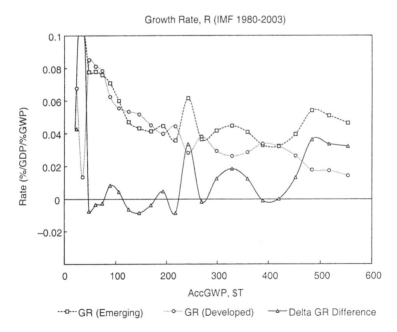

Fig. 6.8   The differential decline of rates of GDP growth

experience and risk exposure in the global trade between the two groups, and of the total available pie.

What is seen is illuminating: the two growth rates (top dashed lines) are in antiphase or negatively correlated: when one goes up, the other goes down, and vice versa. One grows literally at the expense of the other. There is also some periodicity in the divergence pattern, and evidence of emerging positive divergence in growth rates toward $600T in 2003+. The opposite correlation between the growth rates is clear—the developing economies have a positive correlation of ~+0.9 and the developed economies a negative correlation of about –0.7, with increasing accumulated GWP. As world wealth increases, one is declining, and the other is increasing in growth rate. The implication is that the relative growth shares part of the global economy pie growth, and hence the economies themselves are indeed closely coupled, which is perhaps obvious in hindsight.

The prediction is clear based on these trends. The developed world economies would actually go into near zero or into negative GDP growth rate in 2003+ (the projection is around 2005 to 2006 when GWP exceeds $600T), after many years of decline. The emerging economies would continue to grow positively at 5 percent or more. The difference in rates was highly oscillatory and perhaps not stable, as the liquidity (credit) needed to fund growth in emerging economies cannot come from those developed economies whose available assets and economies are in decline. So the implication is that—in a globalized economy where all the individual economies are linked or "tightly coupled"—there are unknown feedback and stability relationships at work that we need to examine.

A very first attempt was also made to predict the actual rate of the known global fiscal crises, where the key is again finding the relevant units for the measure of the risk exposure/experience, τ. For the preliminary results shown in figure 6.9, as listed in the IMF's WEO2009, the experience was taken as GWP-years for the interval 1870 to 2009, with eight nonwartime crises. The resulting global crisis rate, λ_G, is

λ_G = (Number of crises, per accumulated risk exposure years from 1870,

$accY$).

The theory line also shown in figure 6.9 is derived from a MERE failure rate, which is firmly based on human learning, so that the equation is:

$$\lambda_G = 0.059 + 0.2 \exp -\left(\frac{accGWPy}{230}\right),$$

with a correlation of $r^2 = 0.958$.

Clearly the predicted tail is nearly constant with the lowest presently attainable crisis rate of about 0.06 per year (or averaging one every seventeen years), suggesting a plateau in the finite minimum rate due to human

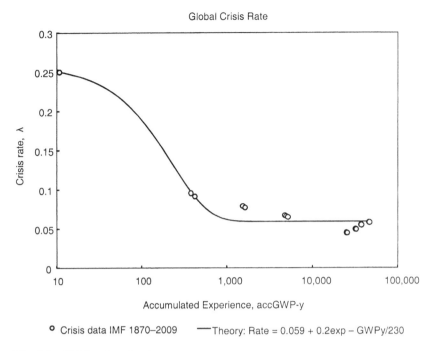

Fig. 6.9   Crisis rate estimate

involvement. Crises are occurring much faster than might have been expected using simple extrapolation with a power law: the number and rate of crises increases with risk exposure (i.e., with increasing GWP), which might seem to be rather obvious, producing yet another fat tail. Despite the overall theoretical trend suggesting the crisis rate is at best constant and not decreasing further, the last four data points indicate that the crisis rate is actually slightly increasing and may constitute a new dynamic prediction of more frequent crises. While not asserting completeness at this early stage of the analysis, it is possible and highly desirable in the future to further examine the trends in these crisis data in more detail.

6.9   Risk: Quantifying the Uncertainty

How can we estimate the stability of a global or national system? The whole system is too complicated to predict its every move, behavior, or state, so how do we proceed? How can we estimate and predict the stability of a system when it is unpredictable? Here we introduce the only known objective measure of uncertainty, complexity and randomness, and illustrate how it can be used to predict system stability.

Early work on economic stability (Solow 1956, 65) focused on presumed and arbitrary functional growth relationships between labor (employment) and wealth generation (capital) for determining equilibrium conditions.[11] The actual form of the economic growth function was not given or known, but using simple analytical functions, the possibility was shown for the existence of multiple alternate steady-states or equilibria. But as clearly stated by Soros (2009): "The financial system is far from equilibrium. . . . The short term needs are the opposite of what is needed in the long term."

Since financial markets are actually unstable and dynamic and not in equilibrium, the real need is to determine and predict the instant of and conditions for instability, not whether some ideal equililibria or new steady state is achievable. Markets just like the entire physical world are random, chaotic, and unpredictable, so predicting frequent and rare events is risky and uncertain.[12] Learning and randomness are powerful and unpredictable issues for risk prediction because we tend to believe that things behave according to what we know and, consciously or unconsciously, dismiss the risk of what we have not seen or do not know about. *After all, we do not know what we do not know.* We, as humans, are the very product of our norms and patterns, our knowledge skills and experience, our learning patterns and neural connections, our social milieu and moral teachings, in the jobs, friends, lovers, lives, teachers, family, and managers we happen to have. We perceive our own risk based on what we think we know, rightly or wrongly, and what *we* have experienced. But in key innovations and new disciplines, where knowledge and skill is still emerging—areas like terrorism, bioengineering, neuroscience, medicine, economics, computing, automation, genetics, law, space exploration, and nuclear reactor safety—we have to know and to learn the risk of what we know about what we do not know. We cannot possibly know everything, and these are all complex systems, with new and complex problems and lots of complexity, with much uncertainty.

The way to treat randomness and uncertainty has been solved in the physical sciences, where it was realized that unobserved fluctuations, uncertainty, and statistical fluctuations govern and determine the actually observed behaviors and distributions. Events can happen or appear in many different ways, which is literally the "noise" that surrounds and confuses us, whereas what we actually observe is the most likely but also contains information about the signal that emerges or is embedded as order emerges from disorder, and we process and discard the complexity. In fact, not just the physical world but the whole process of individual human response time and decision making has been shown to be directly affected by randomness, in the so-called Hick-Hyman law (Duffey and Saull 2008). As individuals and as collectives, we do and must process complexity, both in our brains and in our behavior, seeking the signal from all the noise, the learning patterns from

11. The author is grateful to Ms. Christina Wang for pointing out both this reference and its relevance: for the present discussion we presume that "wealth creation" can be related or correlated to GWP and GDP.

12. The inherent randomness is often termed the aleatory uncertainty by statisticians.

the mistakes, and the information from all the distractions. Systematic processing and the perverse presence of complexity are essential for establishing learning distribution patterns.

The number of different ways something can appear or be ordered in sequence, magnitude, position, and experience, is mathematically derivable and is a measure of the degree of order in any system (Duffey and Saull 2008). The number of different ways is a measure of the *complexity*, and is determined by the Information Entropy, *H*, which is also a measure of what we know about what we do not know, or the "missing information" (Baierlein 1971), which is a measure of the risk. The relation linking the probability of any outcome to the entropy is well known from both Statistical Physics and Information Theory, and is the objective measure of complexity:

Information Entropy, $H = \text{Sum}(p \times \text{natural logarithm}, p) = -\Sigma p\, lnp$.

Note that the units adopted or utilized for the entropy are flexible and arbitrary, both by convention and in practice as being a *comparative* measure of order and complexity. So this measure of uncertainty requires a statement of probability. Now Taleb (2007, 315) noted that "I am purposely avoiding the notion of entropy because the way it is conventionally phrased makes it ill-adapted to the type of randomness we experience in real life." We dismiss this assertion, and proceed to make this very subtle notion applicable to financial systemic risk simply by rephrasing it.

To make the entropy concept adaptable and useful for "experience in real life," all we have to do is actually relate and adapt the information entropy measure to our real life experience, or risk exposure interval, as we have already utilized (Duffey and Saull 2002, 2008) and have also introduced earlier. So we can now change the phrasing and the adaptability, since before we unconventionally phrase entropy as being "an objective measure of what we know about what we do not know, which is the risk." In support of this use and phraseology, other major contributors have remarked:

> Entropy is defined as the amount of information about a system that is still unknown after one has made . . . measurements on the system. (Wolfram 2002, 44)

> This suggests that . . . entropy might have an important place in guiding the strategy of a business man or stock market investor. (Jaynes 2003, 343 et seq.)

> Entropy is a measure of the uncertainty and the uncertainty, or entropy, is taken as the measure of the amount of information conveyed by a message from a source." (Pierce 1980, 23)

> The uncertainty function . . . a unique measure for the predictability (uncertainty) of a random event which also can be used to compare different kinds of random events. (Greiner, Neise, and Stocker 1997, 150)

There is no other measure available or known with these fundamental properties and potential, particularly for handling uncertainty and randomness, the processing and influence of complexity, and providing the objective measure of order. This measure also has direct application to the subjective concept of resilience engineering, where "resilience is the intrinsic ability of an organisation (system) to maintain or regain a dynamically stable state, which allows it to continue operation after a major mishap and/or the presence of a continuous stress" (Hollnagel, Woods, and Leveson 2006, 9). But resilience, just like culture, has not been actually measured or quantified anywhere: it is simply a desirable property. We have developed the numerical and objective system organizational stability (SOS) criterion that incidentally unifies the general theory and practice of managing risk through learning (Duffey and Saull 2008). This criterion is also relevant to crisis management policies and procedures, and emergency response centers in major corporations, facilities, and industries.

6.10   System and Organizational Stability: SOS

The function of any management system is to create order from disorder, be it safety, regulatory, organizational, or financial and hence to reduce the entropy. Thus, for order to emerge from chaos, and for stability in physical systems, the incremental change in entropy, which is the measure of the disorder, must be negative (Kondepudi and Prigogine 1998). Our equivalent SOS criterion or indicator then arises implying from the fact that the incremental change in risk (information entropy, H) with changes in probability must be negative, or decreasing with increasing risk exposure. In any *experience* increment we must have the inequality, expressed in differential form to reflect dynamic change:

$$\frac{dH}{d\tau} \leq 0.$$

Stated in words, for financial systems and markets, this SOS criterion states that there must be an incremental decrease in complexity with increasing or changing risk exposure. Conversely, increasing complexity with incremental risk exposure is systemically unstable.

This key condition or indicator also requires that a maximum (peak) exists in our changing missing information or state of order as a function of experience and/or risk exposure, equivalent to a meta-stable condition. To illustrate this variation, consider the limit cases of concern of the probability/possibility/likelihood of another collapse event, having observed a similar one already, considering all our previous knowledge. From the past experience we showed that the prior probability for REP is, with little learning, $p \approx (1 - 1/e) = 0.63$, and also this same value holds for novice mistakes with little experience (when $\tau 0$). For the future risk, the posterior probability,

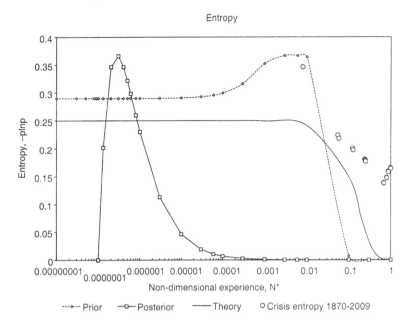

Fig. 6.10   Entropy variations with experience, knowledge, and risk exposure: Stability indicator

with little learning, is $p \approx 1/\tau$ for rare events and also for highly experienced systems (when $\tau \to \infty$).

For the two *limited learning* cases of the prior (past MERE) and posterior (future rare event) the entropy increment, $dH = -plnp$ in any risk interval can be calculated. The results are shown in figure 6.10 as a function of the experience or risk exposure interval, N^*, which purely for convenience has been nondimensionalized to the maximum experience or risk exposure. For the example known prior case, entropy is calculated from the MERE probability result with little learning ($k = 0.0001$); the decrease in entropy at larger experience or risk exposure for the prior case is due to the probability of an outcome finally reaching a certainty, $p \sim 1$, as ultimately there is no uncertainty. For the unknown posterior case, the entropy is calculated from $p = 1/\tau$; the peak in entropy at small experience is simply due to the greater uncertainty, which decreases as experience is gained.

Also shown in the figure 6.10 is the purely theoretical prediction obtained from SEST, the statistical error state theory (Duffey and Saull 2008), which treats outcomes as appearing randomly. The theory derives the most likely statistical distribution of outcomes, and relates the probability of the outcomes with variation in the instantaneous depth of experience or risk exposure in any given risk interval. The information entropy, H, is the measure of the complexity in any interval and is given by integrating the resulting exponential probability distributions, to obtain:

$$H = \frac{1}{2}(p_0 \exp - aN^*)^2 \left(aN^* + \frac{1}{2} \right).$$

At small experience, as $N^* \to 0$, the previous SEST result becomes $H \to 0.25$, which is close to the prior value with little learning of $H \to 0.29$, so the two results are also consistent in their limits, as they should be. The value of the slope parameter or learning exponent, a, is derived deliberately from very diverse prior data sets for failure distributions, which are very detailed and complete.[13] The theory line in figure 6.10 utilizes the "best" $a = 3.5$ in the earlier exponential distribution as a working approximate estimate for comparison purposes, which is close to the learning rate constant value, $k \sim 3$. For most of the experience or risk range shown, the entropy is not decreasing significantly until sufficient experience is attained.

Figure 6.10 itself contains information about what we know about what we do not know, so is worth some more discussion. Knowns (prior or past) apparently contain more uncertainty (H is larger) than unknowns (posterior or future), except at very early or little experience ($N^* < 10^{-4}$). The shapes of the curves are of interest for another reason: for evaluating the system organizational stability (SOS) criterion. By inspection of the two cases in figure 6.10, this stability condition is only met or satisfied at small experience for the unknowns, and at large experience for the knowns.

Basically, at small experience *unless learning is occurring* the existing system is unstable and in danger of repeat events until very large experience is attained. Conversely, any future system is also initially unstable until sufficient post-entry experience has been attained. So learning—or decreasing complexity—is *essential* for stability, and this is plainly relevant to the market stability when introducing the use of new and/or complex financial instruments.

Quoted at the very beginning of this chapter, we can now return to the statement in Soros (2009) that "markets are unstable," a controversial assertion when contrasted with normal economic theory based on near-equilibrium markets (the balance between supply and demand as reflected in price). To test this assertion, the data points shown as circles in figure 6.10 are for the trial crisis entropy estimates calculated using the preliminary probability values for rare events, $p \approx n/accGWP$, where n is simply the number of observed crises, and the risk interval or experience has been nondimensionalized on the basis of the accumulated GWP from 1870 to 2009. The general data trend is downward (i.e., stable) until the last few data points for the crises of 1997 and 2007. Moreover, the greater the GWP becomes, the greater the risk. Importantly, the slope of the last four data points being positive satisfies the formal indicator (the criterion $dH/d\tau > 0$) for inherent global market instability, as has been previously suggested (Soros 2009).

13. Specifically, we used: (a) US commercial aircraft near midair collisions (NMACs) for 1987 to 1998, where experience and risk exposure is measured by total flights; and (b) Australian traffic fatalities from 1980 to 1999, where experience and risk exposure is measured in driver-years (as shown in 5, figure 8.8).

The present results and stability indicator are based on the inclusion of the uncertainty due to human decision making and risk taking, and thus quantifies and supports the idea independently and effectively simultaneously proposed by Soros (2010) of the Human Uncertainty Principle.[14] This principle is firmly based on experience and learning from investment and market behaviors, and proposes that human involvement and risk taking inherently introduces risk due to incomplete knowledge and complexity, resulting in intervention actions in the market based on imperfect understanding that have unintended consequences, in what Soros describes as "reflexivity."

This new data comparison suggests that entropy is indeed a potentially significant indicator that should not be simply avoided as Taleb does, and represents our best and most refined state of knowledge regarding systemic risk. We have now actually quantified the behavior of the chaotic and random financial market. As to regulation of systemic risk, this is really about regulating such unknown uncertainty while meeting the stated goals (Brown 2009; RECP 2008). In fact, Brown (2009, 209) suggests that "to be effective and worthy of public trust, any governance system must be able to demonstrate technical competence. Effective and trustworthy governance arrangements must have four key qualities: informed, transparent, prospective and adaptive." We have provided new technically-founded measures for the basis of a governance system that are: (a) informed by the actual world data and validated; (b) transparent both in their calculation and in using the precepts that describe human learning and risk taking; (c) prospective and future orientated by being able to make actual predictions; and (d) adaptive to generally encompass changes in chaotic markets, risk exposure, and financial systems.

6.11 Concluding Remarks: Our New Methods and Measures Provide This Framework for Objective and Predictive Governance

An exercise such as predicting the next recession or crisis becomes simply equivalent to determining the probability of and risk interval for the next event or outcome. This probability must be based on relevant and correlated measures for experience and risk exposure, which include the presence or absence of learning. We have analyzed the world economic data to make a prediction of the next crisis probability based on the presence and influence of human risk taking and decision making in financial markets.[15]

We have summarized some recent ideas on risk *prediction* for multiple technological systems, using the existing data, and have explicitly included the key

14. By delightful chance, within a week of each other on two continents, the verbal Soros "Lectures" were given on October 26–30, 2009, in Budapest, and the present chapter presented at the NBER Research Conference on Quantifying Systemic Risk on November 6, 2009, in Cambridge.

15. In response to a question raised in discussion at the conference, the present estimate and prediction based on past data is for one global financial crisis occurring at least every eight to seventeen years, becoming more frequent in the future as the GWP and concomitant risk exposure grow. Knowing this fact, the keys are to be prepared for crisis and proactive in risk management.

impact of human involvement using the learning hypothesis, namely that we learn from our mistakes. This ability of homo-technological systems to learn from experience reduces risk and errors, but also produces a fat tail as the processes of learning, making errors, and risk taking persist. We have related these ideas to the prediction of rare events, systemic risk, and organizational stability in global systems and, although we do not pretend to have all the answers, there are clear directions to follow. Risk is caused by our uncertainty, and the measure of uncertainty is probability. The risk of an outcome (accident, event, error, or failure) is *never* zero, and the possibility of an outcome *always* exists, with a chance given by the future (posterior) probability. The key is to include the human involvement, and to create and use the correct and relevant measures for experience, learning, complexity, and risk exposure.

Standard statistical distributions and indicators presently used for financial systems (e.g., as used in VaR, or yield spread) are known to *not* be applicable for predicting rare events, systemic risk, crises, and failures. Because of the human involvement, the risk becomes greater than just by using a Gaussian, normal, or simple power law, until we reach very, very large experience and would have had a prior event anyway. We have a *greater* chance of outcomes and unexpected unknown unknowns if we are not learning than we might expect even from and if using simple scaling or power laws. *This is simply because we are humans who make mistakes, take risks, and cannot be error-free.* In colloquial terms, the human adds another fat tail to an already fat tail.

So the past or prior knowledge indeed informs the future risk: what we know from what we already know from the probability of what were once past unknowns tells us about the probability of the unknown unknowns in the future also.

The measure adopted and used and that is relevant for estimating risk exposure is key. Over some seven to eight decades (orders of magnitude) variation in the rate and in the risk exposure or accumulated experience, for the rare event the negligible learning prediction holds. At any future experience or risk exposure, the error (or uncertainty) in the risk prediction is evidently about a factor of ten in future crisis occurrence probability, and about a factor of two in average crisis frequency.

We have suggested several major factors and useful measures that influence the prediction of risk and stability in financial systems, based on what we observe for all other systems with human involvement:

1. The Universal Learning Curve provides a comparative indication of trends.

2. The probability of failure/loss is a function of experience or risk exposure.

3. The relevant measure of failure is the rate of decline in GDP growth rates.

4. A relevant measure of experience and risk exposure is the accumulated GWP.

5. Stable systems are learning systems that reduce complexity.

6. An absolute measure of risk and uncertainty is the Information Entropy, which reflects what we know about what we do not know.

7. Unique conditions exist for systemic stability.

8. Repeat events are likely.

9. Existing systems are unstable unless learning occurs.

10. New systems are unstable at small experience.

The rare events are essentially all the same, whether they be aircraft crashes, space shuttle losses, massive explosions, or huge financial crises: we know nothing about them until they actually happen, when and if they occur almost magically becoming known unknowns. We learn from them only after they have happened at least once. But based on what we know about what we do not know, we can always estimate our risk and whether we are learning or not. The rare unknown unknowns, or colloquially, the fat tails or Black Swans of the unpredictable rate distributions, are simple manifestations of the occurrence of these outcomes whenever and wherever they happen. We can and must expect them to continue to appear.

In our previous published work (Duffey and Saull 2008), we had quantified the uncertainty or complexity using the information entropy, H, as an objective measure of other subjective organizational and management desiderata of safety culture and organizational learning as a function of experience. This is the first time, to our knowledge, that information entropy has been introduced as an objective prediction of the subjective feeling of risk exposure in the presence or absence of learning. As to regulation of systemic risk, this is about regulating uncertainty, so that we demonstrate technical competence. We provide measures and indicators for the guidance of effective and trustworthy governance arrangements that possess the four key qualities of being informed, transparent, prospective, and adaptive.

The work and concepts discussed in this chapter are only a necessary first step in developing understanding for predicting and managing risk in complex systems with human involvement. This new application to financial systems and markets, and the adoption of new measures requires time, patience, and can also introduce risk. Further work is clearly needed in this whole arena of system stability, the selection of relevant experience measures, and the quantification and prediction of future risk.

Appendix

Probability Definition

The *outcome probability* is just the cumulative distribution function (CDF) conventionally written as $F(\tau)$, the fraction that fails by τ, so:

$$p(\tau) \equiv F(\tau) = 1 - \exp - \int \lambda dt,$$

where the failure rate:

$$\lambda(\tau) = h(\tau) = \frac{f(\tau)}{R(\tau)} = \left\{ \frac{1}{(1-F)} \right\} \frac{dF}{d\tau}, \text{ and the p.d.f. } f(\tau) = dF/d\tau.$$

Carrying out the integration from an initial experience to any interval τ, we obtain the probability of an outcome as the *double exponential:*

$$p(\tau) = 1 - \exp \left\{ \frac{(\lambda - \lambda_m)}{(k - \lambda_m \tau)} \right\}$$

where, from integrating the minimum error rate equation (MERE), $(d\lambda/d\tau)$ $= -k(\lambda - \lambda_m)$, the failure rate is:

$$\lambda(\tau) = \lambda_m + (\lambda_0 - \lambda_m) \exp - k\tau$$

and $\lambda(\tau_0) = \lambda_0$ at the initial experience, accumulated up to or at the initial outcome(s), and $\lambda_0 = 1/\tau$ for the very first, *rare,* or initial outcome, like an inverse power law.

In the usual engineering reliability terminology, for n failures out of N total, the failure probability,

$$p(\tau) = (1 - R(\tau)) = \frac{\#\,\text{failures}}{\text{total number}} = \frac{n}{N},$$

and the frequency is known if, n and N are known (and generally N is not known).

References

Baierlein, R. 1971. *Atoms and Information Theory: An Introduction to Statistical Mechanics.* New York: Dover.

Barthelemy, F. 2001. *Accident on the 21st of September 2001 at a Factory Belonging to the Grande Paroisse Company in Toulouse, Produced Jointly with the Explosives Inspectorate and with Help from the INERIS.* Report of the General Inspectorate for the Environment, Affair no. IGE/01/034. Paris: Inspection Générale de l'Environnement, October 24.

Bayes, Rev. T. 1763. "Memoir Communicated by R. Price, 'An Essay Toward Solving a Problem in the Doctrine of Chances.'" *Royal Society of London* 53:376–98.

Brown, S. 2009. "The New Deficit Model." *Nature Nanotechnology* 4:609–11.

Columbia Accident Investigation Board (CAIB). 2003. "Report, Volume 1." August. "Working Scenario." July. CAIB/NASA/NAIT. http://www.caib.us.

Commission of Inquiry. 2007a. *Report of the Commission of Inquiry into the Collapse of a Portion of the de la Concorde Overpass.* October. Gouvernement de Quebec. http://www.cevc.gouv.qc.ca/UserFiles/File/Rapport/report_eng.pdf.

————. 2007b. *Rapport sur les causes techniques de l'effondrement du viaduc de la Concorde.* Principal report by Jacques Marchand and Denis Mitchell.

Coolen, F. P. A. 2006. "On Probabilistic Safety Assessment in the Case of Zero Failures." *Proceedings, Institution of Mechanical Engineers, Part O, J. Risk and Reliability* 220 (2): 105–14.

Duffey, R. B. 2004. "Innovation in Technology for the Least Product Price and Cost—A New Minimum Cost Relation for Reductions during Technological Learning." *Int. J. Energy Technology and Policy* 2 (1/2): 106–29.

Duffey, R. B., and T. S. Ha. 2009. "Predicting Electric Power System Restoration." Paper presented at the Proc. IEEE (TIC-STH) Toronto International Conference–Science and Technology for Humanity. Toronto, Ontario. September 27–29.

———. 2010. "Human Reliability: Benchmark and Prediction." *Proc. I. Mech. E, Part O: J. Risk and Reliability* 224:186–96. doi: 10.1243/1748006XJRR307.

Duffey, R. B., and J. W. Saull. 2002. *Know the Risk,* 1st ed. Boston: Butterworth and Heinemann.

———. 2008. *Managing Risk: The Human Element.* West Sussex, UK: John Wiley & Sons Ltd.

Duffey, R. B., and A. B. Skjerve. 2008. "Risk Trends, Indicators and Learning Rates: A New Case Study of North Sea Oil and Gas." Paper presented at the Proceedings of the European Safety and Reliability Conference (ESREL) 2008, 17th SRA Conference. Valencia, Spain. September 22–25.

Duffey, R. B., and R. L. Tapping. 2009. "Predicting Steam Generator Tube Failures." Paper presented at the Proceedings of the 6th CNS International Steam Generator Conference. Toronto, Ontario. November 8–11.

Estrella, A., and F. S. Mishkin. 1996. "The Yield Curve as a Predictor of US Recessions." *Current Issues in Economics and Finance* 2 (7): 1–6. Federal Reserve Bank of New York.

Fragola, J. R. 2009. "How Safe Must a Potential Crewed Launcher be Demonstrated to be Before it is Crewed?" *Journal of Loss Prevention in the Process Industries* 22:657–63.

Greiner, W., L. Neise, and H. Stocker. 1997. *Thermodynamics and Statistical Mechanics.* New York: Springer.

Hanayasu, S., and K. Sekine. 2004. "Damage Assessment of Industrial Accidents by Frequency-Magnitude Curve." Proceedings of Probabilistic Safety Assessment and Management (PSAM) 07, paper no. 0229.

Hollnagel, E., D. Woods, and N. Leveson, eds. 2006. *Resilience Engineering: Concepts and Precepts.* Hampshire, England: Ashgate Publishing Limited.

Holton, G. A. 2004. "Defining Risk." *Financial Analysts Journal* 60 (6): 19–25. www.cfa.pubs.

Howlett, H. C. 2001. *The Industrial Operator's Handbook,* 2nd ed. Pocatello, ID: Techstar.

International Monetary Fund (IMF). 2009a. "World Economic Outlook of the International Monetary Fund." Update Table 1.1, January 28. www.IMF.org /external/pubs/ft/weo/2009/update. Washington, DC: IMF.

———. 2009b. "World Economic Outlook: Sustaining the Recovery." Figure 3.1, October. Washington, DC: IMF.

Jaynes, E. T. 2003. *Probability Theory: The Logic of Science,* 1st ed. Cambridge: Cambridge University Press.

Kondepudi, D., and I. Prigogine. 1998. *Modern Thermodynamics: From Heat Engines to Dissipative Structures.* New York: John Wiley & Sons.

Ohlsson, S. 1996. "Learning From Performance Errors." *Psychological Review* 103 (2): 241–62.

Perrow, C. 1984. *Normal Accidents, Living with High Risk Technologies.* New York: Basic Books.

Petroski, H. 1985. *To Engineer Is Human: The Role of Failure in Successful Design.* New York: St. Martin's Press.

Pierce, J. R. 1980. *An Introduction to Information Theory.* New York: Dover.

Royal Commission on Environmental Protection (RCEP). 2008. 27th Report: "Novel Materials in the Environment: The Case of Nanotechnology." Cm7468, HMSO. www.rcep.org.uk/reports.

Rumsfeld, Donald. 2002. US Defense Secretary, quoted from February 12th press conference. Available at http://en.wikipedia.org/wiki/.

Solow, R. M. 1956. "A Contribution to the Theory of Economic Growth." *Quarterly Journal of Economics* 70 (1): 65–94.

Soros, G. 2009. "Do not ignore the need for financial reform." *Financial Times,* Comment section, October 26. www.ft.com/soros.

———. 2010. *The Soros Lectures.* Lecture One, Public Affairs. New York: Perseus Books Group.

Stevens, J. C., and H. B. Savin. 1962. "On the Form of Learning Curves." *J. Experimental Analysis of Behaviours* 5 (1): 15–18.

Sveshnikov, A. A. 1968. *Problems in Probability Theory, Mathematical Statistics and the Theory of Random Functions.* New York: Dover.

Taleb, N. 2007. *The Black Swan: The Impact of the Highly Improbable.* New York: Random House.

US National Commission. 2011. *Deep Water: The Gulf Oil Disaster and the Future of Offshore Drilling.* Report to the President. Washington, DC: GPO.

US Nuclear Regulatory Commission (NRC). 2008. "Davis-Besse Reactor Pressure Vessel Head Degradation: Overview, Lessons Learned, and NRC Actions Based on Lessons Learned." Report NUREG/BR-0353, Rev. 1, August. www.nrc.gov.

Wolfram, S. 2002. *A New Kind of Science.* Champlain, IL: Wolfram Media, Inc.

Woo, G. 1999. *The Mathematics of Natural Catastrophes.* London: Imperial College Press.

World Bank. 2009. "Gross World Product." Available at www.-wds.worldbank.org/WBSITE, GWP 1981–2004.

Comment   Joseph G. Haubrich

In "The Quantification of Systemic Risk and Stability: New Methods and Measures," Romney B. Duffey reminds us that financial markets are complex human systems, and argues that there is a lot to learn from failures in other complex human systems, such as airline flight, power generation, and cardiac surgery. Two key lessons that emerge are the importance of learning and the proper measure of time. Learning has a somewhat paradoxical effect on failures: it is by experiencing failures that humans learn, and in turn adjust the system and create the techniques to prevent failures. This notion

Joseph G. Haubrich is a vice president of and an economist at the Federal Reserve Bank of Cleveland.

The views expressed here are those of the author only, and do not represent the views of the Federal Reserve Bank of Cleveland or the Board of Governors of the Federal Reserve System. For acknowledgments, sources of research support, and disclosure of the author's material financial relationships, if any, please see http://www.nber.org/chapters/c12061.ack.

of experience, Duffey shows, can be a useful corrective for a financial risk-management community that all too often lapses into inappropriate physical analogies, such as hundred-year floods. Duffey shows that calendar time is often a poor gauge for failure probability; rather, what he terms "experience time" is more relevant. Thus the risk exposure for airlines depends on number of flights flown, for trains on miles traveled, and for ships on years afloat.

For financial crises, Duffey argues the relevant experience measure is cumulative Gross World Product. While he presents some evidence that crises match the pattern of failure in other systems, this seems clearly like a first attempt at financial experience time, and it would be interesting to see how other possibilities would work, such as accumulated trading volume or open interest. It may be that the contribution of these techniques is less to systemic (or even market) risk, but more to operational risk: to problems with the "plumbing" of trading and payments. Certainly in times where we have seen a flash crash and electronic trading takes an ever-larger share of the market, understanding "ops risk" becomes vital, as it can become a source of systemic risk itself.

Specific functional forms aside, one possible difference with financial systems is that as purposeful human systems, the innovative activity may not always be on the side of safety. Ed Kane (1981) coined the term "regulatory dialectic" to describe the financial innovation aimed at getting around rules. Certainly firms in other industries seek to minimize compliance costs, but finance may be different in the sense that much of the response is a desire to take on increased risk. To the extent that firms have an incentive to maximize the value of deposit insurance, grow to become too big to fail, or take correlated risk (Penati and Protopapakis 1988), the net effect of learning may be toward increased risk.

References

Kane, Edward J. 1981. "Accelerating Inflation, Technological Innovation, and the Decreasing Effectiveness of Banking Regulation." *Journal of Finance* 36 (2): 355–67.

Penati, Alessandro, and Aris Protopapadakis. 1988. "The Effect of Implicit Deposit Insurance on Banks' Portfolio Choices with an Application to International 'Overexposure.'" *Journal of Monetary Economics* 21 (1): 107–26.

Contributors

Viral V. Acharya
Stern School of Business
New York University
44 West 4th Street
New York, NY 10012

Tobias Adrian
Capital Markets Function
Federal Reserve Bank of New York
33 Liberty Street
New York, NY 10045

Markus K. Brunnermeier
Bendheim Center for Finance
Princeton University
Princeton, NJ 08540-5296

Terence C. Burnham
George L. Argyros School of Business
  and Economics
Chapman University
One University Drive
Orange, CA 02866

Ben Craig
Research Department
Federal Reserve Bank of Cleveland
P. O. Box 6387
Cleveland, OH 44101-1387

Jon Danielsson
Department of Finance and Financial
  Markets Group
London School of Economics
Houghton Street
London, England WC2A 2AE

Gianni De Nicolò
Research Department
International Monetary Fund
700 19th Street, NW
Washington, DC 20431

Mathias Drehmann
Financial Institutions
Bank for International Settlements
Centralbahnplatz 2
Basel CH-4002 Switzerland

Romney B. Duffey
Atomic Energy of Canada Limited
Chalk River, Ontario
Canada K0J 1J0

John Elliott
PricewaterhouseCoopers LLP
7 More London Riverside
London SE1 2RT England

Joseph G. Haubrich
Banking and Financial Institutions
    Group
Federal Reserve Bank of Cleveland
P. O. Box 6387
Cleveland, OH 44101-1387

Henry T. C. Hu
The University of Texas Law School
727 E. Dean Keeton Street
Austin, TX 78705

Sujit Kapadia
Bank of England
Threadneedle Street
London EC2R 8AH England

Andrew W. Lo
MIT Sloan School of Management
100 Main Street, E62-618
Cambridge, MA 02142

Marcella Lucchetta
Department of Economics
University of Venice Ca' Foscari
Cannaregio 873
30121 Venice Italy

Bruce Mizrach
Department of Economics
Rutgers University
75 Hamilton Street
New Brunswick, NJ 08901-1248

Hoai-Luu Q. Nguyen
Department of Economics
Massachusetts Institute of Technology
50 Memorial Drive
Cambridge, MA 02142

Mikhail V. Oet
Supervision and Regulation
    Department
Federal Reserve Bank of Cleveland
P. O. Box 6387
Cleveland, OH 44101-1387

Lasse H. Pedersen
Stern School of Business
New York University
44 West 4th Street
New York, NY 10012

Thomas Philippon
Stern School of Business
New York University
44 West 4th Street
New York, NY 10012

Matthew Richardson
Stern School of Business
New York University
44 West 4th Street
New York, NY 10012

Hyun Song Shin
Department of Economics
Princeton University
Princeton, NJ 08544

Gabriel Sterne
Exotix Limited
1st Floor, Watson House
54 Baker Street
London W1U 7BU England

Hao Zhou
Risk Analysis Section
Board of Governors of the Federal
    Reserve System
Mail Stop 91
Washington, DC 20551

Jean-Pierre Zigrand
Department of Finance
London School of Economics
Houghton Street
London WC2A 2AE England

Author Index

Subject Index